CHILD AS CITIZEN

ChLA
Children's
Literature
Association

Children's Literature Association Series

CHILD AS CITIZEN

Agency and Activism
in Children's Literature and Culture

Edited by Giuliana Fenech

University Press of Mississippi / Jackson

The University Press of Mississippi is the scholarly publishing agency of
the Mississippi Institutions of Higher Learning: Alcorn State University,
Delta State University, Jackson State University, Mississippi State University,
Mississippi University for Women, Mississippi Valley State University,
University of Mississippi, and University of Southern Mississippi.

www.upress.state.ms.us

The University Press of Mississippi is a member
of the Association of University Presses.

Publisher: University Press of Mississippi, Jackson, USA
Authorised GPSR Safety Representative: Easy Access System Europe -
Mustamäe tee 50, 10621 Tallinn, Estonia, *gpsr.requests@easproject.com*

Library of Congress Control Number: 2025936710

Hardback ISBN 9781496858405
Paperback ISBN 9781496858412
Epub single ISBN 9781496858429
Epub institutional ISBN 9781496858436
PDF single ISBN 9781496858443
PDF institutional ISBN 9781496858450

British Library Cataloging-in-Publication Data available

CONTENTS

Part III. Childhood Ecologies and the Agency to Act and Heal

Part IV. Systemic Agency and Sites of Recognition and Engagement

ACKNOWLEDGMENTS

I offer my gratitude to our editors, Roxanne Harde, Katie Keene, and Katie Turner at the University Press of Mississippi, as well as their teams.

Thanks also go to the Advisory Board of The Child and the Book conference for their collegiality and support, and to all the contributors to this collection, who approached the project with enthusiasm and dedication throughout the publication process. The memory of us engaged in discussion and basking in inspiration at the 2022 Malta edition of the conference, postpandemic, will remain a fond one for years to come. I offer my gratitude to our editors, Roxanne Harde, Katie Keene, and Katie Turner at the University Press of Mississippi, as well as their teams. Special thanks go to Corley Longmire for her dedication and work on the manuscript.

CHILD AS CITIZEN

AGENCY, ACTIVISM, AND CITIZENSHIP IN CHILDREN'S AND YOUNG ADULT LITERATURE AND CULTURE

GIULIANA FENECH

This book discusses children's and young adult agency and activism across literature and culture, demonstrating how they influence child citizenship. It engages with agentic voices and practices across multiple spheres of young people's lives, as well as the challenges to active citizenship faced by children. The collection establishes both agency and citizenship to be relational. We consider agency as a system of relations between children themselves, between children and adults, children and institutions, children and nation-states, as well as children and the nonhuman. We discuss citizenship as an entanglement, a process of becoming rather than an awarded status experienced passively. Across the essays included in *Child as Citizen*, we review the interconnectedness that emerges from these relationships and attempt to untangle some of the complications. How can we truly position children as cocreators within institutions and systems that do not share our values? How do we balance individual and collective agency? How can citizenship become a vehicle for care-full activism rather than a passive status? To respond, we adopt an interdisciplinary approach, drawing on the sociology of childhood, children's literature studies, youth culture studies, media, technology and cultural studies, and Anthropocene, ecofeminist, and disability studies. Brought together into a single volume, we hope that these essays become a point of reference in establishing how children's and young adult texts bring their readers closer to embodied participation in political processes of positive change toward social justice.

The role of the child in society has been a matter of interest for centuries (James and Prout 1990, Milne 2013, Gubar 2009 and 2016, Cummings 2020) but the historical categorization of the child as innocent and in need of protection,

3

or evil and in need of discipline (Crawley 2010, Spyrou 2018), is no longer valid. Likewise, the more modern notion of the child as victim and subject to multiple pathologies (Cavazzoni et al. 2022), or its antithesis framing the child as uncaring and detached (Nance Carroll 2021), are inadequate pictures of the childhood realities that we encounter both in life and in literary representation. Together with the contributors to this book, I am thinking of child and young adult agency as multidimensional and based on the possibility to engage in a broad range of entangled civic systems and processes. Spanning the personal, the familial, the social, and the political, these systems and processes are predicated on (but are not restricted to) the right to access knowledge and resources and the right to use that knowledge to participate in dismantling ideological hierarchies of power that no longer serve well. The impetus of this form of agency is resistance, social justice, and activism (recognized as movements rather than moments) that is not "predetermined by inherent biological or physiological factors," such as age, and is not "an essential, transhistorical or transcultural continuity" (Lesnik-Oberstein 2011). Changes that occur on personal, familial, social, and political levels may look and sound different depending on the geopolitical context that children inhabit (Percy-Smith and Thomas 2009). In fact, the intersectional and intergenerational sense of agency at play in children's claims towards more active forms of citizenship is recognized as crucial to understanding their role as citizens (Hardman 2001). At the heart of the changes we see forming around cultural constructions of childhood is a generational gap that fails to acknowledge the power that children have to act upon their own situation and the context around them. For this to shift, it is necessary to destabilize "power relations between adults and children" and, as the essays in this collection demonstrate, this also means "destabilising power relations between misogynistic patriarchal societies and more equitable ones" (McDowell 2002).

Forming communities of their own, often online, young people experiment with different forms of relational and social agency, enacting change through deeper inclusion and more distributed forms of power. The multiplicity of voices that are entering the public sphere (as we learn to harness the positive power of the internet even more than ever before) is enriching. Is it fully representative? No, not yet. Is internet use unproblematic? Certainly not. We have a long way to go. It is, however, more vocal about injustice and well-connected than was historically possible before the digital age. The degree to which young people are challenging the "more traditional, developmental discourse of children's incompetence" (James in Flynn 2016: 266) is perhaps the most fundamental change we have noticed in our research on the role of the child as citizen.

Instead of labeling children and young people as snowflakes (Fox 2017), authors in this book recognize them as active citizens. Instead of describing children and young people as a narcissistic, selfish, disrespectful cohort of human students, we acknowledge their interest in the local, the sustainable, the folk, and the digital as a different mode of being in the world that goes beyond a simple, or for that matter defeatist, reaction to the biggest problems in the global political situation. Having said that, we are not advocating here for the glorification of a whole generation; in fact, many of these essays emphasize the importance and influence of collaboration and learning across generations. As Meg Rosoff reminds us in her essay on the value of books in today's climate, being oblivious is dangerous and the antidote to that is being aware and agentic. A hopeful position is one that "assumes competency, that promotes an ethic of care and cooperation, and that recognizes young people as co-producers and coperformers [sic] rather than passive recipients" (Flynn 2016: 263). This volume therefore explores young people's engagement in solution-building toward climate change, unsustainable housing markets, rising levels of debt and subsequent financial hardship, modern-day slavery, the constant threat of far-right politics and the long shadow cast by dictatorships that cling to power, causing so much harm to communities along the way. The onus to provide solutions is not placed fully on young people, of course, but the passionate desire to contribute is definitely a trait that emerges in the studies on young people included in this volume.

In view of this, or perhaps as a result of it, the "care-full" (Motta & Bennett 2018) activist approach coupled with the decolonization project spreading across children's literature and its associated academic circles is commendable and is placed at the forefront of the methodologies underlying the research and writing of this book. Justyna Deszcz-Tryhubczak describes how research in children's literature and childhood studies is meaningful and can have social and political impact. It can also generate the multiplier effect discussed by Farriba Schulz when discussing the impact of academic research on cultural and political changes instituted in society, but not unless there is commitment across the whole community of stakeholders. Decentering the white, male, ageist, Western gaze is important, as is uncovering the injustices and suffering on which much of today's prosperity is built. No longer content to accept the status quo or even the fait accompli sense of business as usual (is that interchangeable with a sense of despair?) that young people are often presented with, they seek to understand the processes behind the products, the systems beneath the societal norms they are told they "should" endorse, and the injustices inherent in our institutions perpetrating systemic abuse of person, policy, and politics (op de Beeck 2020). As both Rosoff and Schulz point out, there is a sense of anger growing toward political complacency around social inequity and injustice, and rightly so. And, out of this anger, new forms of activism emerge. As Naomi Hamer and Ann Marie Murnaghan claim, young people are becoming more aware that it is not enough to be a passive citizen—we all need to be actively engaged in society for real change to be affected. Our engagement needs to be cooperative, intergenerational, embodied, and spanning multiple social and cultural platforms. It is only through a remembered interwoven culture of care and community that we can move through, and beyond, the numerous global crises currently knocking at our door (Soep 2014; Jenkins et al. 2016; Scolari et al. 2018). This is what lies at the heart of child citizenship in a post-9/11, (post) "ecostable," (post)pandemic, and mass-displaced world.

Child as Citizen addresses the culture of care and community directly through "the right to culture" (Harde and Kokkola 2018; Moylan 2020; Castro and Clark 2021; Reynolds 2022). Expanding on UNESCO's definition of the right to cultural life, we use the word "culture" to refer to the right to live by your chosen identity, alongside your inherited one. This could include (but is not restricted to) revisions to your ethnic, racial, and religious customs, assigned gender and imposed sexuality, body apology/autonomy, the practices associated with your socioeconomic class and the (non)geographical place you call home. Again, none of these are new concerns. Historical, comparative studies of children and young adult literature demonstrate how young people are framed in society and the roles they are asked to take on (Gubar 2010; Joy 2019; Slavtcheva-Petkova 2023). What is new, however, is the way in which we are connecting these epistemic frameworks and roles to daily life and coupling this work to the drive for a more simple, scaled-down, and sustainable way of life, as well as a more representative and empowering literary and cultural landscape. Children and young adult involvement in the public sphere demonstrates a desire for "a richer sense of self" (see Hamer and Murnaghan in part IV) and a richer "emotional geography" (see Murphy in part IV). Our work explores how this desire traverses the literary, cultural, and media landscape, gaining traction as it grows.

THE URGENT NEED FOR CARE-FULL ACTIVISM:
AN AUTHOR, ACTIVIST, AND ACADEMIC'S PERSPECTIVE

In line with its objective of representing agency, activism, and citizenship from multiple perspectives, part I of this volume features essays by a renowned children's author, an activist, and an academic. It begins with a manifesto on the value of books, penned by none other than Meg Rosoff. Rosoff laments the current state of affairs: "Children in the twenty-first century are being groomed by education [and governments] to conform to a standard capitalist model that favors self-interest, consumption and economic growth over the creation of a better world." Childhood reading is in sharp decline. Where, if anywhere, do books enter the conversation in a world where barely anyone reads anymore? And what role do we need them to play? Ranging from a broad overview of her own experience with reading and writing children's books, to the motivation behind some of the most needfully troubling stories she has written, Rosoff delivers a scathing yet deeply moving account of why children need books, now more than ever. Children's role in society is dependent on their knowledge of what matters and why. But not only, Rosoff reminds us: their society and ours depend on what they choose to do with that knowledge. Failing to equip young people with a meaningful education will have a detrimental effect on us all. We used to say children are the future. Rosoff reminds us that there is a strong case to make for acting as though children are the present because the future itself is at stake here. The second chapter of part I offers Nicola Parker's practitioner's perspective of developing Amnesty International's work on children's literature and human rights. For over two decades, Amnesty International has used story, poetry, illustration, and nonfiction to support children and young people in developing knowledge, building empathy, and gaining the confidence to stand up for themselves and others. Parker guides us through "a three-stage evolution: firstly, using stories to explore human rights; secondly, supporting young people's freedom of expression through a poetry and spoken word education resource; and thirdly, upholding children's participation rights in a book creation process." The essay raises key questions about the nature and extent of child participation in democratic processes and how these may be affected by geopolitical context. It offers important insights into "a dynamic use of literature, where adults' challenge is not to be didactic but to embrace freedom of expression, to listen to and trust the children." The sense of urgency at the heart of this work is also present in Justyna Deszcz-Tryhubczak's essay on academic activism. In spite of institutional structures that become more and more commodified and service based, Deszcz-Tryhubczak reminds us that academia can still be engaged in "implicit or small activism." Here, small does not mean insignificant. Deszcz-Tryhubczak outlines the multiplier effect that university classrooms can have. Adopting a feminist ethics of care framework, she advocates for "care-full activist onto-epistemological commitments in our scholarship and other professional activities," which allow us to resist oppression and participate in the younger generation's rebellion against systemic silencing and injustice.

LITERARY AGENCY AND A RECASTING OF EQUITABLE CHILD CITIZENSHIP

Chapters 4, 5, and 6 demonstrate how relational social agency is narrativized across different literary genres and forms, as well as periods, for children and young adults. Juxtaposed to one another, the three essays highlight difference as an onto-epistemic opportunity for increased equity that helps us to imagine and execute the right to citizenship beyond traditional notions of conformativity (see Christensen) and productivity (see Leach-Leung, Coste). In chapter 4, Nina Christensen explores how agency works in relational systems of influence. Analyzing elements of a picture book, a project in which authors and children coproduce stories for children, and an autobiographical account of children and adult relationships in the nineteenth century, Christensen demonstrates how children are capable of acting with others. She observes that while able to harness a more powerful form of action through connection, they remain true to their own identities, even though these may still be developing. Each of the analyses presented in the essay allows the reader to think through the ways in which children are allowed to act and what resources they draw on in order to affect the change that they feel is necessary, both in themselves and in the context or people around them. Change often requires destabilizing current worldviews in a movement toward more inclusive, stable, and just ones. In her essay on disability, Elizabeth Leach-Leung extends this argument to the types of agency afforded to children with disabilities in cultures that promote citizenship measured by old forms of material and economic productivity. Through her analysis of eugenic legacies in children's literature, she reminds us of the systemic changes needed for children's books to become more diverse and demonstrates how to read for eugenic legacies and resistance in children's and young adult literature featuring disabled characters. She identifies its impact on disabled citizenship alongside the promotion of agency in disabled and able-bodied children in these narratives. Angled differently through a discussion of ageism, Jill Coste discusses agency and citizenship in the same terms. Her essay is a moving plea to continue believing in the power of children's literature to elevate its readers and empower them to act against systemic injustice. By looking at multiethnic writers who began their work as teens and whose novels address social concerns that push back on hegemonic norms, Coste demonstrates how "these young writers challenge aetonormativity and prove their might by prioritizing and amplifying the conversations that can help change our world for the better." Systemic injustice is a key focus both in the writing of these teenagers, as well as in Coste's own work, as she foregrounds the emotional needs of teenagers who are dissatisfied with the civic cultural practices they find themselves forced into and are seeking to change them. All three essays highlight a desire to build childhood ecologies founded on care, curiosity, connection, and courage despite oppressive structures pushing us in the opposite direction. They highlight the fact that children do not simply have or possess citizenship but rather that citizenship is an entangled relationship based on interconnectedness and cooperation across all spheres of life—intellectual and embodied experiences across cultural, social, and political contexts. Therefore, as elaborated in the next section on childhood ecologies, agency is framed here as a "working with" rather than a "working on" issues, or even people, so that within collective systems, everyone maintains the right to meaningful participation without compromising their identity. This, we argue, also requires acknowledgment of historical and systemic trauma and a consideration of how corporeal aspects of children's everyday geographies affect agency.

CHILDHOOD ECOLOGIES AND
THE AGENCY TO ACT AND HEAL

In chapter 7, Daniela Brockdorff and Katrin Dautel focus on young adult literature that demonstrates children and young adults working through trauma while harnessing individual and relational agency to mitigate their disturbing situations. Like Leach-Leung and Coste, they emphasize the fact that young people resist victimization and almost always perform better under duress than we may expect. Trauma, "narrated in its raw form through stories of abuse and neglect, challenges agentic paradigms of the child as powerful," but this research shows that even young people subject to abuse are resourceful. Often, they are able to "expand" the space around them by using the imagination to interact with objects and creatures in their environment. Introducing Lambros Malafouris's notion of "creative thinging" as a making of "new things that scaffold the ecology of our minds, shape the boundaries of our thinking and form new ways to engage and make sense of the world" (2014: 140), Brockdorff and Dautel demonstrate how storytelling is a way of exploring human-nonhuman relationality and the ways in which this can be a tool to promote agency (Raithelhuber 2016; Spyrou, Rosen, and Cook 2018). Taking this discussion further, Irena Barbara Kalla links the discourse on trauma, environment, and relational agency to literature on the Holocaust, showing that failure to recognize the interconnectedness of all things leads to tragedy. Kalla finds a useful set of analytic tools within ecocriticism and encourages us to think more deeply about postcatastrophic literature and its revelations on the role children may take when society is in crisis. Building on Parker's essay, she notes that the suppression of young people, leading to a lack of agency and therefore citizenship, is "intertwined with other exigencies of the twenty-first century, such as poverty, hunger, migration, and human rights issues." Thus, exploring child agency and citizenship as an "ecology" can be a powerful method to describe the relationships of young people with literature, culture, society, and nature. In chapter 9, Anne Klomberg develops this discussion further by exploring corporeal citizenship as an ethics of care that encompasses all life on earth. As Coste does in part II, Klomberg delves more deeply into the ecofeminist ethics of care principle to show how teenage activism is embodied rather than abstract. She argues that "adolescent bodies are always, already, somewhat out of place as a result of aetonormativity," emphasizing their "outsiderhood." Like Leach-Leung and Brockdorff and Dautel, among other authors in this collection, Klomberg insists that this does not necessarily mean that young people are disempowered. Embodied activism allows us to appreciate that adolescents' materiality can become a source of power, enabling them to challenge aetonormativity, and reject the hopeless world image that adult characters envision. Literature provides examples of ways in which this can foster more meaningful experiences of citizenship. Through all these chapters, we understand why citizenship cannot merely be awarded but must emerge from a cultural ecology that fosters the "richer sense of self" that Hamer and Murnaghan describe, as well as the richer "emotional geography" outlined by Murphy. Additionally, as discussed by Rosoff and Parker, the function of books in children's lives and how they do, or may, leverage their readers into higher positions of civic power, generating real (legal and long-lasting?) change, is an area that deserves sustained attention.

SYSTEMIC AGENCY AND SITES
OF RECOGNITION AND ENGAGEMENT

In this section, Schulz, Murphy, Hamer and Murnaghan, and Kulkarni and
Owens explore how children's and young adult literature is produced and
received within sites of "agentic relation and recognition"—the places and
spaces where children encounter power and may choose to adopt it. As
discussed throughout this volume, the encounter with power can come in
the form of adult and/or systemic intervention attempting to raise them
up or, equally, oppress them. This section of the book considers four of the
most significant cultural and educational sites through which literature is
positioned to help young people negotiate their relationship with power—
schools, archives, museums, and online platforms. In chapter 10, Schulz
focuses on the role teachers play in establishing the literary classroom as a
space in which to rethink the children's relationship to/with/in nature and,
through that, to consider the implications of childhood ideologies to understand what is oppressed or leveraged in the process of representation. Schulz
draws on ecocriticism to ask what agency means at the interstice of nature
and culture and how the agentic child is framed through that perspective.
The social/pedagogical angle of this chapter is important as it outlines the
"multiplier" effect that so many activists name as a crucial aspect of their
work. As Deszcz-Tryhubczak also points out, pushing back and rework-
ing old systems requires high levels of momentum to sustain and, in turn,
this requires more people (and diverse demographics) to get on board with
the work. In chapter 11, Murphy frames "emotional geography" (mapped
throughout the objects and memorabilia in the archive) as a way of discovering lost children's voices while better understanding the role of children in
society historically. Working through archives with an open mind allows us
to study children's experiences based on their own account, alongside that of
those observing them. Importantly, as Christensen observes in her essay too,
it invites us to replace the predominantly white, male accounts of children's
restricted social roles with more relational and interconnected relationships.
Likewise, in chapter 12, Hamer and Murnaghan explore museums as a site
for adventure, agency, and independence that can, and often do, function
as liberatory sites for imagined futures. Studying child-adult relationships
through museums efficiently exposes a tension between adults and children.
The children form their own real and imagined relationships to the objects
and collections on display, but they are also very tightly controlled and monitored when spending time in these spaces. This seems to be an anomaly that
is dismissed by cultural phenomena like *Night at the Museum* but reemerges

whenever past histories are challenged and called out as being inadequately framed. Like Brockdorff and Dautel, Hamer and Murnaghan study the relation of reality and fantasy as ways of expanding space to amplify children's voices. Standing more firmly in their own worldviews and becoming active agents of change is a topic picked up by Kulkarni and Owens, who expand the discussion to include digital practices as they play out in the world of TikTok. As Coste and Klomberg also observe in their essays, Kulkarni and Owens note that nurturing subcultures as a way of democratizing critique leads to the onto-epistemic redefining of (in)justice and generates positive change from the inside out.

CONCLUSION

Generating positive change from the inside out is a powerful tool against oppression and this collection explores both the nature of that change as well as its literary, social, and political manifestations. The fight for justice and healthier, more inclusive, societies is both personal and collective. As authors, academics, teachers, and curators study and create the changing conditions of child agency, activism, and citizenship, it is important to adopt the curiosity and spirit of collaboration that we see emerging in young people. Their desire to tell their own story, to claim their own identities and have them represented in books, films, and digital and social media worlds is, or must be, at the heart of efforts to democratize children's literature, media, and culture. While acknowledging the absence of children's voices represented directly in this volume, we hope that our scholarship still provides a step in that direction as it outlines the complex, care-full changes that are already taking place, and those that still need to happen.

REFERENCES

Castro, Ingrid, and Jessica Clark, editors. *Representing Agency in Popular Culture: Children and Youth on Page, Screen, and in Between*. Mayland: Lexington Books, 2018.

Cavazzoni, Federica, Alec Fiorini, and Guido Veronese. "Alternative Ways of Capturing the Legacies of Traumatic Events: A Literature Review of Agency of Children Living in Countries Affected by Political Violence and Armed Conflicts." *Trauma, Violence, & Abuse* 23, no. 2 (2020), 555–66. doi:10.1177/1524838020961878.

Crawley, Heaven. "'No One Gives You a Chance to Say What You Are Thinking': Finding Space for Children's Agency in the UK Asylum System." *Area* 42, no. 2 (2010), 162–69. doi:10.1111/j.1475-762.2009.00917.x.

Cummings, Michael. *Children's Voices in Politics*. Oxford: Peter Lang, 2020.

Flynn, Richard. "What Are We Talking About When We Talk About Agency?" *Jeunesse: Young People, Texts, Cultures* 8, no. 1 (2016), 254–65. doi:10.1353/jeu.2016.0012.

Fox, Claire. *I Still Find That Offensive*. London: Biteback Publishing, 2018.

Gubar, Marah. *Artful Dodgers: Reconceiving the Golden Age of Children's Literature*. New York: Oxford University Press, 2010.

Gubar, Marah. "The Hermeneutics of Recuperation: What a Kinship-Model Approach to Children's Agency Could Do for Children's Literature and Childhood Studies." *Jeunesse: Young People, Texts, Cultures* 8, no. 1 (2016), 291–310. doi:10.1353/jeu.2016.0015.

Harde, Roxanne, and Lydia Kokkola editors. *The Embodied Child: Readings in Children's Literature and Culture*. London: Routledge, 2019.

Hardman, Charlotte. "Can There Be an Anthropology of Children?" *Childhood* 8, no. 4 (2001), 501–17. doi:10.1177/0907568201008004006.

James, Allison. "Agency." In *The Palgrave Handbook of Childhood Studies*, edited by Jens Qvortrup et al., 34–45. Houndmills: Palgrave, 2009.

James, Allison, and Alan Prout, editors. *Constructing and Reconstructing Childhood: Contemporary Issues in the Sociological Study of Childhood*. London: Routledge, 2003.

Jenkins, Henry, Sangita Shresthova, Liana Gamber-Thompson, Neta Kligler-Vilenchik, and Arely Zimmerman. *By Any Media Necessary: The New Youth Activism*. New York: NYU Press, 2016.

Louise, Joy. *Literature's Children: The Critical Child and the Art of Idealization*. London: Bloomsbury Academic, 2019.

Lesnik-Oberstein, Karin, editor. *Children in Culture, Revisited: Further Approaches to Childhood*. London: Palgrave Macmillan, 2011.

Malafouris, Lambros. "Creative Thinging." *Creativity, Cognition and Material Culture* 22, no. 1 (2014), 140–58. doi:10.1075/pc.22.1.08mal.

McDowell, Kelly. "*Roll of Thunder, Hear My Cry*: A Culturally Specific, Subversive Concept of Child Agency." *Children's Literature in Education* 33, no. 3 (2002), 213–25. doi:10.1023/a:1019634116385.

Milne, Brian. *The History and Theory of Children's Citizenship in Contemporary Societies*. New York: Springer, 2013.

Motta, Sarah C., and Anna Bennett. "Pedagogies of Care, Care-full Epistemological Practice and Other Caring Subjectivities in Enabling Education." *Teaching in Higher Education* 23, no 5 (2018): 631–46. doi:10.1080/13562517.2018.1465911.

Moura, Pedro. "Children and Youth Cultures Meet the Challenges of Participation—Interview with Henry Jenkins." *Comunicação e Sociedade* 37 (2020), 187–99. doi:10.17231/comsoc.37(2020).2657.

Moylan, Tom. *Becoming Utopian: The Culture and Politics of Radical Transformation*. London: Bloomsbury Academic, 2020.

Nance-Carroll, Niall. "Children and Young People as Activist Authors." *International Research in Children's Literature* 14, no. 1 (2021), 6–21. doi:10.3366/ircl.2021.0374.

op de Beeck, Nathalie, editor. *Literary Cultures and Twenty-First-Century Childhoods*. London: Palgrave Macmillan, 2020.

Percy-Smith, Barry, and Nigel Patrick Thomas, editors. *A Handbook of Children and Young People's Participation*. London: Routledge, 2009.

Qvortrup, Jens, and William A. Honig, Michael-Sebastien, editors. *The Palgrave Handbook of Childhood Studies*. Houndmills: Palgrave, 2009.

Raithelhuber, Eberhard. "Extending Agency. The Merit of Relational Approaches for Childhood Studies." In *Reconceptualising Agency and Childhood: New Perspectives in Childhood Studies* edited by Florian Esser et al., 89–101. London: Routledge, 2016.

Reynolds, Kim. "Culture for All: Why Children's Literature Matters." Accessed October 11, 2022. https://www.culturematters.org.uk/index.php/arts/fiction/item/3942-culture -for-all.

Scolari, Carlos, editor. "Teens, Media and Collaborative Cultures: Exploiting Teens' Trans- media Skills in the Classroom." Accessed July 20, 2020. www.transmedialiteracy.org.

Slavtcheva-Petkova, Vera. *Young People, Media and Politics in the Digital Age*. London: Routledge, 2023.

Soep, Elizabeth. *Participatory Politics: Next-Generation Tactics to Remake Public Spheres*. Massachusetts: MIT Press, 2014.

Spyrou, Spyros. *Disclosing Childhoods: Research and Knowledge Production for a Critical Childhood Studies*. London: Palgrave Macmillan, 2018.

Spyrou, Spyros, Rachel Rosen, and Daniel Thomas Cook, editors. *Reimagining Childhood Studies*. London: Bloomsbury, 2018.

Part I

The Urgent Need for Care-full Activism: An Author, Activist, and Academic's Perspective

Chapter 1

"DO YOU THINK YOU'LL EVER WRITE A REAL BOOK?"

Troubled Children and the Trouble with Writing for Children in 2022

MEG ROSOFF

This talk was delivered as a keynote address
at The Child and the Book Conference in Malta in 2022.

People get very excited when they hear I'm a novelist. An actual novelist! How thrilling!

Then comes the inevitable follow-up—what sort of books do you write?

Telling people that I write books for children is nearly always met with a tolerant smile and the end of the conversation.

At this point, I force myself not to stutter and prevaricate not to say:

Well, my subject is adolescence so my books are frequently categorized as YA, but mainly the people who read them are creative writing students or adults who are interested in coming-of-age stories, the bildungsroman, so I'm not only a children's writer, per se, I mean, I'm exploring what adolescence means and have also written for adults, and the children's and adult books are more or less on the same subject, i.e., what it means to be a person.

What I'm trying to say, in the most embarrassing way possible, is that I write SERIOUS books. Literary books. For children.

Most of the time I don't try to explain, which is good, because it sounds a) incredibly defensive and b) totally pathetic.

In the end, however, it doesn't matter much. Once I mention that I write for children, everyone starts to look over my shoulder, hoping to meet someone who does a "real" job, not the equivalent of working at a cat rescue.

Because writing for kids isn't like writing proper books—to the general public, and sometimes even to publishers, it's barely a real job at all. Writing children's books is the sort of thing anyone can do for a hobby, like baking cakes or designing hats for dogs, something innumerable people have told me they'd really love to try.

"Oh, you're a children's writer! How interesting. If all else fails, I think I'll write a children's book too."

It is fashionable these days to become a children's writer in your spare time because after all, how difficult can it be? A bit of rhyming or alliteration for your main character: Squishy the Squid, Peppy the Puppy, or Buddy the Bear, and presto, you're in.

Of course if you're lucky enough to be a pop star, a famous footballer, or an Instagram influencer, your book will not only get published, but you probably won't even have to write it yourself, and you might also get a huge advance.

Celebrities, influencers, minor royalty. The idea that you need any particular skill to write for children seems to have gone out of fashion, skewing the market toward a kind of amateur story-making based on achievement in other fields or on your number of Twitter or Instagram followers.

It's all part of the process of commodifying children's books, stuffing them into the sausage machine of commerce, where a few huge publishers make bigger and bigger profits and the books become more and more anodyne.

I am not the first person to complain about this. Perhaps it's what writers do.

In 1980, Maurice Sendak wrote, "We are flooded with books; books come pouring out of the publishing meat grinder. And the quality has dropped severely. I'd much rather we just took a year off, a moratorium: no more books. For a year, maybe two—just stop publishing" (Sendak 1980).

But the publishing goes on. And the theory is this . . . .

Children are idiots anyway; it's not like you need any special talent to write for them.

And the corollary to that? Children's writers are not REAL writers because they only write for idiots.

There are two problems here. The first is that children are not idiots and they are not simple versions of adults. They are possibly more complex versions of adults, though they know a good deal less about finance and politics.

The second problem with writing mediocre books for children is that it makes children think that's what books ARE. A bit samey, a bit dull, not nearly as much fun as the internet or Fortnite.

It's an adage among writers and librarians that if you give a child the wrong book, they won't tell you they don't like the book, they'll tell you they hate to read.

I do not belong to the contingent of outdated English public school boys, most of whom serve in Boris Johnson's cabinet, who believe that eight-year-olds should read Charles Dickens and Walter Scott. Fashions in books change, language changes, the world changes—how many adults have the attention span for Dickens anymore?

But to write well for children requires skills at least as sophisticated as those required to write well for adults—the ability to construct a good story, originality of thought, a talent for writing—but the additional ability to tap into the psyche of young people—their sense of humor, what worries them, what frightens and delights them, the extremity of their brains.

Children are hardwired to investigate the world. To try to understand it. The first independent travel a small child will do is in his or her own head.

I read last weekend that a famous British actor joined forces with his sister to write *The Fart That Changed the World*. Which should not surprise me. There have been at least ten thousand children's books written on the subject of bottoms and poo. Because don't all children get a kick out of poo?

But there is one classic book on the subject, a really good book, one you can bear to read over and over, that adults like as much as children—a book that is more than an exercise in sniggering. *The Story of the Little Mole Who Knew It Was None of His Business*, written in 1989 by Werner Holzwarth and Wolf Erlbruch, is a strange, subtle, anarchic book. For starters, the Mole himself is an angry picture book character, which is not something you come across very often—in picture books, children are almost never depicted as having strong emotions. In addition, the illustrations are powerful, not pretty or cute. It is not an exercise in "children are idiots anyway."

Neither is *Duck Death and the Tulip* (2007) also by Erlbruch—the finest treatise on death that I have ever read by anyone for any age group. It is one of my favorite picture books because it tackles the most difficult subject in all of literature—death—without a trace of sentimentality. There are no sweet funeral scenes in this book, no sparrows in boxes, no meaningful chats with mother about heaven. *Duck Death and the Tulip* is a classic piece of literature—so challenging and thought-provoking that I'm pretty sure nine out of ten parents would want nothing to do with it. But they would be wrong. It is a subject that begs discussion, even with small children. Particularly with small children.

Another great literary children's book is Sendak's strange, almost deliriously dreamy *In the Night Kitchen* (1970), which has been subject to extensive

Freudian analysis and is one of the most banned books of all time. It is a much weirder book than any child could fully appreciate, which may be why it upsets adults so much. It is full of references to Hitler, Stan Laurel, and the strange unconscious world of dreams. It is frightening and compelling at once. And worse! IMAGINE! It features full frontal nudity. In a drawing. Do children have genitals? Not in picture books they don't. "Contrary to most of the propaganda in books for the young," Sendak wrote, "childhood is only partly a time of innocence. It is, in my opinion, a time of seriousness, bewilderment, and a good deal of suffering" (Sendak 1980).

Roald Dahl, whose books have sold 250 million copies and often feature difficult families, neglect, cruelty, underdog, and revenge scenarios, would agree. He's been canceled—rightly or wrongly—for his antisemitism, but he sure knew how to write for children.

Sean Tan's *The Arrival* (2006) is the very definition of mute eloquence—a beautiful, tragic, hopeful book about being a refugee. When it won overall book of the year at the 2006 Sydney Writers' Festival, I overheard two publishers expressing outrage: "It isn't even a proper novel!" Imagine, I thought at the time, how difficult it must be to write a proper novel without using a single word.

If anything, classic literary children's books are **more** fierce and **more** radical than literary novels published for adults. Go back to Beatrix Potter some time if you want a truly terrifying read.

I'm not arguing that you can't sit and read *Guess How Much I Love You* (1994) to your children occasionally, though I'd rather shoot myself. Not every book you pick up has to be a literary masterpiece.

But the point about these books, the ones that will endure, is that the writers respect the curiosity and intelligence of children. Their job, as they see it, as we see it, is to live up to that challenge.

Unfortunately, the number of children reading books is declining steadily. We all know this. And we all know why. Children are gaming, watching TV, and spending more and more time online. Literacy across the world is up, but reading for pleasure is down across all age groups and continues to decrease year after year.

According to research carried out by the National Literacy Trust in the UK in 2020, "Children today read less frequently than in any previous generation and enjoy reading less than young people in every past year."

To make matters worse, enjoyment now dwindles with age: nearly twice as many five to eight-year-olds as fourteen to sixteen-year-olds said they took pleasure from reading.

Some of this trend has to do, quite simply, with access.

In the UK, as of six months ago, nearly a third of children were living in poverty. According to the Child Poverty Action Group, nearly 50 percent of children in single-parent families and 46 percent in Black and minority ethnic families were living in poverty. And if families can't afford food, they can't afford books.

Never mind, we think. They can always go to a library.

But eight hundred libraries in the UK have closed in the past decade. That's one in five.

As a final insult, government guidance puts pressure on schools to teach children to read via Synthetic Phonics, which separates the technical aspects of reading from books and storytelling. "Since the introduction of the phonics screening check in 2012, the percentage of Year 1 pupils meeting the expected standard in reading has risen from 58% to 82%, with 92% of children achieving this standard by Year 2," crows a Department for Education spokesperson (Weale 2022).

Standards in reading, however, have no correlation with enjoyment of reading. And though they may learn to read faster, they are taught to read via methods that do not involve books. The government makes it very clear that it is interested in attainment, not stories. Not enjoyment.

It's like teaching someone to cook without ever allowing them to taste the food.

It has struck me on repeated occasions that the British government hates children.

Some of us, however, value children—if not for themselves, as individuals, then for the fact that each generation of children represents the future of humanity.

Which is why we bang our heads against the wall and swim against the vast tide of library attrition, a failing interest in good quality children's books, and a decline in reading.

I've spent the past twenty years writing books, endlessly visiting schools to talk about reading, attending book festivals, holding workshops, recommending books to kids, and writing books as fiercely as I can.

At the same time, I tell myself that history moves on, that the world changes. That perhaps reading is an outdated form, destined for extinction like so many other forms of human behavior. Do you know anyone who can fix a car anymore?

My husband and I returned to the place he had worked in Nepal after eighteen years away, in the middle of the Nepali election of 1994. We were walking in relatively unpopulated country scattered with tiny remote villages, and one night we heard a traveling bard—an actual bard like something out of a Shakespeare play. He had arrived at the village to sing the election. As everyone in the village gathered round, my husband, who speaks Nepali, said he was describing the various positive and negative characteristics of the different parties and candidates.

You wouldn't find anyone singing an election anymore, even in Nepal, where mobile phones have reached even the most remote villages. But we accept the loss of oral culture and oral storytelling with relatively good grace and no particular sense of cultural catastrophe.

We are told the quality of digital programming is better than ever. So why do we catastrophize the loss of reading?

I am always careful about my generation's (and any older generation's) propensity to romanticize the past. Like most writers, I was a zealous reader as a child—but even back in the 1960s, I was unusual. Not all children—and of course not all adults—engaged with books, then or now, just as not all people engage with football or mathematics.

I constantly wonder whether I am like some old farmer in 1900 standing with a horse and a plow in a field, bemoaning the invention of the tractor. "It will be noisy and dirty and lead to a polluted, intensively farmed world!" I—and Luddites like me—shout. And even if I am right—and I believe I am right—catastrophizing the future doesn't stop it happening—it just makes you look like a crazy old fool.

So why SHOULD children be encouraged to read?

Over the past three and a half millennia, humans have been entirely at peace for only 268 years, or 8 percent of recorded history. This is not a good record.

We are a species of warmongering, compulsive consumers; we reliably choose greed, tribalism, and violence over altruism and peace, and within a couple of hundred years of inventing the power loom, we are in the process of making life on earth uninhabitable.

Against all odds, however, we retain the hope that things might get better. I would call that the triumph of hope over experience, but it is one of the most enduring and necessary stories we tell ourselves about being human. The story of hope. It is the reason we go on.

Tipping the scales toward optimism requires immense fine tuning of the human brain. It requires education and imagination, compassion, self-discipline, the emotional and intellectual tools at least to TRY to improve life on earth.

It requires the ability to visualize a better world.

At a publishing dinner during the US election campaign of 2016, I told the assembled audience that if you want to know what a nonreader looks like, look at Donald Trump. He lacks education, imagination, compassion, and curiosity about other people. He has no personal morality, no respect for history, no respect for other people's knowledge and experience, no respect for the rule of law, no respect, in fact, for anything other than power and money. He is a liar and a cheat, a man who, famously and proudly, has never read a book. He cares nothing for the future of the planet or of humanity.

He says he wants to make America great again, but his story is entirely about himself. He has no story of hope for the future.

Would it make a difference if he read books? Maybe. It could be argued that it is impossible to view the world entirely in black and white if you have read Shakespeare or Hilary Mantel or George Eliot. Or Sendak. Or Tan. The scientific method would suggest that we are not looking at the individual, we are looking across populations.

A friend of mine taught Boris Johnson classics at Oxford. He said he rarely showed up to class and slept through the classes he did attend.

This does not surprise me.

It seems to me, and to almost everyone I know, that we are living in a world on the brink of something bad, whether that something will be another world war, catastrophic species extinction, or mass migration due to climate change. We already have widespread social deprivation.

As a society, we have canaries in our coal mine who detect poison gas, who warn us that we will all die if we do not stop doing what we are doing.

The canaries are children.

And the canaries are showing the strain.

The incidence of mental illness among young people is at an all-time high.

The Millennium Cohort Study, carried out in 2021 and published in the *British Journal of Psychiatry*, followed the lives of about nineteen thousand young people born at the start of the millennium in Great Britain.[1]

Its results told us that 7 percent of children have attempted suicide by the age of seventeen and almost one in four says they have self-harmed in the past year.

Violent pornography is now a standard form of sex education for children as young as eight or nine. And in October 2019, according to an article in *Forbes* magazine, "[T]he UK Government abandoned its plans to introduce a nationwide age verification system for online pornography. This despite agreeing that adult content is too easily accessed online and more needs to be done to protect children from harm" (Ochab 2020).

Today more than ever it seems, children are overprotected by their parents and underprotected by governments—funneled by schools and groomed by education to conform to a capitalist model of attainment that favors self-interest, consumption, and economic growth over the creation of a better world.

Meanwhile, the climate crisis, passive screen culture, fake news, and the rise of online pornography have quietly become the major behind-the-scenes influencers on everything from brain development to body image to gender dysphoria.

A great many children feel hopeless. They lack hope. And they lack the tools required to imagine a better future.

For someone who writes books and whose major mechanism of understanding the world has always been reading, the decline of reading for pleasure seems particularly cruel. I have spent entire weeks and months of my life in retreat from the world, buried in a book, thinking. While I was in that other place, I was building a bank of knowledge courtesy of other people—people older and wiser than myself, people whose job it is to think and to turn that thinking into a story. It is, for me, a glorious respite and a glorious education in one.

And yet THINKING goes against the grain of a docile capitalist society.

Governments do not want citizens to THINK, they want citizens to work, to follow the rules, citizens who don't ask too many questions or make difficult demands. Faced with the gap between rich and poor, soaring energy and food prices, a racist police force, our abysmal policy on refugees, the last thing power wants is people on the street. The very last thing they want is revolution.

How do governments create a compliant population?

They start with children.

In a 2014 book, *Excellent Sheep: The Miseducation of the American Elite and the Way to a Meaningful Life*, award-winning American essayist and educator William Deresiewicz addressed what's going at the top level of American education: "Our system of education manufactures young people who are smart and talented and driven, yes, but also anxious, timid, and lost, with little intellectual curiosity and a stunted sense of purpose . . . great at what they're doing but with no idea why they're doing it."[2]

These talented children grow up with no motive to question the status quo, no motive to question the structure of society or the emphasis society puts on a certain kind of success. If you win a beauty contest, you don't dedicate your life to challenging society's perceptions of beauty. Deresiewicz points out that "kids who get into elite colleges have, by definition, never experienced anything but success. The prospect of *not* being successful terrifies them, disorients them. The cost of falling short, even temporarily, becomes not merely practical, but existential. The result is a violent aversion to risk" (2014).

It's a kind of brainwashing.

And it's happening at exactly the moment at which the world most needs risk-takers: individuals willing and able to retell the story of society in a more positive way, to take risks with social, political, and scientific change, to find solutions and reasons for hope.

Hardly anyone would disagree that our political system needs changing— free market capitalism has led to terrifying extremes of wealth and poverty. The legal system favors those with money, as does policing, education, housing, and medical care. In the meantime, there is, if it can be believed, STILL little financial motive to stem—or even acknowledge—the devastating effects of global warming.

I had an extraordinary conversation last year with the man who invests my retirement funds.

"I'd like to sell all my holdings in fossil fuels," I told him.

"But they're making you so much money!" The pain in his voice was evident.

"Still," I insisted, "I want to sell."

He had one last plea. "Think of your daughter," he said. "How can you justify reducing her inheritance?"

And I wanted to say, "How can I justify investing in companies who have, for decades, continued knowingly to destroy the future of the planet?" But I didn't. Because it wouldn't have impressed him.

I, like most members of my generation, are carrying the guilt for a lifetime of heedless over-consumption, and most of us want to do something. Even something as small as not investing in fossil fuels.

It is difficult to think of a single aspect of life on earth today that couldn't do with rigorous deconstruction and rethinking.

If schools are going to train a better class of political leaders, entrepreneurs, scientists, parents, and social policymakers, they—WE—have to ask ourselves which qualities we want to promote. If we require a more compassionate, more radical, less class-driven and self-centered definition of success, where does it begin?

I am hopelessly prejudiced, but I believe that at least some of it begins with books.

We can be lectured till the cows come home about the dangers of right-wing, paternalistic power structures, but Margaret Atwood's book *The Handmaid's Tale* (1985) instantly allows us to imagine EXACTLY where those power structures might lead us.

Everyone should read Ursula Le Guin's story, *The Ones Who Walk Away from Omelas* (1973). It's only five pages long. Omelas is about a perfect utopia in which everyone lives in contented bliss—thanks to the perpetual and horrible suffering of a single child. Read Le Guin's story and you will never think about the "civilized" world again without also thinking about the scapegoats.

Each person who reads *Catch-22* (1961), *Beloved* (1987), *Anne Frank's Diary* (1947), or *Wolf Hall* (2009) takes a step closer to leading an examined life—a step away from living as an excellent sheep.

I have frequently wished that a successful person could be redefined as a person who thinks creatively and laterally, who questions authority and accepted wisdom, who lives thoughtfully, generously and not entirely for personal gain. Whose goal is to leave the world a little bit better.

How do we do this? By encouraging each new generation to read history and philosophy and fiction—to think big, dangerous thoughts about religion, politics, ethics, love, passion, life and death and the origins and future of the universe. Change will not happen by thinking about what we are but what we might be.

Humanity's story can be redeemed only by a story of hope.

At the start of lockdown, I gave an entire month over to the last of Hilary Mantel's Wolf Hall series—*The Mirror and the Light* (2009–2020). As I neared the end of the book, I read late into the night until at 2 a.m. Thomas Cromwell was betrayed and arrested.

My husband had gone to bed hours ago, and I didn't have the heart to wake him. But I was devastated. I lay staring at the ceiling in a state of shock and despair at this turn of events, despite knowing perfectly well from the beginning of book 1 what happens at the end of book 3—Thomas Cromwell is executed by order of Henry VIII; it's history. But the suddenness of the arrest felt like a punch to the gut. It turned my heart over and my emotions upside down in a way that the real world rarely does.

The ability to engage in the ideas of history is one of the great gifts of reading. And as we all know, those who do not study the past are doomed to repeat it.

Meanwhile, publishers turn out books whose sole purpose is to offer children a momentary jolt of sugar without thought, without real content, without intellectual nutrition.

My hope is that children will continue to learn about anarchy from *The Cat in the Hat* (1957), injustice from *The Story of the Little Mole* (1989), about friendship from *The Secret Garden* (1911), about good vs. evil from the Harry Potter series (1997–2007). That they will read *Noughts and Crosses* (2001–2021) or *The Giver* (1993) and imagine a different world.

The books you read as a child teach you about the forces of darkness and goodness. They tell you how important it is to think uneasy, difficult thoughts and to change the world. They teach you not to be helpless.

The older I get, the more I realize that engagement with real life is great and important, but engagement with the inside of your head is the most important part of being human. It's subversive and dangerous and it's where the really deep ideas are born.

My favorite children's books all talk about the same things my favorite adult books talk about—power, love, identity, friendship, sex, war, inequity, death. Kids are desperate to understand all these things. They seek intensity—big emotions, big ideas.

As I settle into my sixties, the intensity in life comes unsought from parents and partners and friends who are ill or dying, friends with too much money or not enough, divorces, from children or grandchildren with autism or addictions or mental health issues.

These days, in other words, though I appreciate books for any number of reasons and read a great deal with great pleasure, it is a very rare book that affects me to the degree that most of what I was reading when I was fifteen did. It's not that books have lost their power, but rather that my relationship with them has become less urgent.

When I was five and ten and fifteen, I read books over and over again. Hundreds of times. They carved deep roads in my brain that determine who I am now.

So I try to pass it forward. As a writer, I can explore all those deep, dark issues like war and love, and existential angst, and sex, and identity, and the future of the planet, offering readers a place where they can consider how difficult the world is, feel the pain, but also feel the consolations of love, and work, friendship, and the power of change.

"Think harder," I try to say with my books.

And I try to remember what C. S. Lewis said about books for children: "No book is really worth reading at the age of ten which is not equally (and often far more) worth reading at the age of fifty. The only books we ought to grow out of are those which it would have been better not to have read at all" (2002).

How the future of the planet looks depends on children. It is vitally important to take their minds seriously. We know that if you fill a child's mind with pornography, conformity, and lies, it will stick. Garbage in, garbage out.

But bring them up to question authority, to understand the power that resides in their own heads, the power to write a new story for the future—and the world has a chance.

I am trying to teach children to be anarchists.

There can't be a job more important than that.

NOTES

1. Millenium Cohort Study. University College London. https://cls.ucl.ac.uk/cls-studies/millennium-cohort-study/. Accessed May 28, 2023.

2. William Deresiewicz. "Don't Send Your Kid to the Ivy League." *New Republic*. https://newrepublic.com/article/118747/ivy-league-schools-are-overrated-send-your-kids-elsewhere. Accessed May 28, 2023.

REFERENCES

Clarke, Christina, and Irene Picton. "Children and Young People's Reading in 2020 Before and During the COVID-19 Lockdown." National Literacy Trust. Accessed May 28, 2023. https://literacytrust.org.uk/research-services/research-reports/children-and -young-peoples-reading-in-2020-before-and-during-the-covid-19-lockdown/.

Deresiewicz, William. "Don't Send Your Kid to the Ivy League." *New Republic*, July 22, 2014. Accessed May 28, 2023. https://newrepublic.com/article/118747/ivy-league-schools -are-overrated-send-your-kids-elsewhere.

Lewis, Clive S. *Of Other Worlds: Essays and Stories*, 2nd ed. San Francisco: Harper One, 2017. Kindle edition.

"Millennium Cohort Study." University College London. Accessed June 14, 2024. https://cls.ucl.ac.uk/cls-studies/millennium-cohort-study.

Ochab, Ewelina U. "We Must Protect Children from Online Pornography." Forbes. Last modified February 28, 2020. https://www.forbes.com/sites/ewelinaochab/2020/02/26/we-must-protect-children-from-pornography-online/.

Sendak, Maurice. "Maurice Sendak." In *The Openhearted Audience: Ten Authors Talk About Writing for Children*, edited by Virginia Haviland. Washington: Library of Congress, 1980. Kindle edition.

Weale, Sally. "Focus on Phonics to Teach Reading is 'Failing Children,' Says Landmark Study." *The Guardian*. Accessed May 29, 2023. https://www.theguardian.com/education/2022/jan/19/focus-on-phonics-to-teach-reading-is-failing-children-says-landmark -study.

Chapter 2

A HUMAN RIGHTS
PRACTITIONER'S PERSPECTIVE

How Children's Literature Can Support Their Rights
to Justice, Dignity, and Voice

NICOLA PARKER

> Adults never listen to kids—especially kids like me.
> But we have important things to say.
> —DUJUAN HOOSAN, AUSTRALIAN ARRERNTE AND
> GARRWA BOY (AMNESTY, JOLIE AND VAN BUEREN 2021: 143)

In this essay, I share a practitioner's perspective of leading Amnesty International's work on children's literature and human rights for over two decades, mostly at its UK national office (AIUK) and later at its International Secretariat (AIS). In my work, I sought to encourage the exploration of story, poetry, illustration, and nonfiction through a human rights lens with the objective of supporting children and young people to develop knowledge, build empathy, and gain the agentic confidence to stand up for themselves and others. Amnesty is a campaigning organization, so the term "activism" is more commonly used than "agency," but there is a clear overlap in terms of active citizenship.

Arguably, my work saw a three-stage evolution: firstly, using stories to explore human rights; secondly, supporting young people's freedom of expression through a poetry and spoken word education resource; and thirdly, upholding children's participation rights in a book creation process. In this chapter, I consider all three approaches both at AIUK and AIS, paying particular attention to the most recent participatory project. Work of this nature within a nongovernmental organization (NGO) faces many challenges. Unless children are the main target audience for NGOs, charities, and indeed, companies, they do not usually receive the same level of attention that is given to adults. This is for a range of possible reasons, including the social disenfranchisement of under-eighteens; that children's participation rights are not embedded across society; that children cannot be paid-up members of any NGO or charity; and that privacy and safeguarding laws make it hard to develop and target communications to this audience. At an operational level, all these factors make it easier to sideline children. On top of this, for an NGO facing daily human rights crises, it may seem frivolous to invest time and budget in culture, even if this too is a human right (Article 27, UDHR).

WHY CHILDREN'S LITERATURE AND HUMAN RIGHTS?

Amnesty's logo of the candle in barbed wire goes with the motto "it is better to light a candle than curse the darkness." Since its foundation in 1961, the spoken and written word have been at Amnesty's core: it gathers people's testimony and tells their stories as a means of bearing witness and campaigning for justice. Many of those it campaigns for are writers and artists imprisoned, tortured, or killed because of the power of their words and pictures to stir emotions and liberate ideas. Amnesty takes pains to gather facts and establish the truth. In its work with children's literature, I would argue that it is still telling the truth but through metaphor. Familiar recurring literary themes such as fairness, identity, and equality are human rights values, and many children's storytellers are expert at communicating them simply. Some children's literature can be compared to the Amnesty candle: it lights the darkness, safely reveals the monsters, and supports young readers to a position of greater understanding and strength.

For those who read through a human rights lens, it's easy to see that most good children's stories already revolve around a human rights value, including protagonists whose actions (or lack thereof) invite rich inquiry. Amnesty UK's literature program has used a range of fiction, nonfiction, picture books, poetry, and spoken word in order to provoke thoughtful engagement in topics that might otherwise be regarded as dull or frightening. The indirectness and nuance of fiction and poetry provide safe spaces and journeys of the mind for children who might struggle with more didactic classroom learning or who have experienced abuse that they do not wish to discuss. In fiction, they can find themselves in unexpected places, discover that they are not alone, and feel hope. The greatest children's literature offers the "mirrors, windows, and sliding glass doors" described by Rudine Sims Bishop in her seminal call for representation in children's books, which also speaks to children's rights to equality, knowledge, and freedom of thought (1990: ix–xi).

The creation and enjoyment of literature depends on the realization of rights. Authors and artists need freedom of expression if they are to thrive. In exchanging ideas and feelings with readers—a kind of call and response—their work stimulates empathy, imagination, and freedom of thought. Readers temporarily occupy the same worlds as the protagonists and antagonists, then reflect, discuss, and even do something differently in a story-inspired form of freedom of expression. These are participation rights and they are essential to being an active citizen and laying the foundation for a strong society. After all, if we can't imagine a better world, how can we create one? The human rights lens is thus a dynamic use of literature, where adults' challenge is not to be didactic but to embrace freedom of expression, to listen to and trust the children. For a period of about two decades (2001 to 2020), AIUK commissioned story collections and picture books and endorsed other books that were considered to uphold or celebrate human rights. It entered into book partnerships with commercial publishing houses where there was mutual benefit: AIUK benefited from their specialist editorial, design, production, marketing, and sales infrastructure; they benefited from AIUK's content expertise, large supporter base, high profile contacts and specialist networks. The partnerships meant that both parties could reach a far bigger audience than either could achieve alone. This mattered, not just to generate sales but to bring awareness of human rights to more people. As time went by, strict principles were adhered to: Amnesty ran an ethical screening into all potential publishing partners, paying particular attention to labor, environmental, and any human rights policies, how and where they printed, what paper they used, what working conditions there were, and so forth.

The literature program developed after I started at Amnesty UK in 2001, when its publishing program was almost exclusively devoted to human rights reports on specific countries, serving a niche but influential audience of lawyers, politicians, and academics. We diversified and independently published two nonfiction books on racial and LGBTQ+ equality for young adults (Szwarc 2001; Baird 2004) that found an audience and were well-reviewed but were labor- and cost-intensive. It was clear that we needed to find another working model if we were to reach more people with limited budget and capacity. My own children were young at the time, and I could see many human rights values implicit in the stories I read to them, but we had no idea if AIUK supporters would be interested. We tested the water by buying fifty copies each of six children's titles that in different ways celebrated human rights values and promoted them in AIUK's members' magazine.[1] They all sold out within two weeks, a clear indicator of interest and a springboard for a new area of work.

The next step was to develop a picture anthology for children in collaboration with publisher Frances Lincoln Children's Books. In *We Are All Born Free: The Universal Declaration of Human Rights in Pictures* (Amnesty 2008), we simplified the complex Articles of the UDHR and commissioned twenty-eight illustrators to interpret them for children ages three and up. The book won awards, was translated into thirty-one languages, and has been reprinted many times. A few months after it was published, the keynote speaker at the 2009 Amnesty UK AGM was Jenni Williams, a Zimbabwean human rights activist and founder of a grassroots organization called Women of Zimbabwe Arise, who had survived significant police brutality. When an Amnesty member asked what she would like the AGM to do, she asked not for money or advocacy but for one hundred copies of *We Are All Born Free* to illuminate human rights for the children of Zimbabwe. An audience member pledged the money, but we knew the books would not be deemed acceptable under Robert Mugabe's government. Somehow, we had to get them over the border from South Africa, so we organized a clandestine delivery and smuggled them across.

More Amnesty-commissioned publications followed, including an anthology for young adults, *Here I Stand: Stories That Speak for Freedom* (Amnesty 2016), which explored rights under threat in the global North (rather than "over there"). A teacher who bought this book for her school library told us about a silent thirteen-year-old student who was often late handing in her homework and never willingly spoke to staff. This girl read *Here I Stand* and was struck by Sita Brahmachari's short story titled "Stay Home" about a child carer. For the first time, the girl voluntarily approached the teacher and confided that she thought she was a child carer too, as she was looking after her mother and younger siblings. She hadn't known the term before, but the story helped her to understand and articulate her experience—it gave her a voice. The conversation helped the school put in measures to support her and build a trusting relationship.

Colleagues in AIUK's human rights education team reported that fiction and poetry are an especially inspiring and accessible way of discussing human rights with children and young people. Over the years, they have developed free fiction resources, such as an origami Story Explorer (www.amnesty.org.uk/story-explorer) that encourages children to ask questions such as "whose story is being told?," "who is telling the story?," and "whose voices aren't being heard?" The clear link between children's literature and human rights education led to a 2016 to 2018 AIUK partnership with CILIP, the library and information association in the UK. It awarded the Amnesty

CILIP Honour to books on the CILIP Carnegie and Greenaway Medal short-list that Amnesty's judges believed best upheld or celebrated human rights and the values that underpin them. AIUK created classroom resources for all shortlisted books to help teachers notice and explore the human rights values in the stories and pictures (www.amnesty.org.uk/cilip).

One of the first Amnesty CILIP Honour winners was the picture book *There's a Bear on My Chair* (Collins 2015). It's the story of a mouse who tries to persuade a domineering polar bear to get off his chair. A secondary school teacher told us of a twelve-year-old student with learning difficulties who picked up this book. They used Amnesty's classroom resources to read and talk about it together, which enabled him to express his sadness about another child who wouldn't let him have his favorite chair in the library. They provided him with another chair of his own and said that this "book talk" helped his literacy progress much faster than anticipated and that he was writing sentences within a year.

VOICE—POETRY AND SPOKEN WORD
BY CHILDREN AND YOUNG PEOPLE

Like adults, children have the right to be active citizens and to express them-selves, to seek out and find information, and to peacefully protest (UNCRC 1989: Article 13 and 15). At AIUK, we began to pay more attention to this when we worked on another picture book anthology, *Dreams of Freedom* (Amnesty 2015). For its launch, we partnered with Chickenshed, an inclusive commu-nity theater company, that workshopped the book with six hundred children in London, exploring what freedom meant to them and what sort of world they would like to see. This culminated in a large-scale performance at the Royal Albert Hall where the children performed their wishes for the world in a spectacular show of dance, music, and art. It spurred us to develop a literary project that would focus on empowering young people's voices. In 2017, we launched a poetry and spoken word project in partnership with Cheltenham Literature Festivals. Words That Burn is a free online education resource that encourages young people to use poetry and spoken word to explore human rights and to express themselves (www.amnesty.org.uk/wordsthatburn). The first challenge was to motivate school students uninterested in poetry (which teachers told us they often viewed as the domain of dead white people) to take part. We created ten teaching sessions that connected chosen poems to different human rights themes, such as "power," with dynamic video clips of spoken word artists performing their work or giving writing tips. In 2021, an independent evaluation of the project was overwhelmingly positive. Teacher feedback included: "Many pupils are more open to poetry as a living, breathing genre with relevance to them." Another teacher spoke of the benefits of using poetry and spoken word to build empathy among young people in rural schools where "lots of the students had very limited knowledge about other cultures and events happening around the world."

In 2022, Amnesty UK commissioned three spoken word artists (Patrick Cash, Deanna Rodger, and Joelle Taylor) for a pilot project exploring the extra value of sending poets into schools. It gave them human rights training to deliver Words That Burn poetry workshops in three schools in the area served by Cheltenham Festival's year-round education program, which targets marginalized communities. As part of their workshops, the poets shared Amnesty's proverb "it is better to light a candle than curse the darkness" as the starting line for a cocreated poem, where each student proposed their own follow-up line. Fifteen of the students performed it at the Cheltenham Literature Festival in October 2022. This is a small part of the whole poem:

> It is better to light a candle than curse the darkness,
> Work together to make a bridge of light
> It is not the strongest threads that define us but the weakest
> If we can connect our weaknesses, we can make the world right.
> Do you let the candle burn, do you let life take its turn?
> Always keep the candle lit.

One of the students (aged twelve) said, "It was a really different atmosphere compared to when you're at school—it's not tense, you feel like you're all part of a family and you can really express yourself. If you mess up it's fine because we all make mistakes. It was amazing to be part of this!" Another student (aged twelve/thirteen) said, "Words That Burn is important because it gives us an idea of the world's problems and how young voices can be heard all around the world. It doesn't matter what religion or race you are or what language you speak, everyone has a voice that should be heard" (Year 8 student, Severn Vale School, Gloucestershire, UK).

For a March 2023 evaluation of this pilot project, teachers reported that they had felt part of a creative community with the poets and noted a change in how students could talk about wider issues with sensitivity and empathy. They described the project as "transformative" for students and their families. The three poets reported a strong sense of collective action and that they felt inspired and rejuvenated by working with the young people. The young people were enthusiastic and energized by the poets entering their spaces, which affirmed to them not just that they have the right to a voice, but that their voices matter. They gained positive feelings about the poetic process and a heightened awareness of the power of their own voice as they experienced what it feels like to be listened to. Sixty percent of the young people said they would continue to write poetry, with 46 percent saying they would continue to take action on human rights, indicating increased agency. The students' newfound confidence in expressing their thoughts and feelings through poetry is a demonstration of citizenship in action.

COCREATION OF LITERATURE—
UPHOLDING CHILDREN'S PARTICIPATION RIGHTS

In 2018, AIUK was approached by actor, film director, and humanitarian Angelina Jolie, who was interested in collaborating on a children's book. We agreed on a book project on children's human rights and invited Professor Geraldine Van Bueren, one of the original drafters of the UNCRC, to join us. Agreed goals were to empower children and young people to know, understand, and claim their rights as defined in the UNCRC, and for adults to support them. To begin with, we envisaged a fiction anthology for middle grade (ages eight to twelve), each story exploring child rights. Most importantly, we agreed that any book on child rights must uphold children's right to participate through an intergenerational rights-respecting project. This represented a challenge as Amnesty does not have a history of working directly with children and young people (our education program works with educators). We therefore approached Professor Liz Chamberlain at the Open University's Children's Research Centre, whose team undertook research with the aim of making visible children's and young people's views about their rights and for their voices to be at the heart of the book creation process.

Over the autumn and spring of 2018 to 2019, the research directly involved one hundred and fourteen children and young people with a further hundred indirectly involved through a school-based, child-led research project. There were eight children in the age range three to four years old, 102 in the range five to thirteen, and four young people ages eighteen to twenty-two. Each of the nine component projects engaged a diverse range of participants, including children from rural communities and those living in urban and peri-urban environments; children from low socioeconomic backgrounds; children from ethnic minority communities; children with learning difficulties; children from vulnerable groups; and care-experienced children and young people. The research approach varied from setting to setting, using drama, song, and dance with Chickenshed, for example, by contrast with child-led research in a primary school in Southampton. The insights gathered were often acute, as, for example, from a ten-year-old girl with Down syndrome, who said, "The right to express yourself is good, but it's not much use if no one listens to you." In a 2019 report by the Open University, *Representing Children's Rights from Discussion Through to Illustration and Interpretation*, Chamberlain et al. write:

> A guiding principle for the design of this study is the recognition of rights as something that cannot be precisely categorised or easily granted, but are fluid, complex, and socially constructed. Such fluidity necessitates a participatory research approach that is responsive to dynamic childhood practices and recognises the different ways in which potential views are shared. Consequently, this research employed a multimodal research design, utilising focus-group interviews, young researcher projects, role-play and drama, and photo-elicitation as the means to engage with and listen to diverse groups of children and young people (C&YP). The aim was to use the multimodal activities as a stimulus for conversation and to provide opportunities for the C&YP to contribute to a shared narrative about rights within the context of their own lives. The research also gathered C&YP's picture book preferences, specifically the kinds of images that attract or interest them.

The children's views and nuanced responses had a significant impact on our thinking. Crucially, their input made us reconsider what sort of book was needed. It was clear that although the children and young people had high levels of understanding of values, their understanding of rights and active citizenship was very low. We therefore transitioned from the idea of a fiction anthology to a nonfiction book that would build knowledge and provide good foundations for later, better-informed fiction. We also decided to start with a book for teenagers so that we could address the more challenging topics in the UNCRC and to follow it up with one for younger children. In 2020, this book project and I were relocated to Amnesty's International Secretariat to maximize the global nature of the project.

ENABLING PARTICIPATION IN THE WRITING PROCESS

In the drafting process, coauthors Jolie, Van Bueren, and I (on behalf of AIS) simplified the fifty-four Articles of the UNCRC into fifteen groups of rights that are easier to understand and remember. We noted that the Open

University report showed children's real concerns about online bullying, which gave us pause for thought, given that the UNCRC dates from 1989, before the rise of social media. We decided to focus on this in the right to privacy. Next, I drafted the book's outline, which we knew we should again sense-check with children and young people. This was not straightforward for a range of reasons, not least because the upholding of children's participation rights is not yet a cultural norm and because Amnesty's outreach to children and young people is mainly conducted via a network of educators. We decided not to revert to the same Open University research cohort, partly because many of them were younger than the book's target market but also because we did not want this to become a burden. The reality is that most children and young people do not have the freedom to choose to participate, rather they are dependent on the knowledge, goodwill, and safeguarding capacity of their supporting adults, often teachers. Children's school timetables are full and circumscribed by other demands, so those who are offered a chance to participate may have to relinquish access to another right, such as that to play. For any few who ultimately make it through, the quality of their feedback likely depends on the skills of their supporting adults to gather thoughts from children unused to being prompted for their opinions, who may say what they think the adult wants to hear.

For quick feedback on the draft outline, we therefore invited expressions of interest through Amnesty's global Youth Power Action Network. In response, eight young people from Burkina Faso, Germany, Hong Kong, Ireland, Nigeria, and the United States offered their time and opinions. It is important both to express our gratitude and simultaneously to note that all were female, all activists (therefore with an existing awareness of human rights), and all between ages nineteen and twenty-two, so not children. This is a further reflection of how hard it is to enable genuine child participation in a society and context where it is not normalized. (It also echoes our experiences in seeking out case studies of child activists to include in the book, of whom the large majority were girls; we had to make a real effort to identify boys to include.) However, we paid close attention to their insights and revised the outline accordingly. Subsequently, I drafted the manuscript and shared it with the coauthors, various human rights experts, and others for their specialist feedback. It remained crucial to share with children and young people, but we had a strict publishing schedule and again struggled to find readers under the age of eighteen, so we reverted to the same group of youth activists who read it. Their comments included:

> I think this book would have brought me a lot when I was a teenager because I have already been helpless in the face of the violence suffered

at school by one of my friends. . . . What seems most relevant to me is to show children and young people how to access / fight for their rights. (Amnesty Archives)

I stumbled a little bit on the [original] working title: *Know and use your rights: A manual for all children and young people.* I know it is about the legal definition, but as far as I remembered teenagers do not like to be referred to as children. So maybe you could think about leaving the term "children" out of the title to make it more appealing to them. (Amnesty Archives)

As we progressed to a second draft in late 2020, we felt it would be irresponsible to place extra burden on the same youth activists in a context of study pressures and the COVID lockdown, so we were delighted when a fourteen-year-old activist from AIUK Children's Human Rights Network stepped forward and went through the entire manuscript with a critical eye and precise feedback. Her overarching comments were reassuring, including: "Just by reading this book I have realised all that I could do—things that are normally believed to be done by adults can be done by so many ordinary kids like myself" (Amnesty Archives).

The coauthors of the book agreed that its narrative voice had to make child rights accessible while upholding the young readers' dignity; it should feel inclusive; it should not patronize or "other" the readers. Use of the first person was clearly inappropriate, while the third person "they" risked children feeling objectified, exposed, or othered. This left the less commonly used second person "you," which we chose to use throughout. The book begins like this: "If you are a child or young person, you have your own set of human rights." The second person was also intended to encourage feelings of togetherness and solidarity, that for any young reader who is experiencing hardship, "it's not your fault" and "you are not alone." However, some adult readers of the first draft expressed concerns that consistent use of the second person was too direct and potentially alarming for young readers, especially in the section on the right to bodily integrity, where text includes, for example, "Your body is yours to enjoy," and "Early forced marriage robs you of your right to take decisions about your own life." Our counterargument was that it is important not to assume that young readers are not already familiar with what is happening in the world. A desire to cocoon our children from the truth does not protect them in the long-term but may in fact make them more vulnerable. Indeed, the fourteen-year-old child rights activist from the UK said, unprompted, "I really love how everything is phrased short and sweet. This is crucial for maintaining the interest and concentration of adolescents. . . . The use of second person makes the message more direct and personal, something we can relate to."

As an aside, we were able to invite the same AIUK child rights activist to join a panel at a UN General Assembly side event in October 2021 on the need for the UN to mainstream child rights. Other speakers included young people from Child Rights Connect and the chair of the UN Committee on the Rights of the Child. The AIUK child rights activist spoke persuasively, held up the book, and quoted Article 42, the right for all children to know their rights. The event contributed to an important breakthrough when the Executive Office of the UN Secretary General responded by saying that it plans to develop a Guidance Note on Child Rights Mainstreaming through an interagency process, which will be a tool to support the inclusion of child rights.

Perhaps the most vibrant aspect of the two child rights books (Amnesty International 2021 and 2024) is the case studies, which, across both books, feature eighty-five child and youth activists from thirty-four countries whose stories of activism bring child rights and notions of citizenship to life. They include girls, boys, and transgender children; LGBTQ+; those with physical and learning difficulties; neurodiverse and neurotypical; from low socioeconomic backgrounds; Black, Asian, minority ethnic and Indigenous; refugees and migrants; those in prisons and refugee camps. They come from Argentina, Australia, Bangladesh, Belarus, Benin, Bosnia, Brazil, Canada, Croatia, Dominican Republic, France, Germany, Hong Kong, India, Kenya, Lebanon, Malawi, Malaysia, Marshall Islands, Kyrgyzstan, Nigeria, Pakistan, Palau, Palestine, Paraguay, Peru, Portugal, South Africa, South Sudan, Syria, Sweden, Thailand, Tunisia, Turkey, United Kingdom, and the United States.

This was not a simple selection process. Finding a balanced set of representative stories from around the world was hampered by linguistic barriers and a media tendency to focus on stories of young victims, "cute" children, or celebrities. On top of this, small Amnesty Sections are often highly stretched dealing with human rights crises; they may simply not have the capacity to work with children. We also needed to ensure the fully informed consent of case study subjects (and their families) before featuring them. This was partly because, in some places, an association with an Amnesty-branded product could represent a risk to their safety and privacy, and also because we wanted to explain the longevity of books and be sure they were comfortable with this level of exposure. In cases where our due diligence uncovered safety risks, we excluded those children from the book. Additional measures included sending a professional interviewer into a refugee camp in Bangladesh to talk to a Rohingya Muslim girl from Myanmar, as well as anonymizing a young Hong Kong activist facing possible life imprisonment because of social media posts. It is important to acknowledge that many young people around the world face real dangers in claiming their rights and being active citizens—this is especially the case for LGBTQ+ young people, girls, children with disabilities, those from minority or Indigenous groups, those who follow a minority faith in their country, or any young activists living under politically repressive regimes.

All the coauthors of *Know Your Rights and Claim Them* hoped to empower children's participation by centering their voices in the book's marketing, but it was not easy. Both AIS and AIUK created free classroom resources to help teachers explore child rights with students as well as online educational content that highlighted young people's voices, but awareness-raising among the general public was crucial. In normal circumstances, there would have been at least one in-person book launch event, but the initial 2021 launch had to be online because of the COVID pandemic. It featured Angelina Jolie in conversation with three child activists from Syria, Nigeria, and the UK. As the international coeditions roll out, media interest is rarely in the young people, child rights, coauthor Geraldine Van Bueren or Amnesty International, but rather on the Hollywood link. Sometimes we have been able to compromise with a joint interview with Jolie and young activists, whereby she uses her profile to amplify their voices. One cost is that Amnesty has had to relinquish PR opportunities, despite being the originator and lead writer.

The second of AIS's nonfiction child rights books, *These Rights Are Your Rights* (2024), is for younger children from ages eight to eleven. It has drawn on the same Open University findings and is also written in the second person, but the language is much simpler, the tone is lighter, and the book is illustrated. It includes case studies of (mainly) younger child activists, and the text is sprinkled with jokes to keep child readers entertained—while upholding their right to play, as the book reminds them. This book has benefited from thoughtful comments from teenagers in Italy, Moldova, and the UK and very useful feedback on text complexity from younger children at schools in Moldova and Italy with whom text extracts were trialed by Amnesty colleagues.

CONCLUSION

Children's literature is rich in citizenship education and human rights values, and Amnesty International's work demonstrates that fiction, picture books, and poetry can communicate them in a simple, sensitive, dynamic, and nonmoralizing way. By holding a human rights lens to literature, it is possible to enhance young readers' understanding of what they are reading, how it relates to them and to the world, and to support a deep-thinking process of critical inquiry with the provision of simple human rights educational resources. We have also learned that poetry and spoken word can empower young people from marginalized communities to explore and express their rights in a way that makes them feel heard.

Notwithstanding, three and a half decades since the adoption of the UNCRC, it remains challenging to uphold children's participation rights in the creation of a book for which they are the target audience. Of course, there is no "one-size-fits-all" process, but from my experience, the Amnesty child rights books were of immeasurably better quality precisely because of children's participation. The ongoing challenge appears to be rooted in societal norms that have not traditionally made time for child participation in decision-making. In a fast-paced adult world of commercial and professional deadlines, people fear any negative impact on costs and schedules; it may be easier to reinforce the infantilizing narrative that children's input is less valuable than that of adults. To paraphrase George Orwell, "everyone is equal, but some are more equal than others" (Orwell 1945).

The UNCRC's General Principles are sometimes simplified as the four Ps: provision, protection, prevention of harm, and participation. There is a risk of being so cautious to uphold children's rights to be protected that we neglect their participation rights. This attitude is further enabled by the commercial needs of businesses who are targeting adults to make the purchase, even if children are the end users. Likewise, NGOs—also chasing short-term income and action—also target adult audiences whom they can more easily and cheaply engage with an ongoing "user journey." In my experience, we have found that even when there is agreement to invite children's participation, there are further hurdles to surmount for which we are not always well-equipped. For example, children and young people may be so delighted to be consulted and so unused to articulating their opinions, that there is a risk that they say what they think we adults want to hear. Mitigating this risk requires particular listening skills and is time-consuming. The starting point may well be—as Eleanor Roosevelt said—in small places, close to home, with values-based book talk that encourages children and adults to share their ideas and feelings and learn how to articulate and how to listen.

The power of children's literature to give children and young people agency needs more focused attention, such as a long-term qualitative study into the lifelong impact of children's literature on their development. Questions that are worth consideration include: What does good, inclusive, and effective child participation look like? Who participates outside the sphere of our own personal and professional cohorts? How do we reach the most marginalized and vulnerable children and young people? What is equitable, given budget constraints and logistics, etc.? What data do we need to create the best products? How do we keep children and young people safe mentally, emotionally, and physically throughout a participatory process? How do we ensure they don't feel exploited but empowered? The answers, surely, lie in better collaboration, carried out with care. We need to work together. All those who care about humanity and a better world—those working in children's rights, literature, education, culture studies, sociology, and more. We need publishing and other businesses on board too, to bring about change in practice. It is children's right to be properly seen and heard in the literary world.

Anyone who has encountered the Amnesty International movement knows that taking action can change lives. And as Greta Thunberg famously said, "No one is too small to make a difference" (COP24 2018). The challenge for everyone with an interest in children's literature is to explore how creative, rights-respecting storytelling with, for, and by children can help all of us imagine and shape a more active citizenship based on equitable human rights for all children and young people everywhere.

NOTE

1. The books distributed were Quentin Blake, *Loveykins* (London: Random House, 2003); Sharon Creech, *Love That Dog* (London: Bloomsbury, 2001); Christopher Gregorowski and Niki Daly, *Fly, Eagle, Fly* (London: Frances Lincoln Children's Books, 2003); Pratima Mitchell and Caroline Binch, *Petar's Song* (London: Frances Lincoln Children's Books, 2004); Caroline Pitcher and Jackie Morris, *Mariana and the Merchild* (London: Frances Lincoln Children's Books, 2000); and Louis Sachar, *Holes* (London: Bloomsbury, 1998).

REFERENCES

Amnesty International, Angelina Jolie, and Geraldine V. Bueren. *Know Your Rights and Claim Them*. London: Andersen Press, 2021.
Amnesty International. *These Rights Are Your Rights: An Empowering Guide for Children Everywhere*. London: Andersen Press, 2024.
Amnesty International UK. *Dreams of Freedom*. London: Walker Books, 2015.

Amnesty International UK. *Here I Stand: Stories That Speak for Freedom*. London: Walker Books, 2016.

Amnesty International UK. *We Are All Born Free: The Universal Declaration of Human Rights in Pictures*. London: Frances Lincoln Children's Books, 2008.

Baird, Vanessa. *Sex, Love and Homophobia*. London: Amnesty International UK, 2004.

Bello, Armando, Marta Martinez Muñoz, Iván Rodríguez Pascual, and Maria Soledad Palacios Gálvez. *Small Voices, Big Dreams 2019: Violence Against Children as Explained by Children*. Spain and New York: ChildFund Alliance and Educo, 2019. Accessed March 24, 2024. https://reliefweb.int/report/world/small-voices-big-dreams-2019 -violence-against-children-explained-children.

Chamberlain, Liz, Jiniya Afroze, Victoria Cooper, and Trevor Collins. *Representing Children's Rights from Discussion Through to Illustration and Interpretation*. Milton Keynes: The Open University and Amnesty International, 2019. Accessed March 10, 2024. https://oro.open.ac.uk/68276/.

Chambers, Aidan. *Tell Me: Children, Reading, and Talk with The Reading Environment*. Stroud: Thimble Press, 2011.

Collins, Ross. *There's a Bear on My Chair*. London: Nosy Crow, 2015.

Jerome, Lee, Anna Liddle, and Helen Young. "Talking About Rights Without Talking About Rights: On the Absence of Knowledge in Classroom Discussions." *Human Rights Education Review* 4, no. 1 (2021), 8–26. doi:10.7577/hrer.3979.

Roosevelt, Eleanor. "The Great Question." United Nations. Accessed March 10, 2024. https://www.un.org/en/teach/human-rights.

Sims Bishop, Rudine. "Mirrors, Windows, and Sliding Doors." *Perspectives: Choosing and Using Books for the Classroom* 6, no 3 (1990), ix–xi.

"Story Explorer: Questions for Exploring Fiction." Amnesty International. Accessed March 24, 2024. www.amnesty.org.uk/story-explorer.

Szwarc, Josef. *Faces of Racism*. London: Amnesty International UK, 2001.

Tibbetts, Felisia. "Evolution of Human Rights Education Models." In *Human Rights Education: Theory, Research, Praxis*, edited by Monisha Bajaj. Philadelphia: University of Pennsylvania Press, 2017. Kindle edition.

"Universal Declaration of Human Rights." United Nations. Accessed March 10, 2024. https://www.ohchr.org/EN/UDHR/Documents/UDHR_Translations/eng.pdf.

"Words That Burn." Amnesty International. Accessed March 10, 2024. https://www.amnesty .org.uk/wordsthatburn.

Chapter 3

LABORS OF CARE

A Proposition of a Care-full Children's Culture Studies

JUSTYNA DESZCZ-TRYHUBCZAK

CARING APPROACHES IN CHILDREN'S CULTURE STUDIES

The conceptualization of children's literature scholarship as a "joint venture," proposed by Helma van Lierop-Debrauwer (2022), accurately summarizes numerous approaches interrogating the field's preoccupation with child-adult binary, intergenerational power imbalance, and aetonormativity (Nikolajeva 2009). These research directions include childist criticism, launched by Peter Hunt and continued by Sebastien Chapleau, who both argued for taking children's perspectives and experiences, including children's criticism, into account in critical practice. Drawing among others on Hunt and Chapleau, Michelle Superle (2016) proposed the child-centered critical approach to children's literature, which advocates valuing young readers' critical and creative responses to what they read and acknowledges works by child authors. More recently, Vanessa Joosen (2022) and Macarena García-González (2022) have also relied on the notion of childism to explore ageism in children's texts and affective children's literature criticism, respectively. Mary Galbraith proposed a general emancipatory model of childhood studies that would include children's literature criticism and identify *"ways to admit childhood desires, experience, and predicaments into all practices of the human community"* (2001: 194, emphasis original). Karen Coats argued for taking into account the "material, effective force" of love, manifested in "the scholars' genuine care for children and their futures" in research involving real child readers (2001: 143, 149). Andrew Melrose proposed looking at a children's book as the closest "we can get to a critical, visual, literary and literal hug," stressing the nurturing and community-building potential of children's literature (2012: n.p.).

An especially important contribution to this direction in children's literature and culture studies has been Marah Gubar's kinship model of child-adult relations, which has replaced the deficit and difference paradigms with an emphasis on agency and experience as something shared across generations, even in various forms or degrees. Gubar's proposition has also inspired an interest in children's creativity and (co)authorship, exemplified in studies by Elisabeth Wesseling (2019), Rachel Conrad (2020), and Helma van Lierop-Debrauwer and Sabine Steels (2021). The kinship model has also facilitated the emergence of interest in the notion of intergenerational solidarity as an important theme in texts addressed to young readers and a result of children's and adults' joint engagements with and collaborations on children's culture (see Deszcz-Tryhubczak and Jaques 2021, Deszcz-Tryhubczak and Kalla 2021). Both the kinship model and childism have catalyzed an interest in participatory research with young readers, including child-led research (see Aggleton 2018, Aggleton 2022, Deszcz-Tryhubczak 2016, Deszcz-Tryhubczak 2019, Chawar et al. 2018, Deszcz-Tryhubczak et al. 2019, Joosen 2019). Finally, García-González and Deszcz-Tryhubczak (2019, 2022) have explored posthumanist and new materialist perspectives to conceptualize children's literature and culture as relational networks and assemblages that include more-than-human agencies and forces.

Diverse as all these approaches are, they share what Gubar refers to as "a perspectival flip" (Gubar 2016: 300) from perceiving children and adults as separate species toward noticing, appreciating, and fostering the full continuum of child-adult relationships as they emerge among other relationalities constituting assemblages of children's culture and the world at large. In other words, they recenter the child from the position of the political, epistemological, and ethical exclusion toward an entity that is a part of the human and more-than-human relational networks in which the adult/child binary no longer holds (Murris and Kuby 2022: 4). Importantly, they also shed new light on the child's agency: It is neither an individual's ability to act intentionally, to make choices, or to self-initiate action to shape one's social environment nor a right that might be given to or possessed by the child. It is not a form of the child's becoming empowered by adults, either. It is rather a capacity that is shared and distributed as it emerges from ever-shifting relationalities and entanglements involving both children and adults in specific contexts. These "entangled relations which materialise, surround, and exceed children [and adults] as entities" unfold diversely across time and space (Spyrou 2018: 8) and may involve nonhuman materialities, agents, entities, forces, and intensities such as books, toys, classrooms, and institutions. Significantly, such a conceptual recentering of the child is not intended to reduce children's status but to create a flat or horizontal approach to agency that may facilitate our understanding of multiple relationships children (and adults, for that matter) have with/in the world around them. Furthermore, following up on the relational framing of (children's) agency, the child's citizenship is not "a status to be acquired, lost or refused by an individual" (Fox and Alldred 2019: 290); it is rather an emergent, fluid, and "relational capacity produced and reproduced in everyday material interactions, across a spectrum of activities" and "interactions between humans and nonhuman materialities" including "spaces and places, objects such as passports, ballot boxes and work credentials, as well as abstract concepts such as nationality and democracy" (Fox and Alldred 2019: 690, 692). Hence, we can view a child, as well as an adult for that matter, as constantly involved in an ongoing material and affective process of becoming-citizen (Fox and Alldred 2019), which in turn is just one of many other becomings we experience in our lives.

I suggest that the massive change in the scholarly perspective described above has been mobilized by care—for young and adult readers, for children's books and other media, for our scholarship, for the professional and public communities we participate in, and for the world around us—which in turn makes our field an example of caring research; that is, research trying to ensure the well-being of people and societies (Uusiautti and Määttä 2016: 4–5). It is this caring attitude shaping our work that is also indispensable in our commitment to do justice to the emergent nature of children's agency and citizenship—a commitment shaping this edited volume as well. I base my proposition on feminist scholars' work on relationalities as always involving care and on care as always relational and all-pervasive and, hence, a meaningful component of agency—an understanding of care that departs from viewing it as a matter of moral norms. As expressed in the definition of care by Berenice Fisher and Joan Tronto, caring can "be viewed as a species activity that includes everything that we do to maintain, continue, and repair our 'world' so that we can live in it as well as possible. That world includes our bodies, our selves, and our environment, all of which we seek to interweave in a complex, life-sustaining web" (Fisher and Tronto 1990: 41). Moreover, as stressed by feminist scholars working with posthumanism and new materialism, attentiveness, responsiveness, and responsibility involved in caring are also enacted in more-than-human-worlds with the human being as one of the many active participants in caring relationships. For María Puig de la Bellacasa (2017), care is networked and "distributed across a multiplicity of agencies and materials and supports our worlds as a thick mesh of relational obligation" (20). A number of feminist scholars also stress the importance of care ethics and relationality in contemporary academia and higher education, which are increasingly being subjected to neoliberal imperatives of competitiveness, performativity, and (self-)audit.

In this chapter, I rely on feminist accounts of care to reflect on how care and knowledge production in children's culture scholarship come together to make more just worlds possible. As our work centers on children and childhoods, we are inevitably involved in social, cultural, and political debates, for the child is central to adults' efforts to preserve the past, define the present, and determine the future (see Lee 2013). Childhood and children are repositories of adults' anxieties, frustrations, hopes, fantasies, and ambitions. They are also linked to the survival of our species. As Meg Rosoff puts it in her chapter in part I, "How the future of the planet looks depends on children." She also professes that, through her craft, she tries to assume the responsibility for helping children "understand the power that resides in their own heads, the power to write a new story for the future." Following up on Rosoff's commitment to counteract the cultural, social, and political negligence of children as critical thinkers, agents, and citizens, I propose that children's literature and culture scholars' choices concerning what, who, why, and how we research also have an ideological impact on broader issues concerning childhood, including how children's agency and citizenship are mobilized, produced, and perceived in our societies and communities.

I invite the reader to reflect on care by sharing my own experience of practicing caring research. I also comment on the lack of understanding and acknowledgment of its care-fullness caused by limited accounts of what knowing can be and create, which in turn results from neoliberal ideas of impact and research use when we experience the pressure toward narrowly understood dissemination or translation of scholarly research to public spheres. I also speculate about the possibility of research with children and more-than-human others that moves away from the human-centered and individualistic conceptualization of the child reader/viewer/user/creator/agent/citizen, toward the child as always already situated in relational entanglements and as becoming attuned to new more-than-human relationalities through encounters with texts of culture. I see this approach as an example of caring research as it both strengthens child-adult relations and foregrounds children's and adults' learning with and caring for one another and for the complex and interdependent more-than-human worlds cocreated by various other beings, entities, and forces on earth.

However, caring research is also about cultivating spaces to care for our colleagues and students through positive relationships in research collectives; that is, through mutual engagement, collaboration, trustworthiness, and constructiveness. Moreover, as Puig de la Bellacasa points out, care is "unthinkable as something abstracted from its situatedness" (2017: 7). Therefore, my reflection on care in children's culture studies also needs to bring attention to how we work and interact with each other by highlighting examples of current initiatives in the field that facilitate a culture of solidarity as an antidote to the individualist competitive model of scholarship promoted by universities in neoliberalism. I argue that by modeling care-full practices in our institutions and thus transforming them from within, we may also produce caring exchanges between academia and society, including attentiveness to children's agency.

Making visible the work done is a care-full act in itself (Mol 2008: 2). Yet this interest in various aspects of children's culture scholarship is also to develop a general metanarrative of our field that centralizes care as holding potential for a better future for ourselves, our colleagues, our students, societies, and the earth. It is to show that the intellectually flourishing enterprise of children's culture scholarship is an important academic field propagating an ethos of empathy, openness, collectivity, and collaboration between scholars and the intergenerational public and among scholars themselves. As such, our practices of thinking, knowing, and doing in research, as well as our pedagogies, supervision, and mentoring, can substantially contribute to the imperative of addressing the uncertain futures of the planet and to coping with the urgent challenges of today's societies. Ultimately, they may help us imagine and build the human-more-than-human communities of which we wish to be a part. In part I, Rosoff writes that

> [i]f schools are going to train a better class of political leaders, entrepreneurs, scientists, parents, and social policy-makers, they—WE— have to ask ourselves which qualities we want to promote. If we require a more compassionate, more radical, less class-riven and self-centered definition of success, where does it begin?
>
> I am hopelessly prejudiced, but I believe that at least some of it begins with books.

As I propose in this chapter, some of it also begins with children's literature and culture scholarship.

AN ORIENTATION TOWARD CARE

Why and how should we care at all? How can we care in the contemporary world? How are care and knowledge production connected? What kind of knowledge should we produce, and how do we create more just worlds? And why should we bother at all? Monika Rogowska-Stangret suggests that such questions, which I believe we should ask ourselves relentlessly, direct us toward a general understanding of care as a prerequisite for any ethics, "that is, any engagement in the world" (2020: 19). Rogowska-Stangret's conclusion follows from earlier feminist accounts of care. Below, I present a brief and selective overview of feminist approaches to care that inform my further discussion of children's culture scholarship as a practice motivated by and promoting care-fullness including caring attention to children's emergent capacities for agency and citizenship (Fox and Alldred 2019: 690).

Tronto and Fisher's definition of care quoted earlier is explicitly focused on values and practices of fostering relationalities. Care can thus be conceptualized as a disposition, a practice, and a process (Bozalek 2016: 84) aimed at creating a better world in situated contexts. Tronto (2013) further develops her notion of care by distinguishing five phases of caring activity. The first such phase is *caring about*, which means becoming aware of and paying attention to the needs of the care receiver. The second phase is *responsibility* that calls on the caregiver to respond to the care receiver's needs. The third phase involves *competence* and the provision of adequate care. The fourth phase—*responsiveness*—refers to how care receivers respond to the care provided to them. Finally, the fifth phase—*caring-with*—draws attention to the development of trust and solidarity over time. Importantly, for Tronto, the notion of caring-with may serve as an alternative to *caring-for*, the latter of which distances caregivers and care receivers. In contrast, caring-with reflects the fundamental relationality of care. As Vivienne Bozalek comments on caring-with, "Conditions of trust are created where reliance can be developed through the caring practices of others. Solidarity develops when people realise they are relational beings who are better off engaged in such processes of care together rather than alone" (2016: 18; see also Romano 2020).

Tronto's approach has become the basis of a renewed interest in care as a prerequisite for relations between humans, more-than-humans, and the earth. Feminist new materialism and posthumanism, in particular, draw attention to care as vital for respectful, responsive, and attentive relationships through which the world comes into being. Karen Barad argues, for instance, that ethics "is a matter of the ethical call that is embodied in the very worlding of the world" (2007: 160), thus alerting us to our shared ethical engagements with the world around us, including, in our case, children's culture and its young audiences. For Donna Haraway, "caring means becoming subject to the unsettling obligation of curiosity, which requires knowing more at the end of the day than at the beginning" (2008: 36). This care-full curiosity drives us to become attentive to and appreciate the world in its ongoing becoming. Puig de la Bellacasa proposes that caring and relating are connected on the ontological level as "to care about something, or for somebody, is inevitably to create relation" (2012: 198). Hence, care is "concomitant to life—not something forced upon living beings by a moral order; yet it obliges in that for life to be livable it needs being fostered" (2012: 198). Such understandings provoke questions about what it means to care about human-more-than-human worlds and how we can persevere in the practical labor of care-full relations.

Many scholars in feminist new materialism and posthumanism also comment on ethics of care in practices of knowledge production and in academia in general. Barad (2017) proposes the term ethico-onto-epistemology to show that knowledge, ethics, and being coconstitute one another and that knowledge is not something we acquire on our own but something we engage with ethically because ethics constitutes us rather than being an external norm we follow. According to Puig de la Bellacasa, as "knowing and thinking are inconceivable without a multitude of relations that also make possible the worlds we think with," "relations of thinking and knowing require care" as well (2012: 198). Importantly, this integration of care into knowledge production allows for affectionate and emotional knowing that opposes the notion of the objective and value-free or neutral inquiry. Thinking with care in research acknowledges feelings—of researchers and nonacademic research participants—and may bring about substantial positive transformations, such as the formation of nurturing researcher communities (Staffa et al. 2021: 51) and the cultivation of mutual trust and respect in research with humans and more-than-humans.

An exceptionally productive concept developed in feminist new materialism and posthumanism in relation to ethics of care and knowledge production is the notion of response-ability, which links responsibility and accountability with an ability and willingness to respond. It is also closely related to curiosity, attentiveness, trust, and rendering each other capable (Bozalek 2020). Bozalek helpfully brings together various theoretical understandings of response-ability that all see it "as being central to flourishing or living and dying in the world well, or as well as possible" (2020: 142). For Haraway, it is "the cultivation of the capacity of response in the context of living and dying in worlds for which one is for, with others" (2015: 257). Barad sees it as "differential responsiveness (as performatively articulated and accountable) to what matters" (2007: 380), while, in Vinciane Despret's work, it is connected to "rendering each other capable," that is, enlarging each other's potential and competences (see Despret 2008, 2016). In another account of response-ability, Vivienne Bozalek and Michalinos Zembylas also refer to "the practice of attentiveness" (2017: 67). In order to cultivate our ability to respond, we need an attentiveness, close and careful engagement, and sensibility enabling us "to pay due attention" (2017: 67). We also need to listen with "discernment and care to what is and what is not being expressed" and open ourselves "to being affected by another" in order to notice what is significant for them (2017: 67). Finally, Haraway also talks of cultivating curiosity, which means finding others interesting without assuming that one already knows about others, and instead letting oneself be surprised and intrigued by them—often through unanticipated encounters (2016: 27). Bozalek and Zembylas stress that cultivating curiosity is a practice that changes those involved in it, often in unpredictable ways. When seen in the context of research, response-ability is then "not just about what an ethics committee instructs you to do in research" (Bozalek 2020: 142); it is rather about respectful, receptive, and reciprocal encounters with others. It is also about posing questions that "would interest both the respondents and the researcher, questions that matter to the respondents," as well as about being attentive to how the participants are responding to the research process and about being ready to modify it in order to respect their needs. These ideas are echoed in Rogowska-Stangret's proposition of care as a methodology, which encourages a reflection on learning "how to hear, read, engage, negotiate, [and] ask the right question" in our research engagements (2020: 3).

The above account of care seems relevant to children's literature and culture scholarship if we conceive of it as practiced as a joint child-adult venture dependent on intergenerational and human-more-than-human kinships. These kinships, in turn, rely on response-ability and care as prerequisites for promoting epistemic justice through collective knowing, being, feeling, and doing that shifts the child-adult binary toward an intergenerational rendering each other capable and a mutual curiosity regarding children's and adults' lifeworlds. In the following section, I provide examples of such research, commenting on institutional contexts devaluing care. As I show further in the chapter, care-full processes and acts also occur among scholars in our field. While they may seem only indirectly related to actual research, I argue that they are indispensable for creating an environment that enables the development of caring approaches to children and childhood, including issues of agency and citizenship, within and outside academia.

CARING CHILDREN'S CULTURE RESEARCH
AT CARE-LESS UNIVERSITIES

Thinking back to the participatory research projects I coconducted with child researchers in the years 2016 to 2018, I have come to see them as practices aimed at fostering and responding to the process of children's becoming-citizen and at translating research findings into outcomes that make a positive, imaginative, affirmative, and hopeful contribution to society (see Chawar et al. 2018 and Deszcz-Tryhubczak et al. 2019). The successful collaboration with children motivated Mateusz Marecki, my colleague and coresearcher, and myself to think of ways in which we could further democratize academic practices in children's literature studies. We achieved this goal by publishing two peer-reviewed articles coauthored with the young researchers. Although research participants often produce the research itself and are usually involved in data collection or research dissemination, academics usually write down the results on their own. We concluded that to build positive relationships with children, we needed to create opportunities to establish such relationships in our work with them. Joint academic writing seemed to us a promising approach to do so (see Deszcz-Tryhubczak and Marecki 2021). Thinking about this venture with care ethics, I also see it as a sincere attempt to care for the child participants. In the research process itself, we cocreated safe and nonhierarchical spaces in which both the children and the adults were able to reflect on matters that concerned them the way they wanted to. The collaborative writing itself represented a form of mutual empowerment and rendering each other capable across age and professional divides. It also counteracted adult-centered knowledge production in children's culture studies and provided a model for intergenerational response-able collaborations and epistemic justice.

Despite the academic interest following our articles coauthored with the young researchers, for a long time, we had found little institutional understanding and support for our research, as it was perceived as public outreach. The situation changed during the recent national evaluation of Polish universities conducted by the Polish Ministry of Education and Science and completed at the beginning of 2022. Importantly, the impact of scientific activities on the functioning of society and the economy was taken into account for the first time and constituted as much as 20 percent of the whole evaluation. Universities were required to provide tangible evidence of the relationship between the results of research and the economy, the functioning of public administration, health protection, arts and culture, environmental protection, national security and defense, or other factors affecting the civilizational development of society. To me, the evaluation of social impact was a bold attempt at changing our academic culture toward accountable knowledge construction, toward research addressed to audiences beyond the university, and toward bridging the gap between scholarly expertise and public interests and needs. In care-full terms, it also promised attention to the voices of "those who have the most to say [but] may not be those who speak the eloquent language of the academy or of . . . public policymakers" (Tronto 1995: 145). I was thrilled to learn that children's culture research projects at my university, and especially the activities of the scholars from the Centre for Research on Children's and Young Literature at the Faculty of Letters, were selected as one of the fields that could provide evidence of their social impact. My colleagues and I saw that decision not only as a useful opportunity to highlight our joint and individual work at our university but also as an avenue for drawing attention to the role of children's culture scholarship and academia more generally as vital elements of assemblages that contribute to the emergence of children's agency and citizenship.

As I was assigned the task of providing evidence of the social impact of the aforementioned participatory research projects, I decided to highlight the two peer-reviewed articles coauthored with the child researchers as proof of both how intergenerational knowledge production may impact members of society and how it may question adultism entrenched in academia: those articles were not only scholarly publications documenting research but also a form of children's participation in academic knowledge-making, thereby standing for possible transformations it might undergo. In other words, they enabled a two-directional movement animating our research as not only remaining for public use but also returning to academia and changing it into an institution responsive and attentive to various kinds of knowledge, ways of being and working, and experiences.

I presented this argument to show the articles' viability as evidence of social impact, but it was not appreciated by the expert evaluators. As I read in their comments, shared with me by the university administrators, they insisted that the articles are unusual forms of public outreach and that they document our scholarly activities. However, as such, they do not constitute the evidence for a change resulting from the research and do not testify to their social impact in the form of new attitudes, decisions, or behaviors of children and young people as representatives of civil society. I believe that in this logic, academia and the university are very visibly separate from society and cannot be transformed as a consequence of interactions with the general public. I find such thinking hard to accept as, to me, it negates the sense of the university as a space of deliberation, compromise, and accountability. It also denies the role of research in creating opportunities for generating spaces of equality and widening the sense of what the common good might entail for various parties and stakeholders. Finally, it testifies to a very restricted and restrictive understanding of academia's social impact that, as our case indicated, may constrain rather than enable individual and collective children's civic capacities and bring their citizen capacities into effect. Yet a care-full university depends on society and on the work from the ground up. Dismissing the situated work of care, as it happened in our case, contributes to what Puig de la Bellacasa refers to as "building disengaged versions of reality that mask the 'mediations' that sustain and connect our worlds, our doings, our knowings" (2012: 210) through the relational practices of response-ability. Becoming response-able also necessitates "altering one's power" and developing vulnerability: "It requires that the kinds of boundaries and divisions that allow academia to thrive be dissolved. It requires not only a patience to engage with the world more broadly, but the courage to face uncertain, imprecise, hidden and complex realities that are in flux and that are all implicated in contemporary practices of power, care and knowledge production and transmission" (Tronto 2020: 159).

The evaluation we received discredited the care-full effects of our child-adult collaboration, thereby excluding a critical reflection on and possibly a radical disturbance of "the hierarchies that elevate theory, research, and academic knowledge production to a higher plane than method, community-based dialog, and non-conventional academic writing" (Nagar 2013: 3). It is perhaps also telling that the university administrators were not interested in an in-depth discussion following up on the experts' comments.

Ours might be an isolated case, but it reveals the difficulty of disrupting standardized evaluations and normative conceptualizations of research. Thinking with care ethics requires a sustained effort of "seeking inventive ways to disrupt . . . normative logics and practices of research" (Shefer 2020: 112). Taking into account the proximities of children's culture scholarship, education research, and childhood studies, as well as societies' dependence on children and childhoods, we certainly have a lot of avenues for engaged, ethical, and caring scholarship based on collaborations across academia and various nonacademic communities in which we belong. I would like to think that the growing interest in children's agency and participation, as well as in intergenerational research and creative ventures as clearly visible in this volume, signals that our field is gaining momentum in the search for ways to promote care-full knowledge-making that can help us create an academia open to inner transformation and, in particular, to the generative processes of children's citizenship as decentering traditional knowledge production.

My own interest in continuing the caring research into children's literature and culture originates from my response-ability regarding the ontological and epistemological challenge of the Anthropocene as the concept that defies our current perception and understanding of reality. I would venture that—in light of the planetary risks of the Anthropocene—it is our responsibility as scholars to identify practices that let multiple entanglements of the human and the more-than-human move to the foreground over the humanist notions of agency. As we are all, regardless of age, facing the progressing destruction of our planet as a multispecies habitat, we need to confront it not just by hoping for a better life in the future but also by noticing and cherishing small-scale possibilities for refiguring our place in the anthropogenically damaged world and by learning to live well in it here and now. Hence, my research endeavors have transitioned toward possible ways in which children's literature and culture studies could move beyond human-centered knowledge production, as well as humanist understandings of children's agency, in order to appreciate and respond to human-more-than-human relationalities that enliven our worlds, including children's experiences of texts and our research practices. How could scholars studying children's culture and young audiences become attentive to knowledge generated through dynamic interactions among multiple beings, entities, and forces on our shared planet, including the lively common worlds which children, adults, and texts coconstitute with other beings and entities? Could we think of citizen formation taking place in the context of human-more-than-human entanglements?

As I suggest elsewhere (2023), one way of developing such projects is worlding (see Haraway 2008, Haraway 2016, and Malone and Murris 2020); that is, enabling the emergence of a common world of relations and interdependencies based on responsiveness and respect. Affrica Taylor and Miriam Giugni emphasize "[l]earning how to 'world,'" which means learning "how to be responsible in and for our common worlds; how to bring others into our common worlds; how to form 'questioning relationships' with these others; how to negotiate common interests in common worlds; and how to practise a relational ethics" (2012: 117). Motivated by such matters of care, projects premised on children's participation in and interactions with culture and society could move toward more-than-human participatory research, which is done *with* rather than *on* more-than-humans and relies on methods that invite them to participate actively in the research process. More-than-human participatory research is then about living with various creatures and entities and learning with and from them instead of approaching them as objects of knowledge (see Bastian et al. 2017). Such a research framework applies to almost anything because it insists that human social worlds are always more-than-human social worlds; that is, they are composed of relations between humans, nonhuman life, and nonhuman forces (see Noorani and Brigstocke 2018). If children can be key actors with expert knowledge, perhaps this status could indeed be extended to more-than-humans, which, of course, requires asking anew how knowledge is produced, by whom, for whom, for what interests, and for what purposes. What might plants and animals seek from participatory research? What about rivers, mountains, or seas? How could we care for such participants? How would children's culture matter in such projects? And, most centrally for the concerns raised in this volume, how could we conceive of becoming-citizen as a collective process emerging from the ever-changing human-more-than-human interdependencies rather than, for example, from "individual rights and responsibilities and shared national values" (Mulcahy and Healy 2023: 9)? I have not yet tried implementing research methods that would bring together children's culture, children and more-than-human beings, forces, and entities. Yet the sheer entertainment of the possibility of such openings prompts a reflection about ways of creating new forms of knowledge-making that would enable cultivating "the openness and the sensitivities necessary to be curious, to understand and respond in ways that are never perfect, never innocent, never final, and yet always required" (van Dooren and Rose 2016: 90), and, as I would like to add, always demand care.

COMMUNITIES OF CARE IN CHILDREN'S CULTURE STUDIES

While the above examples of children's culture scholarship emphasize care as an object of study and a methodological concern, I now discuss initiatives that engender an ethos of care, relationality, and reciprocity in our scholarly lives, thereby working against the care-less subjectivities imposed on us at neoliberal universities. These hospitable spaces foster dialogical cocreation of knowledge, enable us to enact caring relationalities in teaching and networking, and offer support in our academic career development. Ultimately, they are also instrumental in promoting care in societies.

One such care-full environment is the International Research Society for Children's Literature, established in 1970, bringing together scholars working on children's literature and culture from all over the world. "The Statement of Principles of The International Research Society for Children's Literature," as well as the IRSCL statements on the climate emergency and the war in Ukraine, is a tangible example of response-ability and accountability to colleagues and society in general. Moreover, when I served on the IRSCL board in the years 2017 to 2021, I took part in endeavors caring for colleagues, such as providing travel and research grants. As the coordinator of the IRSCL mentoring program in my time on the board, I also witnessed diverse practices of attentiveness, curiosity, and rendering each other capable taking place between the mentors and the mentees as, in the course of the program, they were becoming more and more entangled in a relation with each other, which involved not only an exchange of ideas or creating academic alliances but also developing trust, kindness, and sometimes friendships well exceeding the requirements of networking. The mentoring program has been successfully continued by other colleagues and offers a number of new activities integrating the mentees and mentors, including a reading group. Mentoring is also an important part of the editorial process in *International Research in Children's Literature*, the Society's journal. As the reviews editor since 2014, I have solicited reviews of non-Anglophone scholarly publications in children's literature studies to ensure better visibility of colleagues publishing in their native languages. I have also encouraged early career scholars to submit reviews as a way for them to hone their academic writing skills. It must be stressed that it is emerging researchers and nontenured scholars that especially benefit from such affirmative practices and spaces, as they may feel pressured to conform to their institutional contexts and act care-lessly, for example, through self-promotion that disregards their relationalities with colleagues. Being faced with constant (self-)audit of quality and success, the individualization of academic labor, as well as growing workloads, scholars are bound to find committing to peer-to-peer care increasingly difficult.

An important caring endeavor of the IRSCL is its biannual congresses, which bring together numerous scholars from all over the world and provide a welcoming forum for early career researchers. The challenging, and indeed care-related, dilemma facing the Society at the moment is whether to continue organizing onsite congresses or move to hybrid or fully virtual conferencing. While it is obvious that we all need opportunities for in-person interactions with our colleagues—whether for work purposes or to satisfy our need for companionship—we have to weigh our preferences against our care for planetary health and equity, especially in times of the energy crisis resulting from Russia's war on Ukraine. Participation in onsite academic conferences, including participants' long-distance aviation travel, is expensive, emissions-intensive, and inequitable. There is ample research indicating that online formats of conferences of a global reach do not necessarily compromise the perceived quality of scholarly exchange and social interaction, the latter being continuously improved thanks to technical innovation (see, e.g., Yates et al. 2022; Niner and Wassermann 2021). Finally, online congresses would probably be a welcome option for all those researchers (often women) who are unable to travel as they take care of their small children, elderly relatives, or family members with chronic diseases or disabilities. Yet online conferencing also has its problems, such as time zone limitations, digital divides, and technical obstacles, such as website overloads and bandwidth issues. There is no straightforward answer as to whether moving the IRSCL congresses online ultimately is a more care-full practice than organizing them onsite. Hopefully, the issue of making the congresses sustainable and equitable becomes a matter of broader discussion among the IRSCL members not only because of the prohibitive costs of air travel, accommodation, and congress fees but also in light of the IRSCL statement on the climate emergency and the declaration that "[a]s scholars, we are well positioned to use our privilege to amplify the voices of young people who are demanding immediate change" (https://www.irscl.org/statements). Again, we can see how the choices we make in our institutional lives may have an impact beyond academia, including children's participation in political and social life.

Another important and most promising care-full community-building initiative is the establishment of the European Children's Literature Research Network in 2022, which indicates that scholars in our field continue to need supportive professional spaces beyond their institutions. The Network's manifesto, authored by scholars from Croatia, Germany, Italy, Montenegro, Norway, and Poland and first announced at The Child and the Book Conference 2022, itself an initiative aimed at fostering exchanges of expertise among early career and senior researchers, emphasizes the intention to promote research on European children's literatures, especially by scholars who have difficulties accessing international journals and conferences and whose work is thus visible only or mostly in their own countries (Cackowska et al. 2022). An important goal of The Network is also to support initiatives involving early career scholars, such as summer schools, graduate conferences, and joint publishing. As highlighted in the manifesto, such endeavors often occur "against the backdrop of the typical institutional marginalisation of children's literature research at universities" (Cackowska et al. 2022). While such professional ghettoes (Coats 2001: 409) are, fortunately, gradually ceasing to exist, the formation of The Network addresses the persistent need for enacting care and kinship as attuned to the specificities of our institutional and national circumstances in order not to further entrench economic, social, and political divides among scholars, which may also translate into how much and what kind of attention and recognition are given to children's agency and citizenship in more and less privileged parts of the world.

An example of a venture combining care-full scholarly and administrative interdependencies with caring pedagogies is The Erasmus Mundus International Master: Children's Literature, Media and Culture program (2018 to 2024), created by a consortium of six universities and attracting hundreds of students from all over the world. Its success can be ascribed not only to the high quality of the scholarly contents, teaching, and administration but also to the response-ability shared across the program, both between the staff and the students and within these two groups. The mutual support and openness regarding the participants' individual predicaments related, for example, to the COVID-19 pandemic or the Russian war against Ukraine; the encouragement for the students' initiatives, such as their own scholarly events and curatorial projects; mentoring them regarding their participation in conferences, publications, and PhD applications; and shared learning as the students and their supervisors collaborate on MA dissertations have resulted in the emergence of a unique, like-minded, and nurturing community that has overcome cultural and institutional gaps. Such communities are a precondition of a knowledge production that can offset the alienating conditions of the neoliberal higher education. More fundamentally, as most of the program alumni become, or in some cases already are, professionals working with children, they have the potential and opportunities to introduce caring practices they experienced in the CLMC in their work outside it.

The above are only selected examples of care-full ventures integrating scholars of children's culture. Caring acts also sustain joint editorial projects, research centers, summer schools (e.g., The Children's Literature summer school at the University of Antwerp), and conferences, including graduate student conferences (e.g., the biennial Master of Arts in Children's Literature conference at the University of British Columbia). There is no doubt that we need to persevere in developing socially just and collaborative communities, especially when most of us experience fear and insecurity related to competition for grants, publications, and constant review and audit processes that characterize the neoliberal knowledge economy, which in turn, as I have tried to show, also affect how children's agency and citizenship are mobilized, produced, and valued in societies at large. Importantly, as most of the above-mentioned initiatives have been undertaken to respond to situations unfolding in front of our eyes, they are response-able actions that have come into being through our relational capacities. While we can choose to pursue an ethos of care, caring acts often emerge and evolve *in situ*, sometimes as a response to an emergency or as a subtle form of resistance and not as intentional acts directed toward a particular end. We become care-full whenever we are ready to respond to ethical calls that we receive practically all the time as academics. This process is never finished; it is always in-between, and it is happening all the time. Peer-to-peer care and caring pedagogies thus constitute a vital element of our academic subjectivities that may, in turn, translate into research and, more broadly, social practices addressing children's agency and their citizen subjectivities.

CONTINUING TO CARE

I was writing this chapter at the time of the continuing coronavirus threat, the intensifying climate emergency, the appalling brutality of Russian aggression against Ukraine, and the harrowing Israeli–Palestinian conflict, all of which affect current and future children. I cannot overemphasize the significance of collective caring for human-more-than human worlds, including our research practices and professional lives, themselves often situated in inhospitable environments. I have, therefore, relied on feminist thought to elaborate forms of commitment to care ethics in current children's culture studies, highlighting the role of care as a salient, if not fundamental, aspect of agencies emerging in our field—both those of adults and of children. To conclude, I would like to reiterate the importance of children's culture scholarship as modeling and contributing to care-full research and pedagogical approaches and community practices as ways to sustain hope and resilience in the face of global, national, and local challenges we face in our scholarly lives and elsewhere and which we often share with children. One of these challenges, let me stress again, is the divisive and competitive academia, in which success often hinges on our self-governmentality and conformity to institutional demands, normativities, and hierarchies. Care-full knowledge-making and pedagogies may help us resist its damaging pressures. Simultaneously, they may help us to promote care and response-ability, including attentiveness to children's agency, as an important contribution to our societies. While I was able to refer to only a few examples of caring scholarly practices, there is no doubt that children's culture scholarship abounds with such projects, and I strongly encourage colleagues to seek ways to render them more visible as they will serve as an inspiration both in our community and elsewhere to cultivate commitments to care and to imagine alternative, sustainable, and creative ways of doing scholarship for the sake of a more just and livable world for younger and older generations alike.

REFERENCES

Aggleton, Jen. "Where Are the Children in Children's Collections? An Exploration of Ethical Principles and Practical Concerns Surrounding Children's Participation in Collection Development." *New Review of Children's Literature and Librarianship* 24, no. 1 (2018), 1–17. doi:10.1080/13614541.2018.1429122.

Aggleton, Jen. "Pictures and Picturing: Mental Imagery Whilst Reading Illustrated Novels." *Cambridge Journal of Education* 53, no. 1 (2022), 79–95. doi:10.1080/030576 4x.2022.2081669.

Barad, Karen. *Meeting the Universe Halfway: Quantum Physics and the Entanglement of Matter and Meaning*. Durham: Duke University Press, 2007.

Bastian, Michelle, Owain Jones, Niamh Moore, and Emma Roe, editors. *Participatory Research in More-than-Human Worlds*. Abingdon: Routledge, 2017.

Bozalek, Vivienne. "The Political Ethics of Care and Feminist Posthuman Ethics: Contributions to Social Work." In *Rethinking Values and Ethics in Social Work*, edited by Richard Hugman and Jan Carter, 80–96. London and New York: Palgrave Macmillan, 2016.

Bozalek, Vivienne. "Rendering Each Other Capable: Doing Response-able Research Responsibly." In *Navigating the Postqualitative, New Materialist and Critical Posthumanist Terrain Across Disciplines*, edited by Karin Murris, 135–49. London: Routledge, 2020.

Bozalek, Vivienne. "Towards a Response-able Pedagogy Across Higher Education Institutions in Post-Apartheid South Africa: An Ethico-Political Analysis." *Education as Change* 21, no. 2 (2017), 62–85. https://eric.ed.gov/?id=EJ1156440.

Bozalek, Vivienne, and Michalinos Zembylas. "Towards a Response-able Pedagogy Across Higher Education Institutions in Post-Apartheid South Africa: an Ethico-Political Analysis." *Education as Change* 21, no. 2 (2017), 62–85. https://eric.ed.gov/?id=EJ1156440.

Cackowska, Małgorzata, Marnie Campagnaro, Anna Czernow, Nina Goga, Svetlana Kalezić Radonjić, Smiljana Narancic Kovac, Bettina Kümmerling-Meibauer, and Jörg Meibauer. European Children's Literature Research Network. Manifesto Presented to The Child and the Book Conference, Valletta, Malta (2022).

Chapleau, Sebastien. "Childist Criticism and the Silenced Voice of the Child: A Widening Critical and Institutional Re-Consideration of Children's Literature." In *Stories for Children, Histories of Childhood*, edited by Rosie Findlay and Sébastien Salbayre, 85–106. Tours: Presses Universitaires François-Rabelais, 2007. Accessed January 8, 2023. https://books.openedition.org/pufr/4946.

Chapleau, Sebastien. "Work in Progress: Children's Literature and Childist Criticism— Towards an Institutional Re-Consideration." PhD diss., University of Cardiff, 2009. Accessed January 8, 2023. https://orca.cardiff.ac.uk/id/eprint/54518/.

Chawar, Ewa, Justyna Deszcz-Tryhubczak, Katarzyna Kowalska, Olga Maniakowska, Mateusz Marecki, Milena Palczyńska, Eryk Pszczołowski, and Dorota Sikora. "Children's Voices in the Polish Canon Wars: Participatory Research in Action." *International Research in Children's Literature* 11, no. 2 (2018), 111–31. doi:10.3366/ircl.2018.0269.

Coats, Karen S. "Keepin' It Plural: Children's Studies in the Academy." *Children's Literature Association Quarterly* 26, no. 3 (2001), 140–50. doi:10.1353/chq.0.1324.

Coats, Karen. "Fish Stories: Teaching Children's Literature in a Postmodern World." *Pedagogy* 1, no. 2 (2001), 405–9. doi:10.1215/15314200-1-2-405.

Conrad, Rachel. *Time for Childhoods: Young Poets and Questions of Agency*. Amherst: University of Massachusetts Press, 2020.

Despret, Vinciane. "The Becomings of Subjectivity in Animal Worlds." *Subjectivity* 23, no. 1 (2008), 123–39. doi:10.1057/sub.2008.15.

Despret, Vinciane. *What Would Animals Say If We Asked the Right Questions?* Minneapolis: University of Minnesota Press, 2018.

Deszcz-Tryhubczak, Justyna. "Using Literary Criticism for Children's Rights: Toward a Participatory Research Model of Children's Literature Studies." *The Lion and the Unicorn* 40, no. 2 (2016), 215–31. doi:10.1353/uni.2016.0012.

Deszcz-Tryhubczak, Justyna. "Thinking with Deconstruction: Book-Adult-Child Events in Children's Literature Research." *Oxford Literary Review* 41, no. 2 (2019), 185–201. doi:10.3366/olr.2019.0278.

Deszcz-Tryhubczak, Justyna. "Research with Children, Weeds, and a Book." In *Children's Cultures After Childhood*, edited by Justyna Deszcz-Tryhubczak and Macarena García-González, 122–36. Amsterdam: John Benjamins Publishing Company, 2023.

Deszcz-Tryhubczak, Justyna, and Macarena García-González. "Thinking and Doing with Childism in Children's Literature Studies." *Children & Society* 37, no. 4 (2022), 1037–51. doi:10.1111/chso.12619.

Deszcz-Tryhubczak, Justyna, and Zoe Jaques, editors. *Intergenerational Solidarity in Children's Literature and Film*. Jackson: University Press of Mississippi, 2021.

Deszcz-Tryhubczak, Justyna, and Irena Barbara Kalla, editors. *Children's Literature and Intergenerational Relationships: Encounters of the Playful Kind*. Cham: Palgrave Macmillan, 2021.

Deszcz-Tryhubczak, Justyna, and Mateusz Marecki. "A Meta-Critical Reflection on Academic Writing with Child Researchers." In *Ethics and Integrity in Research with Children and Young People*, edited by Grace Spencer, 213–27. Bingley: Emerald Publishing, 2021.

Deszcz-Tryhubczak, Justyna, Mateusz Marecki, Ewa Chawar, Magdalena Kaczkowska, Katarzyna Kowalska, Aleksandra Kulawik, Maja Ożlańska, Milena Palczyńska, Natalia Parcheniak, and Eryk Pszczołowski. "Productive Remembering of Childhood: Child–Adult Memory-Work with the School Literary Canon." *Humanities* 8, no. 2 (2019), 74. doi:10.3390/h8020074.

Fisher, Berenice, and Joan Tronto. "Toward a Feminist Theory of Caring." In *Circles of Care: Work and Identity in Women's Lives*, edited by Emily. K. Abel and Margaret K. Nelson, 35–62. Albany: State University of New York Press, 1990.

Fox, Nick J., and Pam Alldred. "Assembling Citizenship: Sexualities Education, Micropolitics and the Becoming-Citizen." *Sociology* 53, no. 4 (2019), 689–706. doi:10.1177/0038038518822889.

Galbraith, Mary. "Hear My Cry: A Manifesto for an Emancipatory Childhood Studies Approach to Children's Literature." *The Lion and the Unicorn* 25, no. 2 (2001), 187–205. doi:10.1353/uni.2001.0019.

García-González, Macarena. "Towards an Affective Childist Literary Criticism." *Children's Literature in Education* 53 (2022), 360–75. https://doi.org/10.1007/s10583-022-09500-0.

García-González, Macarena, and Justyna Deszcz-Tryhubczak. "New Materialist Openings to Children's Literature Studies." *International Research in Children's Literature* 13, no. 1 (2020), 45–60. doi:10.3366/ircl.2020.0327.

Gubar, Marah. "The Hermeneutics of Recuperation: What a Kinship-Model Approach to Children's Agency Could Do for Children's Literature and Childhood Studies." *Jeunesse: Young People, Texts, Cultures* 8, no. 1 (2016), 291–310. doi:10.1353/jeu.2016.0015.

Haraway, Donna. *When Species Meet*. Minneapolis: University of Minnesota Press, 2008.

Haraway, Donna. "Anthropocene, Capitalocene, Chthulucene: Donna Haraway in Conversation with Martha Kenney." In *Art in the Anthropocene. Encounters Among Aesthetics, Politics, Environments and Epistemologies*, edited by Heather David and Etienne Turpin, 255–70. Accessed January 8, 2023. http://www.openhumanitiespress .org/books/titles/art-in-the-anthropocene/.

Haraway, Donna. *Staying with the Trouble: Making Kin in the Chthulucene.* Durham: Duke University, 2016.

Hunt, Peter. "Childist Criticism: The Subculture of the Child, the Book and the Critic." *Signal* 43, no. 1 (1984), 42–59.

Hunt, Peter. *Criticism, Theory, and Children's Literature.* Oxford: Blackwell, 1991.

International Research Society for Children's Literature. Statements of Principles. Accessed January 8, 2023. https://www.irscl.org/about.

Joosen, Vanessa. "Children's Literature in Translation: Towards a Participatory Approach." *Humanities* 8, no. 1 (2019), 48. doi:10.3390/h8010048.

Joosen, Vanessa. "Connecting Childhood Studies, Age Studies, and Children's Literature Studies." *Barnboken* 45 (2022). doi:10.14811/clr.v45.745.

Lee, Nick. *Childhood and Biopolitics: Climate Change, Life Processes and Human Futures.* Basingstoke: Palgrave Macmillan, 2013.

Määttä, Kaarina and Satu Uusiautti. "Time for Caring Research, Time for Well-Being." In *The Basics of Caring Research*, edited by Satu Uusiautti and Kaarina Määttä, 3–18. Rotterdam, Boston, Taipei: Sense Publisher, 2016.

Malone, Karen, and Karin Murris. "Wording." In *A Glossary for Doing Postqualitative, New Materialist and Critical Posthumanist Research Across Disciplines*, edited by Karin Murris, 144–45. London: Routledge, 2022.

Melrose, Andrew. "The Hidden Adult and the Hiding Child in Writing for Children?" Accessed January 8, 2023. https://textjournal.scholasticahq.com/article/31128-the -hidden-adult-and-the-hiding-child-in-writing-for-children.

Mol, Annemarie. *The Logic of Care: Health and the Problem of Patient Choice.* London: Routledge, 2008.

Mulcahy, Dianne, and Sarah Healy. "Citizenship Matters: Young Citizen Becoming in the Posthuman Present." *Educational Philosophy and Theory* 55, no. 12 (2023), 1363–74. doi: 10.1080/00131857.2022.2161892.

Murris, Karin, and Candace R. Kuby. "Adult/Child." In *A Glossary for Doing Postqualitative, New Materialist and Critical Posthumanist Research Across Disciplines*, edited by Karin Murris, 4–5. London: Routledge, 2022.

Nagar, Richa. "Storytelling and Co-Authorship in Feminist Alliance Work: Reflections from a Journey." *Gender, Place & Culture* 20, no. 1 (2013), 1–18. doi:10.1080/0966369x.2012.731383.

Nikolajeva, Maria. "Theory, Post-Theory, and Aetonormative Theory." *Neohelicon* 36, no. 1 (2009), 13–24. doi:10.1007/s11059-009-1002-4.

Niner, Holly J., and Sophia N. Wassermann. "Better for Whom? Leveling the Injustices of International Conferences by Moving Online." *Frontiers in Marine Science* 8 (2021). doi:10.3389/fmars.2021.638025.

Noorani, Tehseen, and Julian Brigstocke. "More-Than-Human Participatory Research." In *Connected Communities Foundation Series*, edited by Keri Facer and Katherine

Dunleavy. University of Bristol/AHRC Connected Communities Programme, 2018. Accessed January 23, 2023. https://orca.cardiff.ac.uk/id/eprint/119017/1/J%20 Brigstocke%202018%20more%20than%20human%20report.pdf.

Puig de la Bellacasa, María. "'Nothing Comes Without Its World': Thinking with Care." *The Sociological Review* 60, no. 2 (2012), 197–216. doi:10.1111/j.1467-954x.2012.02070.x.

Puig de la Bellacasa, María. *Matters of Care: Speculative Ethics in More than Human Worlds.* Minneapolis: University of Minnesota Press, 2017.

Rogowska-Stangret, Monika. "Care as a Methodology: Reading Natalie Jeremijenko and Vinciane Despret Diffractively." In *Posthuman and Political Care Ethics for Reconfiguring Higher Education Pedagogies,* edited by Vivienne Bozalek, Michalinos Zembylas, and Joan C. Tronto, 13–26. London: Routledge, 2020.

Romano, Nike. "Aesthetic Wit(h)nessing and the Political Ethics of Care: Generating Solidarity and Trust in Pedagogical Encounters." In *Posthuman and Political Care Ethics for Reconfiguring Higher Education Pedagogies,* edited by Vivienne Bozalek, Michalinos Zembylas, and Joan C. Tronto, 65–78. London: Routledge, 2020.

Spyrou, Spyros. *Disclosing Childhoods: Research and Knowledge Production for a Critical Childhood Studies.* London: Palgrave Macmillan, 2018.

Staffa, Rachel K., Maraja Riechers, and Berta Martín-López. "A Feminist Ethos for Caring Knowledge Production in Transdisciplinary Sustainability Science." *Sustainability Science* 17, no. 1 (2021), 45–63. doi:10.1007/s11625-021-01064-0.

Superle, Michelle. "The United Nations Convention on the Rights of the Child: At the Core of a Child-Centered Critical Approach to Children's Literature." *The Lion and the Unicorn* 40, no. 2 (2016), 144–62. doi:10.1353/uni.2016.0017.

Taylor, Affrica, and Miriam Giugni. "Common Worlds: Reconceptualising Inclusion in Early Childhood Communities." *Contemporary Issues in Early Childhood* 13, no. 2 (2012), 108–19. doi:10.2304/ciec.2012.13.2.108.

Tronto, Joan C. "Care as a Basis for Radical Political Judgments." *Hypatia* 10, no. 2 (1995), 141–49. doi:10.1111/j.1527-2001.1995.tb01376.x.

Tronto, Joan C. *Caring Democracy: Markets, Equality, and Justice.* New York: New York University Press, 2013.

Tronto, Joan C. "Afterword: Response-ability and Responsibility: Using Feminist New Materialisms and Care Ethics to Cope with Impatience in Higher Education." In *Posthuman and Political Care Ethics for Reconfiguring Higher Education Pedagogies,* edited by Vivienne Bozalek, Michalinos Zembylas, and Joan C. Tronto, 153–60. London: Routledge, 2020.

van Dooren, Thom, and Deborah Bird Rose. "Lively Ethnography: Storying Animist Worlds." *Environmental Humanities* 8, no. 1 (2016), 77–94.

van Lierop-Debrauwer, Helma. "Children's Literature: A Joint Venture." *International Research in Children's Literature* 14, no. 3 (2022), 249–63.

van Lierop-Debrauwer, Helma and Sabine Steels. "The Mingling of Teenage and Adult Breaths: The Dutch Slash Series as Intergenerational Communication." In *Intergenerational Solidarity in Children's Literature and Film,* edited by Justyna Deszcz-Tryhubczak and Zoe Jaques, 218–30. Jackson: University Press of Mississippi, 2021.

Wesseling, Elisabeth. "Researching Child Authors: Which Questions (Not to) Ask."
     Humanities 8, no. 2 (2019), 87. doi:10.3390/h8020087.
Yates, Joe, Suneetha Kadiyala, Yuemeng Li, Sylvia Levy, Abel Endashaw, Hallie Perlick, and
     Parke Wilde. "Can Virtual Events Achieve Co-Benefits for Climate, Participation, and
     Satisfaction? Comparative Evidence from Five International Agriculture, Nutrition
     and Health Academy Week Conferences." *Lancet Planetary Health* 6, no. 2 (2022),
     e164–e70. doi:10.1016/s2542-196(21)00355-7.

Part II

Literary Agency and a Recasting of Equitable Child Citizenship

Chapter 4

RELATIONAL AGENCY, CHILDREN'S LITERATURE, AND CHILDHOOD

NINA CHRISTENSEN

Agency has become a central term in children's literature studies. When childhood studies was established as an interdisciplinary field in the 1990s, the term was connected to children as individuals who act, make choices, and express their own ideas, thereby participating in changing society (James and James 2008: 9). During the first decades of the twenty-first century, new approaches to agency have emerged. This chapter discusses these and other nuances to agency as a concept, especially paying attention to relationships and cooperations as important factors in children's agency. Furthermore, the chapter will demonstrate how the term "relational agency" can be used in the analysis of three types of texts related to children's literature. First, "represented relational agency" in the picture book *En fin sten* (*A Fine Stone*, by Allermann and Kjærgaard, 2020) is discussed. Subsequently, children's experiences of relational agency are examined with regard to the project Tiny Voices—Grand Narratives, in which Danish children and professional authors coproduced texts for children from 2021 to 2022. Finally, the chapter focuses on relational agency in childhood recollected, based on the autobiography of nineteenth-century child actor Johanne Luise Heiberg (1812–1890).

In a number of ways, children's literature evolves around relationships. In texts, characters represent children's and young people's interactions with people of different ages, as well as with nonhuman elements (Deszcz-Tryhubczak and Jaques 2021). Across history, the process of producing texts has involved interactions between young people and adults (Gubar 2009; Grenby 2009; Smith 2017; Lierop-Debrauwer and Steels 2021). When books are produced, adult professionals edit, publish, print, and sell texts for children based on ideas of childhood and the needs and interests of actual young readers and customers. Children and young adults produce and coproduce texts for each other in various contexts, including digital platforms (Johansen 2021). Different kinds of relationships arise in the reception of books and texts: among children as well as among children and adults, including parents, caretakers, educators, and librarians.

This chapter discusses the term "relational agency" and possible ways to apply the term in the analysis of texts within children's literature studies. First, the chapter outlines overall changes within the fields of children's literature studies that can be linked to the development of children's rights and childhood studies, leading to an increased focus on children's agency. Second, it presents the current shift in childhood studies from research interest in children's individual rights and agency and the child's voice to "relational agency." Subsequently, relational agency is applied to three different cases in order to explore the relevance of the term when working with literary texts, actual child readers, and lived or recollected childhoods in a historical context. The three cases point to different areas of children's literature studies: textual analysis, empirical research with children, and childhood, as real, represented, and recollected (Westin 2021).

THE HISTORICAL BACKGROUND FOR RELATIONAL AGENCY

Traditionally, scholars and professionals working with children's literature have paid much attention to the character and quality of children's books, a fact that can be linked to the historical development of the field. The Scandinavian context may serve as an example: from around 1920, children's libraries began to be established; in the 1930s, legislation regarding children's right to access libraries was issued; and in 1964, important legislation concerning school libraries followed (Christensen and Appel 2021). Thus, from around 1920 to 1970, politicians and professionals, including teachers and librarians, collaborated in securing children's access to books, education, and libraries as part of the development of the welfare state. Discussions concerning the quality of books bought for public collections were part of this process. When children's literature studies gradually became established as an academic field in the Scandinavian countries from the 1970s onward, increased attention was paid to the special characteristics of children's literature and the writing of the national histories of literature. The establishment of children's literature studies as a field was linked to the idea of adults as responsible, knowing authorities regarding children's texts.

Internationally, since the publication of Jaqueline Rose's *The Case of Peter Pan* (1984), attention across the discipline was directed toward adult constructions of childhood in relation to children's literature but still with a strong focus on texts and the ways in which adults perceived and represented childhood in books for children. A shift began to emerge around the turn of the millennium, when scholars drew more attention to the first word in the term "children's literature." British scholar David Rudd pointed to the fact that children were not only to be considered the passive recipients of the texts (Rudd 2004), but a more fundamental change of approach related to children's agency was most explicit in work by American scholars. One of the pioneers was Marah Gubar, who took as her point of departure "the child as a competent collaborator, capable of working and playing alongside adults" (Gubar 2009: 9). Writing about children and adults as coauthors in nineteenth-century England, Gubar criticized Rose for reducing the child to an abstract "Other," and she ascertained that even authors of the Golden Age "entertain the possibility that children can resist and reconceive the scripts handed to them by adults, participating not only in the production of narrative, but in the drafting of their own life stories" (Gubar 2009: 38). Here, children and childhood are linked to resistance, participation and production, also when it comes to literature, and Gubar uses "agency" as a key term. Another important scholar in this shift was Káren Sanchez-Eppler, who described her research interest thus: "I strive to understand not just the books adults produced for children—that is, what adults thought about childhood and wanted to say to children—but also what children actually did with these texts, how they took possession of them" (Sánchez-Eppler 2011: 151; see also Sánchez-Eppler 2023). When a revised version of *Keywords for Children's Literature* was issued, "agency" was one of the new entries to be included, along with, for instance, "transnational" and "media" (Christensen 2021).

Increased interest in children's agency within children's literature studies can be linked to the development of children's rights and childhood studies. In a study of the history behind the United Nations Convention on the Rights of the Child from 1989, childhood historian Paula Fass describes a shift from the original post-WWI and WWII ambition to protect children from abuse, war, child labor, and related threats, to a view on children both as capable individuals and individuals in need of protection:

Those "rights" have become familiar to us over the past 20 years since they were first set forth in 1989 as a balance between viewing the child as the object of caretaking who requires various services and protections from adults and the rights of the child to act fully in his or her capacity as a person. Throughout most of the century it was the

former rights—to be cared for and protected—that defined the ideals
that international institutions adopted. (Fass 2011: 18)

Childhood anthropologists Myra Bluebond-Langner and Jill E. Korbin
call the convention a "pivotal event, not only in the development of policies for children but also in terms of scholarship" and the establishment
of childhood studies as a field. More specifically, they state that the way
the convention addresses children's right to participation has "stimulated a
research and policy agenda that includes children's views and perspective"
(Bluebond-Langner and Korbin 2007: 24). Key scholars in childhood studies,
childhood sociologist Adrian James and childhood anthropologist Allison
James, include "agency" as a term in *Key Terms to Childhood Studies* (2008)
where they define it as the "capacity of individuals to act independently."
Furthermore, they state that the concept "underscores children and young
people's capacities to make choices about the things they do and to express
their own ideas" and "emphasizes children's ability not only to have some
control over the direction their own lives take but also, importantly, to play
some part in the changes that take place in society more widely" (James and
James 2008: 9). Underlying this approach is the understanding that an agent
or a subject is an individual who acts, makes choices, and expresses his or her
own ideas and thereby participates in changing society. This did not mean,
however, that, for instance, Allison James was not aware of the complexities
in trying to make children's voices heard (James 2007).

REDEFINING AGENCY IN RELATIONAL TERMS

Three publications from childhood studies and childhood history may serve as
examples of new approaches that challenge definitions of "agency" as the one
mentioned above. In the introduction to the anthology *Reimagining Childhood
Studies* (2018), Spyros Spyrou, Rachel Rosen, and Daniel Thomas Cook question what they consider a reductive use of the term "agency" within childhood
studies. In their view, the field has placed "the bourgeois, Global North 'child'"
as "the theoretical center of the field" (Spyrou, Rosen, and Cook 2018: 2) and
valorized "children's agency to the point of a fetish" (Spyrou, Rosen, and Cook
2018: 3; see also Spyrou 2018). Among other things, they claim that this approach
to agency overlooks childhoods' "multiple and connective scales, relationalities
and structural entanglements" (Spyrou, Rosen, and Cook 2018: 4). Inspired,
among others, by Karen Barad, the alternative they propose is to focus on
agency as "a relational dynamic—not so much a property of an entity, but an

element of a complex, an assemblage of sorts" (Spyrou, Rosen, and Cook 2018: 5). Furthermore, they suggest a "relational posture not only toward bodies and persons but also toward objects, technologies, systems, epistemes, and historical eras" (Spyrou, Rosen, and Cook 2018: 6). In sum, they encourage an approach where researchers pay attention to the ways in which identities are negotiated and developed in interaction with discourses, contexts, and relationships. Hereby, they also want to signal "a shift from childhood as an identity category to the practices which enact it as a particular kind of phenomenon: from what childhood is to how childhood is done" (Spyrou, Rosen, and Cook 2018: 8).

The anthology *Reconceptualizing Agency* (2016) represents a related interdisciplinary approach to agency within childhood studies. In his chapter "Extending Agency: The Merit of Relational Approaches for Childhood Studies," German social scientist Eberhard Raithelhuber critiques two basic aspects of the previous use of the term "agency" in childhood studies. Firstly, the idea that children "'have' or 'possess' agency . . . thus being able to bring about change or to make a difference" (Raithelhuber 2016: 91). Secondly, that the intention of such research is to prove and investigate "how individual children can express agency in the context of constraining and enabling conditions" (Raithelhuber 2016: 91). Like Spyrou, Rosen, and Cook, he claims that this approach to agency rests on Western, Eurocentric humanistic views and a basic dualism between "mind and body, individual and society, micro and macro, human and non-human" (Raithelhuber 2016: 91). According to him, an alternative would be to acknowledge that agency "can only exist in interconnectedness and be brought about in relations" (Raithelhuber 2016: 96). Thus, he argues for "a different understanding of agency as social and collective" and for approaches where agents "consist of overlapping entities or fabrics, which are complex and in motion" (Raithelhuber 2016: 89) rather than being perceived as individual, intentional agents. The example he uses is rituals, but I will later discuss a project where children cocreate literature with peers and professional authors as an example of how this idea of social agency might also be relevant in relation to children engaging with literature.

A third and final example of new approaches to agency comes from the history of childhood. In the article "The Kids Aren't All Right" (2020), childhood historian Sarah Maza analyzes the focus on children's agency in historical research. Within her field, she also finds many attempts to look for and find children's "authentic" voices based on definitions and ambitions from the New Sociology of Childhood. Maza writes, "[w]hile *agency* has been variously challenged and redefined by historians in this century, many of those who work on children still see it as one of their central tasks to demonstrate that young people were more than just the objects or victims of their elders' programs" (Maza 2020: 1,268). While she acknowledges that historians can find examples that point to children's abilities "to perform and create, and to alter their environments by disobeying, running away, engaging in delinquency, or ensuring their own survival in various ways" (Maza 2020: 1,269), she also argues for a more nuanced and social approach to agency. Among others, she refers to William Sewell, who includes a focus on agency as "an ability to coordinate one's actions with others and against others, to form collective projects, and to monitor the simultaneous effects of one's own and others' activities" (Sewell 2005, quoted in Maza 2020: 1,269). Interesting in this context is Maza's discussion of autobiographies as a valuable source of knowledge about children's agency in historical contexts. Rather than describing childhood as a fixed lifespan, she refers to Carolyn Steedman and Mary Jo Maynes, who define childhood as "a labile category that exists not just in the time of youth but as it is remembered and recast throughout an individual's life" (Maza 2020: 1,270). Furthermore, she quotes Mary Jo Maynes for stating that "childhood experience functions not just when it happens in real time, but, because of the dynamics of intersecting temporalities and ongoing personality development, as a life-long phenomenon" (Mary Jo Maynes, quoted in Maza: 1,270). This approach to childhood also as an ongoing process resonates with Gubar's kinship model, according to which "children and adults are separated by differences of degree, not of kind, meaning that we should eschew difference-model discourse that depicts children as a separate species in favor of emphasizing that growth is a messy and unpredictable continuum" (Gubar 2013: 254, Gubar 2016).

To sum up, the three publications mentioned here are examples of responses to research that take as a point of departure the individual, agentic child, and situations where that agency is visible in actions directed at oppressive structures or authorities. Instead, researchers suggest a turn toward agency and subjectivity as being embedded in social interactions and relationships in specific social settings and contexts. In addition, this line of research points to the need to listen to the marginalized and silenced children. The question to follow is how such an approach to agency could be applied within children's literature studies.

CHARACTERS, IMPLIED READERS, AND RELATIONAL AGENCY IN A PICTURE BOOK

In 2019, the Danish picture book *En fin sten* (*A Fine Stone*) was published. At first glance, it is quite a traditional picture book in which a short, simple

Figure 4.1. Anne Sofie Allermann (text), Anna Margrethe Kjærgaard (illustrations): *En fin sten* (*A Fine Stone*). Jensen & Dalgaard, 2020. Original in color.

text is told in the third person, with Orla (a boy's name) as the main character. The first scene is set on the beach, where Orla finds a stone that he thinks looks like a small penguin. Orla starts to build a circus in the sand, and then along comes Olivia, and they start playing together. She thinks the stone looks like a seal and explains to Orla, "'Yes, there is the nose, there are the eyes, and the tail is here.' Olivia points and now Orla sees the seal" (Allerman 2020).[1] A boy named Otto comes along and states that he thinks the stone looks like a shark. Again, the text states, "Orla sees the shark, too." Subsequently, Orla lies on the beach and imagines the stone as a penguin, a seal, and a shark. He puts the stone in the middle of his circus arena, "and now he sees that the audience sees something different, depending on where they are placed." The scene shifts as Olivia and Otto jump into the sea, but

Figure 4.2. Anne Sofie Allermann (text), Anna Margrethe Kjærgaard (illustrations): *En fin sten* (*A Fine Stone*). Jensen & Dalgaard, 2020. Original in color.

Orla stands on the dock, not daring to follow them. From the water, Otto encourages him by telling him to imagine that he is a shark. The illustration shows how Orla imagines "the shark inside himself," and he jumps into the water. Unfortunately, his bathing trunks slide down, and he "gets embarrassed and is on the edge of crying."

The reader might fear that Orla is going to have a bad experience, but on the next double spread, the reader is confronted with all three children laughing together. Orla has pulled up his trunks, and Olivia and Otto have put their hands on Orla's arms in comforting and inclusive gestures. In the final scene of the book, a mum shouts: "Olivia, Otto and Olga! Lunch is ready!" and the following conversation takes place:

> "I do not like it when you call me Olga," Orla says, while they eat.
> "But that is your name," Dad says.
> "No, my name is Orla."
> And then Orla shows them the fine stone he has found.

Figure 4.3. Anne Sofie Allermann (text), Anna Margrethe Kjærgaard (illustrations): *En fin sten* (*A Fine Stone*). Jensen & Dalgaard, 2020. Original in color.

The parents do not seem to want to change their perception of his gender by using a boy's name, according to his wishes. Here, when the father addresses the main character with a girl's name, the reader becomes aware of a subtle gender issue in the book in relation to the main character, and when turning to the back cover, the reader is confronted with Orla depicted with his back toward the reader, wearing a bikini top. Since the main character has not worn a top on the other illustrations, the reader is tempted to turn to the first double spread, only to see a bikini top put away discreetly in the margin of the illustration (figure 4.1).

So, how is this picture book linked to children's experiences of identity, approaches to identity formation, and children's agency? First and foremost, agency (or lack of agency) is depicted as arising through relationships. The discussion between the main character and his parents points to the name "Orla" as being the name he uses to refer to himself, while his parents use the girl's name they have assigned to their child. In this case, Orla/Olga tries to have an influence, but a potential conflict and solution are left open.

The conversation between the parents and the child reflects agency, or lack of agency, as being negotiated and developed in discourses, contexts, and relationships. This brings to mind the conceptualization of relational agency by Spyrou, Cook, Rosen, and Raithelhuber. The parents construct Orla as a girl, an identity that is also hinted at in the illustration on the back cover. The illustrations grant the child individual agency by showing that the parents might buy a bikini top for him and make him bring it to the beach, but he can still choose not to wear it.

The interaction between identity and relationship is also very much present in the situation where Orla loses his bathing trunks. Here, the reader does not see his genitals and might think that he is embarrassed because he is naked. But when the final scene with the parents reveals his experience of being uncomfortable being seen/interpreted as a girl, it becomes notable that the children do not problematize his gender identity among them. The facial expressions of Olivia and Otto first reveal surprise, but they do not mock him; instead, they laugh together. While the omniscient narrator refers to Orla in the third person, when his trunks slide down, the illustration positions the reader behind Orla's back so that readers might identify with the feeling of standing naked in front of your friends. In the final illustration, we see the scene from the adults' point of view but also that the children are placed closely together with Orla's friends at his sides, acting as a human shield or a common front, suggesting that this generation will find it easier to support him than his parents. Otto gazes toward the reader in a confident yet gentle way that might invite a child reader into the company of individuals with open minds and adult readers to consider their position in dialogue with child readers.

Another explicit example of relational agency among children is the way in which they support each other in difficult situations. When Orla is scared to jump into the water and Otto tells him to imagine he is a shark, imagination is depicted as a catalyst of action and agency. The fact that Otto, his friend, sees his potential courage leads to Orla's own ability to imagine himself as brave. This scene brings to mind Raithelhuber's description of agents as consisting of "overlapping entities or fabrics, which are complex and in motion" (Raithelhuber 2016: 89). Being timid or being brave and thus able to act is not an inherent, absolute quality in Orla; here agency is depicted as the result of the children's relationships, dialogue, and imagination. But it is important to note that, in the end, the decision is Orla's own.

When the children discuss whether the stone is a seal, a shark, or a penguin, they also point to identity as something that is negotiated, relational, and the result of discourses. The children use their imagination but listen to each other's perspectives and interpretations of the object. They do not argue, and after different possible "stone-identities" have been presented, the text states that "Orla sees" not only a penguin but also a potential seal and shark in the stone. The different species are not presented as inherent or mutually exclusive qualities or identities in the object but depend on the perspective and interpretation of the viewer. One could argue that in this narrative, the stone is also an agent that encourages the characters to think about identity, which would reflect Spyrou, Rosen, and Cook's suggestion of a "relational posture not only toward bodies and persons but also toward objects" (Spyrou, Rosen, and Cook 2019: 6).

Finally, what about the agency of the reader? One could argue that relational agency is inherent in all acts of reading, as illustrated by Wolfgang Iser's concept of "the implied reader" that addresses the interaction and coconstruction of text and reader (Iser 1974). Reading this picture book, readers are expected to be able to deduce a number of things themselves, especially in the interplay between text and images. Few readers would note the bikini top lying on the towel on the first double spread on a first reading. However, having finished the book, they may revisit the cover and notice that there, the main character is depicted as holding his hands in front of his body. Given the young age of the child, in a Scandinavian context, a girl would not be expected to wear a bikini top, and the gender of the main character is not an issue—apparently, a gender-neutral depiction is intended. The question of biological gender versus the individual's experience of gender is referred to, and the reader/spectator is positioned on the side of Orla. While some aspects of the book invite readers to make up their own minds, other aspects restrict the readers' interpretive freedom. For instance, the omniscient narrator's very explicit didactic tone states that "the audience sees something different, depending on where they are placed." While some reflection is left to the reader and to discussions among children and adult readers, the book can also be seen as a didactic and explicit illustration of contemporary ideas of identity formation.

This picture book transmits a clear message about gender diversity and a child's right to decide his or her own gender, which can be linked to the fact that the manuscript won a competition aimed at making LGBTQ+ issues more visible in Danish picture books. This contest was arranged by a Christian organization, and the competition caused a debate in the Christian newspaper *Kristeligt Dagblad*, where a more conservative theologian accused the organization of "bowing to the zeitgeist," while another theologian interpreted the competition as reflecting the need of some Christian institutions to position themselves as free-spirited or liberal (*Kristeligt Dagblad*, January

18, 2019: 5). This debate also points to relational agency as being embedded in larger structural contexts.

RELATIONAL AGENCY ACCORDING
TO CHILDREN IN AARHUS 2022

Ideas of intergenerational cooperation and children's agency lie behind the project Tiny Voices—Grand Narratives (Små Stemmer—Store Fortællinger, 2021–2022), initiated and hosted by Aarhus Libraries. The main activity in the project was a number of workshops in libraries where children ten to thirteen years old coproduced texts with professional authors. The main ambition of the project was to encourage coproduction and to stimulate the production and public dissemination of texts coproduced by children. Children's literature scholar Ayoe Quist Henkel and I were engaged to collect data on children's experiences of creating narratives together and their agency in that process. In this essay, a small selection of data will be used to exemplify how children talk about producing texts together.

In the spring of 2022, we interviewed two eleven-year-old boys who worked together to produce a text based on input from the professional author Dorte Schou. The boys attended the workshop with their classmates and teachers at the biggest public library called DOKK1, in Aarhus, the second biggest city in Denmark. The children were organized in pairs by their teacher, who wanted them to work with someone they did not usually work with. The cooperation between author and children and between pairs of children allows the researcher to pay attention to agency in a relational context. In the following selected parts of the thirteen-minute interview, the boys talk about their cooperation and the context of that cooperation.

At the beginning of the interview, the two boys both state that they enjoyed working with someone they do not usually cooperate with, and when asked explicitly, "[h]ow has the cooperation between the two of you been?" they state simultaneously, "Really good." Interested in knowing more about children's views on cooperation, the interviewer asked:

INTERVIEWER: Why are you good at working together? What is the good thing about working together with Laurits, Viktor?[2]
VIKTOR: He is smart, he is good at writing, and he is very funny. He is also a good friend.
INTERVIEWER: What is a good friend?

VIKTOR: One who supports you, when you need something, and if you are sad, then he comes over and helps you. (Interview DOKK1, April 7, 2022)

Viktor points to his coauthor's intellect, his skills, his humor, but also more personal qualities, such as being supportive, empathetic, and helpful. Even though these two children have not worked much together before, he calls his coworker "a friend." When the interviewer asks Laurits what it is like to work with Viktor, he states, "I think it is really good, [he is] someone who does not give up easily. And he continues to write instead of just saying 'I am fed up with this.' And then he is really nice and kind to you. And good to talk to."

When describing their cooperation, this boy mentions a skill that is useful in the process of writing and cooperating—perseverance—but he also points to relational or social skills. Moving toward their cooperation in relation to the specific story they made, the interviewer asks:

INTERVIEWER: What individual contributions to the story have the two of you made?
LAURITS: One was writing [on the computer] and then one . . .
VIKTOR: [*Interrupts*] provided ideas . . .
LAURITS: Yes, and then, for instance, when Viktor was writing, then I asked, "If you have any ideas, then you just say so." And then halfway through, we switched places, and then I wrote, because it would be a little tough, if Viktor should write it all, and then I just wrote a bit too.
INTERVIEWER: So you have simply taken turns at being . . .
VIKTOR: [*Interrupts*] The author. (Interview DOKK1, April 7, 2022)

As one can see, the boys cooperate in explaining the situation to the interviewer by finishing each other's sentences and sometimes also the interviewer's sentences. The hesitation or silence of one person in the room gives another the chance to cocreate information and interpretations. I find that the two boys in this interview point to cocreation as a creative process that of course depends on skills but also on the relationship between the two coauthor/-agents being good and based on mutual respect and simply caring for each other, making sure that the coworker is okay. Their immediate joy of participating in that kind of cooperation and the way they talk about it makes me think that this is not the kind of cooperation they always experience. The way they talk about their cooperation seems to support the idea of relationships and interaction being an important part of agency from a child's point of view—and more important than individual ownership of the story.

Bearing in mind Raithelhuber's and other researchers' attention toward agency in context, another aspect of the interview is relevant. When asked an open question concerning their overall impression of the workshop, they responded very positively, Laurits saying that he specifically liked:

> LAURITS: That you can choose yourself. . . . You had a lot of spare time and . . . then you could just walk around like you wanted to.
> VIKTOR: [*Interrupts*] Walk around with your friends, play games, *hygge*, go outside. (Interview DOKK1, April 7, 2022)

I interpret this as the children's explicit joy at *not* being subject to very strict structures and of having an influence on and a choice with regard to what they are allowed to do. They contrast this experience in the library with their limited freedom of choice and influence in their normal school context. Asked whether they would suggest if anything should be changed in relation to how the workshop was organized, Viktor repeats that he found it really cool to be at the library for two days in a row. The interviewer asks what the good thing about being away from the school was and the boy's reply:

> LAURITS: That you can try something new, also because at school it gets very much a lot of the same.
> VIKTOR: You know where all the things are.
> LAURITS: Yes, then it is cooler to try to be down at DOKK1, because there are so many more options, you can try, like more spare time, and for instance in the breaks, you can play fussball, arcade machines.
> VIKTOR: [*Interrupts*] VR.
> LAURITS: And try all sorts of funny things.
> VIKTOR: At school, you can just play football, you can only be outside, you must not be inside, it is mega-boring.

The children explain that their experience at school, even in their spare time, is very restricted with regard to where they are allowed to be and what they can do, in contrast to being in the library, where they experienced quite a lot of freedom and influence on their activities. From the children's point of view, this feeling of agency is linked to the context of the library. From an outsider's perspective, agency is also linked to the relationship between the pupils and their teacher. She demanded that they participate in the workshop, but she was also very much aware of when they needed a break, and when they did, she was very trustful. She communicated very clearly about how long they would have a break and told them to set the alarm on their cell phones so that they could be back on time. And they were, thus demonstrating that their agency was linked to the existing relationship and trust between teacher and pupils. When the application and the framework for the project were designed, agency, as defined by James and James in 2008, was one point of departure, but interactions and interviews with the children made relational agency a very relevant term to work with. As my final example, in continuation of Maza's reflections on children's agency in a historical context, I will now turn to the life and childhood experiences of Johanne Luise Heiberg.

NARRATING RELATIONAL AGENCY IN THE PAST: THE CASE OF JOHANNE LUISE HEIBERG

The autobiographies of Danish fairy tale author Hans Christian Andersen (1805–1875) provide insight into the importance of relationships when a very poor boy growing up in a provincial town at the beginning of the eighteenth century wanted to move upward in society. While Andersen is not the only boy who is able to change his living conditions, at this point in history, it was very rare that poor girls were able to do so and even more rare for them to write their autobiographies. The autobiography of Johanne Luise Heiberg, *A Life Relived in Recollection* (1973; *Et liv genoplevet i erindringen*, written from 1855 onward, was first published in 1891/92), allows us a glimpse into the life of a girl with an emigrant, very poor, partly Jewish background, who did not receive any formal schooling but worked and earned her own money from a very young age. In continuation of Maza's discussion of children's agency in historical context, one could ask to what extent it is productive to apply the terms "agency" or "relational agency" to the context of her account of a childhood.

Born in 1812, Johanne Luise Heiberg mainly grew up in Copenhagen at an unfortunate time in the history of the city: In 1807, Copenhagen was bombed by the British army as part of the Napoleonic wars, and in 1813, the Danish state went bankrupt. Johanne Luise Heiberg's parents struggled to be able to pay for food and a place to live for their nine children, among which Johanne was the second youngest. Her talent as a dancer led to an early career as a child actor at the Royal Theatre in Copenhagen, where she soon became an extremely popular young actress. She married the director of the theater, Johan Ludvig Heiberg, who was also a prominent author and thus a member of the cultural elite, and she continued to work as an actress.

The question here is how the adult author addresses the relationship between her own qualities, efforts, and agency and her dependence on others as well as structural elements. Three scenes of her life as a child as it is "recalled, recorded, and commemorated" (Appel, Christensen, Staffensen 2022: 5) will serve as examples. When referring to Johanne Luise Heiberg's experiences as a child, I will use only her first name.

First scene: In 1818, Johanne's parents were not able to make a living in Copenhagen, which made her mother travel with nine children to the far-away provincial town of Aalborg. Here, she established a household in order to earn a living by cooking for the soldiers in the city. Her husband stayed behind, and the children had to take care of themselves. Johanne entertained herself playing in the gutter and writes in detail about the place and her games, including the moment when she realized the shame of being poor: "By then I was between three and four years old. Lying on my knees in the gutter, poking with a stick in it, I suddenly became conscious about my own self in this life. I remember clearly, how I suddenly looked up, shamefully dried my fingers and thought: If someone sees you like this it is shameful for you. From then on I sticked to the stairs" (Heiberg 1973: 19). This scene shows a child being on her own, conscious about the shamefulness of her poverty and the fact that poverty leaves her playing in the gutter. However, referring to the stairs as her "dear stairs" also suggests that she felt that she had a place of her own, and with some satisfaction, she explains how she was able to create what to her was a meaningful and enjoyable activity. One of her favorite plays was to dig up earthworms, wash them, and put them back in the earth again, feeling that she had done a good deed. Her conclusion to the description of this first scene is that "[w]ith such quiet, modest joys, the first years of my childhood passed" (Heiberg 1973:19). In Aalborg, at six years old, she got her first unpaid job as a codance instructor with one of the officers from the regiment. When the family moved back to Copenhagen, an older girl who lived with the family saw her talent and encouraged her and her sister to apply to the Royal Theatre's ballet school for children. Eight-year-old Johanne and her sister were accepted to the school. Here, the two girls "were derided, mocked, and shunned like two ugly trolls who had ventured into this gathering of sylphs" (Heiberg 1973: 22). Johanne's talent for dancing was noticed, and she achieved small child roles at the theater, but her talents also led to a traumatic event.

The second scene, noteworthy in the context of relational agency, took place in a simple inn run by her father and mother. One evening, her father, who was proud of his two girls, wanted them to perform. The adult author describes how she tried to avoid it, how she was shaking when the father came into the room and told them to dance for his customers, and how she declared insistently that she did not want to do it. But her father got angry and forced her up on the pool table, and while the guests were shouting and clapping their hands, her sister started to dance. The author describes how she followed her sister in tears "while the raw cheering of the guests increased" (Heiberg 1973: 25). Help came from a stranger; a person who had been sitting in the corner of the room interfered, went to the table, grabbed her by the waist, lifted her off the table, and told the mob how wrong it was to force a small, timid girl to do this. The stranger brought Johanne and her sister to his table, and when he learned that they did not know how to read or write, he began to teach them.

There is no doubt that the grown Johanne Luise Heiberg also sees the man, "Herman," as a benefactor, and in relation to the scene mentioned above, she calls him a "protector." He invested time and money in the girls' education and bought the family things they needed, including a piano to help in the development of Johanne's career. However, seen with today's eyes, he also seemed to be grooming the girl. She recalls her distress and sometimes shame at being related to this man, who allegedly wanted to bind her with an engagement when she was only twelve years old. She describes her reaction thus: "It appeared to me that I was sold, disgraced, and I prayed intensively to God that he would bring me home" (Heiberg 1973: 41). Her shame developed into a depression-like state of apathy.

Interestingly, these feelings of dependence, lack of agency, and despair are paired with a description of being able to stand up for herself (and her mother). The third scene takes place when, one evening, her father is drunk, abusive, and on his way to beat up her mother. Usually, Johanne hid from him in such instances, but when he suddenly moved toward her and told her to respect him, she rose, stood up right before him, and, full of fear, told her father how miserable a person he was and how miserable he made the family. Her next thought was that "now he will come on to me and beat me to pieces, the blood rushed to my heart, and trembling from fear I stood there straight and stiff, while all my blood ran to my heart" (Heiberg 1973: 38–39). Much to her surprise, her father suddenly comes to his senses and retires to a corner of the room.

Johanne Luise Heiberg depicts a childhood that is obviously constricted by conditions the girl could not change. Poverty led to lack of food, bullying, lack of formal schooling, an unsecure home, and economic dependency on a wealthier man who takes advantage of the family's underprivileged situation. Like Herman, the mother is an ambivalent figure. She was often the one to provide for the most basic needs of the family, and in some cases, she tried to protect her daughter—but she also neglected the damaging consequences of her daughter's suitor's behavior. These are "agents" that help her, and, in that way, provide what we could call "relational agency," but on the other hand, through their actions or their passivity, they limit the child's agency. Johanne Luise Heiberg also depicts a childhood where she was subordinated to her father's wishes and demands and where she was very dependent on support from outside the family. At the same time, descriptions of her early "inner life" and the situation where she stands up against her father show that she was brave and able to stand up against the tyrant. In spite of being born very poor, her talent made it possible for her to earn her own money at an early age, get a room of her own, and slowly get more influence on her life in general.

I find Johanne Luise Heiberg's portrait of girlhood in the early nineteenth century interesting partly due to the description of relationships between children and adults that are simultaneously characterized by conflicts, violence, and implied erotic elements, and at the same time, by adults who tried to care for the child, tried to help and support, but were not always able to do so. Also, the depiction of the child's own agency is complex. Obviously, some scenes describe her individual ability to speak and have an influence on her own life, but just as many times, she describes the injustices, the feeling of shame, and even a wish to die. Again following Raithelhuber, this recollected childlife is an example of agency not as a question of "to have or to have not"—individual as well as relational agency is sometimes present in her life, but it is not always clear whether it will lead to improvements of her life conditions.

CONCLUSION

This chapter has explored the concept of "relational agency" and the differences as well as the interactions between such definitions of agency and the approach suggested by the New Sociology of Childhood that focused more on individual agency and less on structures or contexts. For me, the three cases show that using the term "relational agency" and paying attention to relationships and contexts make it possible to see new aspects of agency. Individual agency and relational agency merge, both in fictional representations of childhood, children's view on their actual experiences in 2022, and when childhood is recollected in a historical context. More nuances appear, but also a higher degree of ambivalence or contradictions in relation to agency, seen from a child's point of view. The picture book *A Fine Stone* represents a childlife where relational agency exists but also where agency is limited through relationships, in this case, when the parents insist on not listening to the child and calling him by a girl's name. For me, this example also shows that relational agency is powerful, but so are the individual's choice and decision. The project Tiny Voices—Grand Narratives was also conceptualized in continuation of agency as defined by the New Sociology of Childhood. Our empirical research reveals that an approach that pays more attention to the children's experiences of cooperation and relationships when producing texts in a library context together with classmates is very relevant. Yet in spite of the children's joy at creating together, when the book based on mutual efforts is produced, some of them still look for their specific individual contributions to the common product. This shows that discussions of relational agency could and should not exclude individual aspects in contexts.

Finally, the scenes I referred to from Johanne Luise Heiberg's life represent lack of agency and actual agency being present in some of the same situations. The other side of relational agency could be what one might call "relational dependency." This leads me to conclude that while relational agency seems to be a very useful concept in various strands of children's literature and childhood studies, I find it counterproductive to dismiss a focus on individual agency as being a thing of the past and a useless leftover from a Eurocentric, bourgeois way of thinking. Based on children's statements and depictions of children's agency in different contexts, I find it meaningful to combine an approach to agency that includes both a focus on relational and social agency, interactions, contexts, and choices, as well as an approach with a focus on situations that involve the actions and expressions of individuals.

NOTES

Interviews with informants eleven to twelve years old conducted by Nina Christensen and Ayoe Quist Henkel during the project *Små stemmer—store fortællinger* (Tiny Voices—Grand Narratives) at the public Library DOKK1, Aarhus, Denmark, April 7, 2021.

1. All translations from Danish quotes are by the author of this chapter.
2. The names of the boys have been changed for the sake of anonymity.

REFERENCES

Allermann, Anne Sofie, and Anna Margrethe Kjærgaard (illustrator). *En fin sten* (*A Fine Stone*). Copenhagen: Jensen & Dalgaard, 2020.
Appel, Charlotte, Nina Christensen, and Karoline Baden Staffensen. "Children's Books and Childhood Reading in Eighteenth- and Nineteenth-Century Denmark: Memoirs

and Autobiographies as Sources for Children's Media Repertoires." *Mémoires du Livre/Studies in Book Culture* 13, no. 1 (2022), 1–31.

Bluebond-Langner, Myra, and Jill E. Korbin. "Challenges and Opportunities in the Anthropology of Childhoods." *American Anthropologist* 109, no. 2 (2007), 241–46.

Christensen, Nina. "Agency." In *Keywords for Children's Literature*, edited by Philip Nel, Lissa Paul, and Nina Christensen, 2nd ed., 10–13. New York: New York University Press, 2021.

Christensen, Nina, and Charlotte Appel. *Children's Literature in the Nordic World.* Aarhus: Aarhus University Press, 2021.

Deszcz-Tryhubczak, Justyna, and Zoe Jaques. *Intergenerational Solidarity in Children's Literature and Film.* Jackson: University Press of Mississippi, 2021.

Fass, Paula S. "A Historical Context for the United Nations Convention on the Rights of the Child." *The Annals of the American Academy of Political and Social Science* 633, no. 1 (2011), 17–29.

Grenby, M. O. "The Origins of Children's Literature." In *The Cambridge Companion to Children's Literature*, edited by M. O. Grenby and Andrea Immel, 3–18. Cambridge: Cambridge University Press, 2009.

Gubar, Marah. *Artful Dodgers. Reconceiving the Golden Age of Children's Literature.* New York: Oxford University Press, 2009.

Gubar, Marah. "Risky Business: Talking About Children in Children's Literature Criticism." *Children's Literature Association Quarterly* 38, no. 4 (2013), 450–57.

Gubar, Marah. "The Hermeneutics of Recuperation: What a Kinship-Model Approach to Children's Agency Could Do for Children's Literature and Childhood Studies." *Jeunesse* 8, no. 1 (2016), 291–310.

Heiberg, Johanne Luise. *Et liv genoplevet i erindringen (A Life Relived in Recollection).* Vol. 1. Copenhagen: Gyldendal, 1973 (1890–91).

Iser, Wolfgang. *The Implied Reader. Patterns of Communication in Prose Fiction from Bunyan to Beckett.* Baltimore: Johns Hopkins University Press, 1974.

James, Allison. "Giving Voice to Children's Voices: Practices and Problems, Pitfalls and Potentials," *American Anthropologist* 109, no. 2 (2007), 261–72.

James, Allison, and Adrian James. "Agency." In *Key Concepts in Childhood Studies*, 9–12. London: Sage, 2008.

Johansen, Stine Liv. "Münsters Inc. Children as Influencers Balancing Celebrity, Play and Paychecks." In *Cultural and Creative Industries of Childhood and Youth*, edited by Pascale Garnier, Gilles Brougère, and Valérie-Inés de La Ville, 155–71. Brussels: Peter Lang, 2021.

Kristeligt Dagblad (Christian Daily). Jens From Lyng: "Kirkelig bogkonkurrence med LGBT-krav" ("Book Competition in Church Context with LGBT Demands"). January 18, 2019: 5.

Maza, Sarah. "The Kids Aren't All Right: Historians and the Problem of Childhood." *American Historical Review* 125, no. 4 (2020), 1261–85.

Raithelhuber, Eberhard. "Extending Agency. The Merit of Relational Approaches for Childhood Studies." In *Reconceptualising Agency and Childhood*, edited by Florian

Esser, Meike S. Baader, Tanja Betz, and Beatrice Hungerland, 89–101. New York: Routledge, 2016.

Rudd, David. "Theorising and Theories. The Possibilities of Conditions of Childhood." In *The International Companion Encyclopedia of Children's Literature*, edited by Peter Hunt, 29–43. London: Routledge, 2004.

Sanchez-Eppler, Káren. "Methods for an Impossible Subject." *PMLA* 126, no. 1 (2011), 151–59.

Sanchez-Eppler, Káren. "A World of Books: The Transnational Imagination of Child Bookmakers in Late Nineteenth-Century America." In *Transnational Books for Children. Producers, Consumers, Encounters*, edited by Charlotte Appel, Nina Christensen, and M. O. Grenby, 356–76. Amsterdam: John Benjamins, 2023.

Smith, Victoria Ford. *Between Generations: Collaborative Authorship in the Golden Age of Children's Literature*. Jackson: University Press of Mississippi, 2017.

Spyrou, Spyros. *Disclosing Childhoods. Research and Knowledge Production for a Critical Childhood Studies*. London: Palgrave Macmillan, 2018.

Spyrou, Spyros, Rachel Rosen, and Daniel Thomas Cook. "Introduction: Reimagining Childhood Studies: Connectivities . . . Relationalities . . . Linkages . . ." In *Reimagining Childhood Studies*, edited by Spyros Spyrou, Rachel Rosen, and Daniel Thomas Cook, 1–20. London: Bloomsbury, 2018.

van Lierop-Debrauwer, Helma, and Sabine Steels. "The Mingling of Teenage and Adult Breaths. The Dutch Slash Series as Intergenerational Communication." In *Intergenerational Solidarity in Children's Literature and Film*, edited by Justyna Deszcz-Tryhubczak and Zoe Jaques, 218–30. Jackson: University Press of Mississippi, 2021.

Westin, Boel. "Nostalgia." In *Keywords for Children's Literature*, edited by Philip Nel, Lissa Paul, and Nina Christensen, Second Edition, 136–38. New York: New York University Press, 2021.

Chapter 5

RESISTING EUGENIC LEGACIES

Child Agency in Protecting Disabled Citizenship in Children's and Young Adult Literature

ELIZABETH LEACH-LEUNG

Individuals with disabilities, both physically apparent and invisible, trouble ideals of citizenship through the marked difference(s) of their embodiment. Examining landmark American legislation such as the American Rehabilitation Action (1973) and the American Disabilities Act (1990), Emily Russell notes how the ADA acknowledges embodiment as complicated and not wholly medical: "[T]he body is not simply a self-evident, physical truth" (Russell 2011: 2). In her introduction to *The Embodied Child*, Lydia Kokkola echoes the same sentiment that "the body is *not* neutral, and it cannot be separated from the ways in which we think, perceive, and inhabit our environment" (2018: 1, emphasis original). The disabled body has a history of eradication— an embodiment so problematic the only solution was elimination. Eugenics was the sinister solution for the eradication of the undesirable non-white, poor, disabled population. While eugenic practices were applied across various minorities throughout history, this chapter will focus on eugenics as a discrimination against disability, primarily because other ethnic, racial, and sexual minorities were considered a disability within eugenic thinking (Smith 2012: 15). Pitted against eugenic practices of sterilization and execution, individuals with disabilities struggled for their basic rights of citizenship: their right to life. If citizenship is participation in democratic nations (Bérubé 2003) or politics that affect an individual's rights (see Coste below), then how can we protect the disabled voices of children? This chapter demonstrates how to read for eugenic legacies and resistance in children's and young adult literature featuring disabled characters by identifying its impact on disabled citizenship alongside the promotion of agency in disabled and able-bodied children in these narratives.

The history of disability is mired in eugenics: the systematic steriliza-tion or execution of disabled populations following the unscientific and racially biased assumptions that this would strengthen the human gene pool. Believing intelligence was hereditary, Francis Galton is cited as the "father of eugenics." Galton coined the term eugenics—from the Greek *eugenes*—in 1869 to mean "the science of improving stock . . . which, especially in the case of man, takes cognisance of all influences that tend in however remote a degree to give to the more suitable races or strains of blood a better chance of prevailing speedily over the less suitable than they otherwise would have had" (Smith 2012: 9, quoting Galton). The extent of eugenics' cultural resonance can be observed in how it proliferated through children's literature at the turn of the twentieth century. Amanda Hollander observes how children's literature of this time circulated "influential claims by eugenicists that such drastic actions would free the US government from the burden of caring for its own citizens"—claims that also appeared in Nazi prosterilization posters—as "early twentieth-century eugenicists disturbingly aligned liberty with death and sterilization" (2018: 127). Of these undesirable groups, the focus remained on "ostensibly congenital conditions, including intellectual disability, epilepsy, mental illness, 'weakness' or disease, deformity, and sen-sory impairments" alongside the poor and racial minorities (Smith 2012: 13). These eugenic sentiments founded what is known as the medical model of disability (Smith 2012: 4): ideas that disability is an individual problem and that individuals should seek to find a cure. Hollander notes how "the American brand of eugenics would become the most aggressive model until Nazi socialists began their pursuit of the eugenic state" (2018: 135).

The Holocaust has become a cultural touchstone when considering eugen-ics and a turning point for various political issues surrounding this ideology (Herzog 2018: 6). While we vow "never again" and "never forget" (Popescu & Schult 2020), individuals with disabilities have often been forgotten among those sterilized and killed during the Holocaust and throughout the twen-tieth century, a fact Kokkola notes in her survey of Holocaust literature for children (2003: 6). Post–World War II, there was a rise of social activism within the Western world, however, while other rights work such as feminism and antiracism grew postwar, disability rights was a straggler to the human rights canon (Herzog 2018: 11). In fact, much of the early success of feminists and Black rights activists was due to their separation from disability, leav-ing disability as one of the last marginalization to begin conducting its own rights work in earnest in the 1970s (Smith 2012: 16). Disability activists have since succeeded in solidifying rights for individuals with disabilities such as the Individuals with Disabilities Education Act (1975) and Public Law 94–142

(1978), which encouraged children with disabilities to enter mainstream schooling—leading to more representations of children with disabilities within children's literature (Harrill 1993)—and the landmark American Disabilities Act (1990). Yet individuals with disabilities remain haunted by this eugenic past that seeps into the twenty-first-century debates on abortion, to which pro-choice arguments were founded and supported on eugenic sentiments from the 1960s and 1970s (Herzog 2018: 9).

Questions of what disabled citizenship looks like is evoked in Dagmar Herzog's quest to truly unlearn eugenics as he questions how emotional, political, and financial structures of society could be adjusted to provide individuals with disability "dignified rather than demeaned lives" (2018: 12). It involves both understanding how the history of eugenics has seeped into various elements of our contemporary world and how these influence notions of embodied citizenship, as well as creating a future where individuals are no longer stigmatized or viewed as a drain on society. This chapter will evoke two texts on a temporal spectrum—the first, our folkloric past, and the second, our possible futures—which exemplify how eugenics continues to permeate children's literature. Unlike the pro-eugenic sentiments Hollander observed in early twentieth-century children's literature, twenty-first-century texts provide examples of how we can begin to unlearn eugenics and resist its legacies. Kenneth Oppel's *The Nest* (2015) illustrates how eugenic legacies are transmitted into contemporary cultural consciousness through folklore and narratives. Yet, his middle-grade novel demonstrates how one can change this story and fight alongside silenced ghosts to not repeat this eugenic past. On the other side of the spectrum, Corinne Duyvis's *On the Edge of Gone* (2019) depicts how we can create a better, inclusive future. While set in the apocalypse, Duyvis's young adult novel pushes back against the "survival of the fittest" mindset and demands a true democracy.

OUR FOLKLORIC "PAST": CHANGING THE CHANGELING IN KENNETH OPPEL'S *THE NEST*

The history of eugenics ideologies is far older than Galton. Transmitted through narratives, concepts of eugenics are buried within Western mythology and folklore, stories that are retold today. Using the changeling myth as an example, David Mitchell and Sharon Snyder describe how, "even after the professionalization of modern medicine, literature continues to serve an important explanatory function in the cultural understanding of disability" (2014: 26). Also called the substitution story, this folktale acted as a pre-scientific explanation for infants with congenital disability, both physical and intellectual, and provided justification for infanticide. These tales were traditionally a "form of guilt displacement" (Haffter 1968: 58) and a means to justify eugenics. Contemporary retellings such as Oppel's *The Nest* expose how eugenics continues to penetrate our culture through the child substitution story. The perpetually anxious Steve, worried about his sick newborn brother, is visited by an angelic wasp queen in his dreams. She comes with the promise to help "fix" baby Theo by replacing him with her "perfect" child being grown in the wasps' nest outside his window; Steve just has to say yes. *The Nest* reverses elements within the changeling myth to highlight its eugenic themes and provides opportunities for Steve, the child protagonist, to accept his newborn brother's congenital disability alongside his own anxiety, ultimately rejecting the eugenic ideologies presented through history and mythology.

The substitution story is a folktale that describes how fairies would take newborn babies and replace them with their "changeling" or fairy children. Motivated by their quest to obtain an immortal soul, the changeling fey would acquire both beauty and a soul if they were nursed by a human mother while the stolen human child could ennoble fey bloodlines through marriage (Haffter 1968: 56). Naturally, human families did not want a fairy child but their own human baby and many of these stories featured gruesome ends where changelings were beaten, burned, or poisoned to reveal their true fairy nature (Haffter 1968). Scholars as early as 1891 have read the changeling myth as a tale for parents to cope with their children born with disabilities (Renner 2016: 154 citing Munro). From the word's etymological roots, changeling or *cangun/conjeoun* was used as an insult to denote "a dwarf" or "a simpleton" (Sawyer 2019: 65). The descriptions of changeling have been argued to mirror the appearance of various congenital disabilities. Susan Eberly draws connections between these common changeling traits and a wide range of congenital disabilities, including cerebral palsy, Hurler syndrome, cri du chat syndrome, hypercalcemia syndrome, Down syndrome, carp mouth syndrome, sirenomelia, progeria, and achondroplastic dwarfing (1988: 65–66). While physical markers of congenital disabilities clearly align them with the described changeling, there have been disputes over how intellectual disabilities were identified. C. F. Goodey and Tim Stainton argue that changelings were only associated with intellectual disabilities as late as the mid-seventeenth century and that it was indeed Locke—not Martin Luther, who is more commonly cited—who implied the "logical" conclusion that it was only the impossibility of early diagnosis that stopped the "ethical" infanticide on intellectually disabled children (2001: 239). Either way, the idea of the "abnormal" child is paramount to the description of the changeling.

The Nest retains many of the themes and characters of the changeling myth, albeit with a twist. The fairies are reimagined as uncanny wasps: iridescent white—not yellow jackets or hornets that are native to the Ontario setting of the novel—and described as anatomically different from regular wasps: "[I]t might not even be a wasp" (Oppel 2015: 86–87). However, while the changeling myth replaces a "normal/healthy" baby with a "disfigured/disabled" changeling, *The Nest* reverses this substitution. The changeling is still a fairy, grown within the wasps' nest, but it is described as "healthy" and "perfect," whereas Theo, the human child, is sickly. While Oppel does cite his daughter's Down syndrome as the largest influence of *The Nest* (Dror and Bittner 2017), Theo's disability is not specified beyond the term "congenital," although we are told his condition is quite rare (2015: 42).

The largest change Oppel makes to the changeling myth is introducing an intermediary character between the adults, the baby, and fey: the child protagonist, Steve. Steve is placed in an agentic position as a "competen[t] and capabl[e] social acto[r]" (Flynn 2016: 262), a key position the original myth lacks. Unlike other substitution stories, this substitution between the wasp baby and Theo has not yet happened, and Steve becomes a necessary element to continue this narrative: he must help the wasps in their final step, to open the window and let them into Theo's room. It becomes his choice as to whether or not he allows the substitution to take place, for the wasps to "fix" Theo by "replacing him altogether" (Oppel 2015: 68). Commonly used in the medical model of disability alongside "cure" and "ameliorate," the language of "fix" signals the blurred line between medicine and eugenics. If the wasps "fix" Theo, replacing him with their "healthy" wasp baby, then the wasps will eat Theo, thus completing the eugenic death drive of the original changeling myth. Steve is placed on a tipping point: to be passive and allow the substitution to unfold or to "become [an] active participant" (Flynn 2016: 256) and reject the culture of eugenics by changing the narrative.

Yet it is not just Steve's mere presence in the narrative that complicates the substitution story but also his identity as a disabled character that disrupts the key binary between the disabled and changeling child. While the term is not used within the text, Steve displays many traits associated with obsessive-compulsive disorder (OCD): obsessive thoughts, intense anxiety, and compulsive behaviors (NHS 2021). The wasp queen initially weaponizes Steve's fear of his own disabled identity to control him. When Steve says that he's going to tell his parents about the wasps' plan, she replies that his parents will "send [him] straight to the psychiatric ward for assessment and pump [him] full of sedatives and antipsychotics and start debating [his] diagnosis"

(2015: 181). The queen paints a sensationalized and outdated image of modern treatment facilities common in Western media, playing on Steve's fear of being separated from society and locked away in an asylum. John Radford notes how the asylum, as we see depicted in media today, is haunted by its eugenic history: a place where disabled people were segregated from society and often sterilized (1991). The queen also offers to "fix" Steve as his "case isn't so severe . . . a few little tweaks and twokes" (Oppel 2015: 176). Of course, "fixing" is interchangeable with "replacing" for the wasps, and so Oppel changes the substitution story to position multiple disabled characters along the eugenic path of the changeling myth.

There are several other disabled characters within *The Nest* who further complicate the changeling myth: Steve's babysitter has polycystic kidneys; a friend of her uncle's has multiple sclerosis (MS); a door-to-door salesman they refer to as "the knife guy" is missing his fingers from a congenital disability; and the specter of Mr. Nobody. While a cast of disabled characters is not rare within children's literature (see McBryde Johnson's *Accidents of Nature*), the multitude of disabled characters remains a minority to the tokenized disabled child or literary "freak" Abbye E. Meyer describes (2022: 62). As Steve's disabled identity upsets the eugenic drive of the changeling myth, so do the cast of characters supporting him. Notably, Mr. Nobody and knife guy are two somewhat-connected spectral figures who become Steve's greatest allies. Mr. Nobody is described as a shadow, without face or limbs, a shape of nightmares (2015: 223) only present within Steve's dreams or a disembodied voice on the phone. Knife guy is his corporeal counterpart and the bridging figure between the dreamlike wasp world and Steve's reality. He is the one who provides the knife to Steve, which he ultimately uses to defeat the wasps. Together, these figures illustrate how infanticide haunts the changeling story and Western history as Mr. Nobody is the specter of children who were substituted for wasp babies:

> "But who are you really?" I asked.
> "Just Mr. Nobody. I was replaced."
> I staggered after him, stunned. "It . . . it happened to you?"
> "Many years ago."
> A wasp suddenly lunged toward us. My knife flashed out and cut the creature into twitching halves.
> "I'm not alive," said Mr. Nobody. "Scarcely was. The wasps can disperse me. I can't fight them. I can only give you the knife. And show you the way." (2015: 227–28)

Mr. Nobody is the ghost of a disabled child: unnamed, dehumanized, and erased from history by the wasps and their eugenic agenda. Yet this history he (dis)embodies becomes Steve's most powerful weapon. History and knowledge—symbolized by the knife—can provide us with tools we may need to sever one's present from one's eugenic past. However, Mr. Nobody cannot wield the knife: "'It has to be you. I'm nothing'" (2015: 229). Just as how the wasps cannot swap the babies without Steve's help, the battle between knife-wielding Steve and the wasp swarm becomes an externalized battle between Steve and his own internalized ableism. By learning the silenced, eugenic history Mr. Nobody suffered, Steve hopes to change the present and reject the substitution story and its legacy. He uses the knife to cut the metaphorical ties to the past, reject eugenics, and say not Theo, not me, not anyone, never again.

While the changeling myth often presents violent solutions to the changeling problem, *The Nest* centers around a choice: "'Well, there's always a choice,' [the queen] said. 'Always a choice'" (2015: 66). Choice underscores agency for young people, emphasizing their capacities to act and express their ideas (Christensen 2021: 10, citing James and James). For Steve, there is the choice to follow the substitution story or to amend it. There is an ease in allowing the substitution. As the queen postulates, "You think they'll care when they discover [Theo]'s healthy?" (2015: 131). In our world, constructed around the medical model of disability, healthy is undeniably easier, yet health is not an absolute. As Ato Quayson notes, able-bodiedness is temporary and provisional (2007: 14), and disability is an unextractable part of the human condition. Steve comes to this realization as he looks at the wasp baby:

> But I knew, absolutely I knew, that this perfect baby didn't care about our little Theo. It didn't care about me or anyone else. It couldn't, because it was so perfect that it wouldn't even understand what it was like not to be perfect. It would never know weakness or fear. But I could. Because I was broken inside too. And in that instant I decided that this perfect baby would never replace my brother. (Oppel 2015: 179–80)

Steve, initially caught up in what Quayson calls the "subliminal fear and moral panic" (2007: 14) of disability, ultimately disentangles himself from the eugenic themes of the substitution story and becomes both Theo's and his own champion for disabled lives.

However, Steve's victory is a single battle within a war. While Steve prevents the wasp queen from "Lay[ing] one last egg. [To m]ake a new queen"

(Oppel 2015: 220), there are hints that the threat of the wasps remains. After Steve's battle, he asks the exterminator:

> "Have you ever seen that kind [of wasp] before?" I asked.
> He was an older man, said he'd been in the business his whole life. He frowned like he'd tasted something nasty, and gave a grunt. "Maybe just once. A long time ago." (Oppel 2015: 242)

While this interaction is short, it nods to how this nest was one of many. The exterminator's grunt could describe other wasp-like encounters or harken back to the atrocities of the Holocaust a long time ago. Whatever event the exterminator may be referring to, it acts as a warning that Steve must continue fighting against eugenic ideologies that would see him and his brother become Mr. Nobodies.

In their article on disability in changeling stories, Goodey and Stainton end with the thought-provoking phrase, "the concept of the changeling is thus itself a changeling" (2001: 239). The changeling myth, while reworked and reversed, can allow us to investigate ableist constructs built into children's literature and culture. *The Nest* gives its characters agency to reject the substitution plot, engage with the troubled history of eugenics, give Mr. Nobody a voice, and vanquish the changeling without killing the disabled child.

OUR POSSIBLE FUTURES: FIGHTING FOR DEMOCRACY IN THE APOCALYPSE OF CORINNE DUYVIS'S *ON THE EDGE OF GONE*

While books like *The Nest* illustrate how we are still trying to unlearn eugenics and how we are not as far removed from the past as we may like to think, examining futuristic speculative fiction written for children and young adults can enable us to postulate what unlearning we still have to accomplish. Elizabeth A. Wheeler claims that "children with disabilities rehearse their futures as assertive adults and challenge the future to turn partial inclusion into full inclusion," and these rehearsals can play out in science fiction narratives (2019: 179). While some techno futures may feature cyborgs as individuals with prosthetics and physical disabilities as second-class citizens (see Melissa Meyers's The Lunar Chronicles Series) and Afrofutures may sit on positive or negative poles (see Wheeler's discussion of Sherri L. Smith's *Orleans*), there are other futuristic worlds that are welcoming toward its disabled citizens. Yet such inclusive and diverse spaces must be policed by their citizens for, even in the face of the apocalypse, we cannot resort to a eugenic mindset when considering who may survive.

On the Edge of Gone presents a close yet apocalyptic future. In the year 2034, eighteen years after the novel's publication, Earth is hit by an extinction-level comet. Prior to this ecological disaster, many fled Earth on generational spaceships to colonize new worlds, leaving billions behind to chance survival in ill-equipped bunkers. Sixteen-year-old Denise and her mother are two such individuals left behind. By chance, they stumble upon a generational ship, the privately owned Nassau, which has not yet left Earth. Earthbound for repairs after the impact event, Denise strives to convince the captain and crew that she and her family deserve a coveted spot onboard—a real chance to survive.

It is worth noting that Denise embodies various marginalized identities. She is an adolescent female of mixed heritage—Dutch and Surinamese—and is very conscious that she does not look like her white mother and that there are few other brown-skinned bodies aboard the Nassau (Duyvis 2019: 47). She is able-bodied—until she sustains an arm injury at the midpoint of the novel—but is neurodivergent: Denise is autistic.[1] While exploring the full scope of these intersections beyond the space of this chapter, it is worth noting that On the Edge of Gone portrays more diversity than the whiteness of characters present within The Nest and that Denise's intersectional identity permeates her lived experience. The survival novel itself illustrates how Black, disabled women are disproportionately at risk, the environmental disaster metaphorically highlighting the harsh lived experiences of these people within our reality (Wheeler 2019: 180–82).

Concepts of survival, particularly the notion of "survival of the fittest," carry with them a eugenic legacy. The first use of the phrase was recorded in 1864 by biologist Herbert Spencer and later approved by Charles Darwin as an alternative to "natural selection" (Smith 2012: 247). However, "survival of the fittest" was used more by neo-Darwinists "to justify social and economic inequalities as natural and beneficial to humanity and to imagine progression as the continued flourishing of social, economic, and racial elites over the savagery of "primitive" races and ethnicities" (Smith 2012: 7). While Duyvis's novel does not outright discuss eugenics within the human population, especially when compared to The Nest, notions of eugenic thinking are present within flashbacks of Denise's volunteer work at a cat shelter. Wheeler notes that "animals and children have been natural companions in literature for centuries [and that] this companionship takes on particular importance for children with disabilities" (2019: 11). Cats are one of Denise's hyperfixations, and she had one day hoped to become a vet. These hopes are dashed when, leading up to the impact, the shelter she volunteers at decides to euthanize all the rescue cats as an act of mercy as authorities have deemed them not worthy of saving. Indeed, the only animals onboard the *Nassau* are insects and fish that are both necessary resources, and there are few other ships or permanent shelters that would take limited animals (Duyvis 2019: 55, 361–62). The passage wherein Denise oversees the injections draws the reader's attention to many of the misfit cats, such as those who were injured or disabled, as Denise's inner monologue repeats, "*It's necessary. No time for weakness. . . . It's necessary. . . . It's necessary*" (2019: 361). Despite Denise's grief, she consoles herself and the attending vet by saying that euthanizing them is the compassionate action. Yet as Hollander notes in her analysis of the overtly eugenic *Dear Enemy* (1915), misplaced compassion is often a means to justify eugenics as they "consign many to the grave as an act of mercy" (2018: 137).

While the cats' deaths are more of a cull of animals than an example of human gene selection, the thematic links between Denise and the cats she loves carry undercurrents of eugenics. Cats with disabilities and behavioral issues typically proved the hardest to place: "[P]eople don't see them as worth the trouble when there are healthy cats to take" (Duyvis 2019: 74). The experiences of these cats echo Denise's struggles to find belonging as an interracial autistic girl with perceived behavioral issues. To further link the eugenics subthemes, Denise briefly discusses the practice of breeding for desired traits: "I'm against breeding, there are so many great cats already out there, and I really don't like that they're involving wild animals—but it's interesting" (2019: 101). Breeding is a eugenic sentiment and, while one step removed from humans in this instance, there remains a simultaneous distaste yet fascination with the practice. Perhaps the most dangerous thing about eugenics is this fascination with genetics, but this can quickly become problematic and genocidal.

The cats were euthanized because they were no longer deemed useful animals, which provokes the question of whether Denise may face the same fate. As Denise says, "I'm good with cats, but that's not exactly useful" (Duyvis 2019: 74). In the survival genre, it is assumed only the strongest, most useful, will survive. In his chapter on survival, work, and plague, Theodore Martin posits that the contemporary postapocalyptic novel is concerned with the monotony of work. While I would argue young adult dystopias reject monotony in favor of action, Martin notes that the "secretly entwined logics of survival and work afford us a glimpse not of a postcapitalist future but of a contemporary moment shaped by constant yet precarious labor" (2017: 162). Our future is, in many ways, a mirror of our present: the precariousness of employment that plagues young generations within our contemporary neocapitalist world. Neocapitalism naturally derives from its capitalist origins, and Hollander observes, in the eugenic children's literature of the early twentieth century, that "human worth becomes intrinsically tied to the individual's facility to participate in the workforce—a hierarchy in which the able-bodied are designated as the deserving" (Hollander 2018: 129). Work, as measured by capitalistic output, is inherently eugenic: if an individual cannot contribute to society, they are considered lacking—a sentiment likewise shared by the medical model of disability. If the survival genre is "a counter-intuitive form of futurity, [where] survival is desperate for the mere continuation of the present" (Martin 2017: 161), then the neurodiversity paradigm seeks to disrupt this form of futurity and, in turn, disrupt eugenic ideals of "survival of the fittest."

Neurodiversity is a reaction against the medical model of disability and the eugenics it spawned from. It asserts that "[t]here is no 'normal' or 'right' style of human mind, any more than there is one 'normal' or 'right' ethnicity, gender, or culture" (Walker 2021: 15) and that neurodiversity is a type of biodiversity, part of natural human variance (Armstrong 2012; McGee 2012). The neurodiversity paradigm encompasses autism, ADHD, dyslexia, dyspraxia, bipolar disorder, depression, and epilepsy, among other neurominorities, and "acknowledg[es] neurological difference does not imply that all difference is good in itself, or that human traits associated with neurodivergence are always desirable, but it accepts that there are 'good' and 'not so good' traits in all human beings" (Bertilsdotter et al. 2020: 7). Micki McGee argues that "the emergence of the term neurodiversity, and the activism that produced it, may be a symptom of our failure to come up with a theory of personhood that doesn't rest on the faulty premises of individual equality and rational agency, and that doesn't privilege the reasonable, the sociable, and the productive" (2012: 13).

Activist Janine Booth describes these troubles for autistics in particular as they are excluded and disadvantaged in the contemporary workplace. Her monograph *Autism Equality in the Workplace: Removing Barriers and Challenging Discrimination* outlines various ways in which autistics are disadvantaged, including subpar education from delayed diagnosis; overreliance on interviews, verbal communication skills, and teamwork; environments that do not account for sensory issues; and inflexible time management, atop generalized discrimination among coworkers and lack of job security (2016). Duyvis outlines how Denise struggles with many of these, including her late autism diagnosis, as she was written off to be "*[j]ust another maladjusted Black girl from the Bijlmer*" (2019: 60, emphasis original); her struggles with eye contact (2019: 232) and interacting with strangers (2019: 346); and her occasional nonverbal lapses and sensory issues (2019: 409).

While these neurodivergent traits make it challenging to find employment in the contemporary world, this struggle is heightened in the apocalypse.

While social order has basically collapsed postimpact event, power delineations between the working and management classes have become more apparent as Captain Van Zand effectively runs a dictatorship (pun not intended) onboard the *Nassau*. Yet this dictatorship promotes and rewards child agency as opposed to depicting children as "vulnerable and dependent on adult power and protection" (Christensen 2021: 13). Children are expected to be as active in contributing to the ship as the adults, perhaps taking Marah Gubar's "kinship model" (2013) one step further to create an "equality model" (also see Christensen's discussion of "relational agency," above). Age and life experience take a back seat to usefulness. However, while Denise, as a child, may not be discriminated against, concepts of "useful" and "desired traits" become eugenic within the life-or-death situation. "Usefulness" is troubled not by Denise's age but by her autism. Denise is not the stereotypical super-crip: she does not possess unnatural talents or intellect that legitimize or offset her other autistic traits. While it is usual practice within capitalism for the managerial class to "traw[l] the neurodiverse sector for 'talented' neurodiverse individuals" (Adam-Bagley 2022: 123), Denise is "not into literal rocket science" (Duyvis 2019: 67) like her friend Max.

Yet her autism is *not* the overtly limiting factor. Critics have noted the idealistic nature of Duyvis's novel. Sarah Frisch writes that "in the future that Duyvis creates, it is as if the medical model of disability had been rendered all but extinct" (Frisch 2019: 115). Frisch's statement is true to an extent. While there are moments of shock and ideological reorientation when her autism is revealed to other characters, Denise is never explicitly discriminated against because she is autistic; she is allowed the same opportunities to prove herself as everyone else. The *Nassau* even comprises various abilities, including an engineer who is a wheelchair user and another autistic doctor (Duyvis 2019: 275, 282). As Sanne, one of her peers and a homeless teenager who was adopted into the crew, claims, "The *Nassau* doesn't give a damn as long as you contribute" (2019: 275).

Denise recognizes the truth in Sanne's statement, finding the environment on the *Nassau* better than any previous experience she had in school (2019: 283). However, it is the idea of contributing, of being useful to society, that holds onto vestiges of the medical model and its eugenic mindset—not just with Denise's disabled identity, but across other intersections. For example, Denise's sister Iris, despite her youth, is of limited use to a generational ship as she can no longer reproduce as a transwoman (2019: 248). Despite the comparatively welcoming neurodiverse community, the future portrayed in Duyvis's novel still fights against the eugenic mindset of survival: the *Nassau* "judged the applicants' skills, age, health, number of dependents, all that, and made selections" (Duyvis 2019: 73). Ultimately, there remains a "useful" type of neurodivergence.

While initially Denise does not have any "useful" skills, she performs *significantly* better than her neurotypical peers would assume, breaking stereotypes of what an autistic girl is capable of. Her single-minded focus enables her to venture outside of the ship to retrieve lost supplies while looking for her sister and saves many lives from a sudden tsunami (2019: 144). An injury she sustains even becomes a point of pride: "It's proof: *I went out there. I can do more than read about cats*" (2019: 246, emphasis original). She finds a job organizing announcement information onboard, in which she excels (2019: 287). In each instance, Denise fights against the assumptions that she is unable to accomplish these tasks, assumptions epitomized by Captain Van Zand's brother: "She's just being difficult. Have you ever *seen* an autistic kid? Trust me, they're not the kind to take water scooters into the city like she did" (2019: 316, emphasis original). Despite Captain Van Zand's brother, the generally neurodiverse environment allowed Denise to prove her "usefulness" and disprove the assumptions rooted in eugenics.

Yet while Denise proves useful enough to stay aboard the ship—and the ship proves a more welcoming environment to Denise than school ever was—Denise is an exception rather than the rule. There remains a silent population that is unable to work:

> "That wouldn't be fair to the other passengers. It's not about you being autistic—you've seen Dr. Meijer. We treat everyone equally. And everyone works." She [Els] looks to Leyla as if for help.
> "Everyone who *can*." I back away. "I'll talk to the captain myself."
> (2019: 450, emphasis original)

In light of this injustice, Denise becomes an activist for everyone, no matter how "useful" they may be. Denise, alongside Max and Iris, starts a campaign among the crew to demand of the captain that they stay on Earth to help those left behind as "the people on the planet are *part* of that future" (2019: 436, emphasis original). Their campaign ultimately results in a governing shift: "I enjoyed my benevolent Van Zand dictatorship for those few weeks. But I guess we're a democracy now" (2019: 444). Mixing the neurodiverse inclusivity of the *Nassau* in addition to the newfound democracy creates what Michael Bérubé calls "meaningful democracy in which all citizens participate" (2003: 56). A true democracy must account for all voices, even those that might otherwise be considered not fully-able, and Denise pushes for a democracy that accounts not just for those dubbed "useful" but for everyone. While the *Nassau* was relatively welcoming to disabled bodyminds before, democracy improves their situation *and* the situation for all left without a spot on the ship. Bérubé ends his article "Citizenship and Disability" with the sentiment that the betterment of disabled individuals leads to the betterment of all humanity:

> [A] capacious and supple sense of what is to be human is better than a narrow and partial sense of what it is to be human, and the more participants we as a society can incorporate into the deliberation of what it means to be human, the greater the chances that that deliberation will in fact be transformative in such a way as to enhance our collective capacities to recognize each other as humans entitled to human dignity. (2003: 56)

As similar sentiments are evoked in Herzog's notion to unlearn eugenics through the betterment of disabled lives (2018: 12), texts like *On the Edge of Gone* champion disabled citizenship as necessary for the betterment of humanity. As Kit Kavanagh-Ryan states in her article "Who Gets to Survive the Apocalypse?": "The most important part about . . . Duyvis's protagonist, Denise, is that [she] exist[s]. [She] exists, even when parts of [her] world fear [her] or find [her] expendable" (2022: 19). Denise's activism enables neurodiversity to triumph over "survival of the fittest" and for hope of a better future even in the apocalypse.

While *On the Edge of Gone* does not discuss eugenic legacies as overtly as *The Nest*, these legacies still haunt the speculative future. Although the *Nassau* is presented as a generally inclusive, neurodiverse environment, one is only allowed aboard if they are considered "useful" enough to earn their place. But as Iris tells Denise, "Whether someone is useful only matters if you value people by their use" (Duyvis 2019: 447). Inclusivity cannot be a privilege only for those lucky enough to be considered "useful" and win the lottery to board the *Nassau*. Inclusivity must be policed by its abled and disabled citizens, and true democracy must be demanded so people are not—in some cases literally—left behind. *On the Edge of Gone* illustrates how, even in the apocalypse, we need not resort to the "survival of the fittest" to survive.

RESISTING EUGENIC LEGACIES

Legacies of eugenics persist within children's literature as they do within contemporary society. Down to the cores of capitalism and the Western world, there remains the emphasis that one must be "useful" to be worthy of citizenship. As the wasp queen vocalizes, "[W]e want a good orderly society. That's why we make our babies so perfect. Only a perfect baby can make a perfect society" (Oppel 2015: 180). The queen epitomizes the neoliberalist construction of our world as it affects those with disabilities—one must be productive, orderly, to be worthy. But as Steve cuts down the wasp queen, Denise finds environments such as the *Nassau* where "[she] can *thrive*" (Duyvis 2019: 284, emphasis original) as an autistic and advocate for the betterment and survival of all, no matter their "usefulness." Neither book presents a traditional happy ending wherein the disability present is fixed, cured, or ameliorated, resisting Leonard Davis's "sense of ending" that carries with it eugenic principles of elimination (1995: 49). What we see in twenty-first-century novels are a resistance to eugenic "happy endings," a deliberate changing of the narrative, and an aspiration for a better, truly inclusive future.

As eugenics is a part of disability history, overt and subliminal themes of our eugenic past can be read in texts featuring disabled characters. *The Nest* and *On the Edge of Gone* are only two such examples of contemporary children's texts that resist eugenic legacies. They illustrate a spectrum of how this resistance and child activism for disability rights and citizenship may be presented within texts across age categories. By positioning their child protagonists as champions for disabled citizenship—advocating for their right to life—they work toward the process of unlearning eugenics.

NOTE

1. There are ongoing conversations about the preferred use of identity-first—"I am autistic"—or person-first—"I am a person with autism"—language (Dunn & Andrews 2015; Lenny Letter 2018; Sinclair 1999). The NCDJ and APA Style guides suggest that both are accepted by the autism community and that it is a matter of personal identity (APA Style n.d.; *NCDJ Style Guide* 2018). As Denise uses identity-first language to describe herself— "I'm autistic" (Duyvis 2019: 59)—I will do the same in this chapter.

REFERENCES

Adam-Bagley, Chris. "Neurodiversity as Status Group, and as a Class-within-a-Class: Critical Realism and Dyslexia." *Open Journal of Social Sciences* 10, no. 1 (2022), 117–29. Accessed January 14, 2023. doi:10.4236/jss.2022.101009.

Armstrong, Thomas. *Neurodiversity in the Classroom: Strength-Based Strategies to Help Students with Special Needs Succeed in School and Life*. Alexandria: ASCD, 2012.

Bertilsdotter, Hannah, Nick Chown, and Anna Stenning. "Introduction." In *Neurodiversity Studies: A New Critical Paradigm*, edited by Hannah Rosqvist, Nick Chown, and Anna Stenning, 1–11. London: Routledge, 2020.

Bérubé, Michael. "Citizenship and Disability." *Dissent*, Spring 2003. Accessed January 15, 2003. https://www.dissentmagazine.org/article/citizenship-and-disability/.

Booth, Janine. *Autism Equality in the Workplace: Removing Barriers and Challenging Discrimination*. London: Jessica Kingsley Publishers, 2016.

Christensen, Nina. "Agency." In *Keywords for Children's Literature*, edited by Philip Nel and Lissa Paul, 2nd ed., 10–13. New York: NYU Press, 2021.

Davis, Lennard J. *Enforcing Normalcy: Disability, Deafness, and the Body*. London: Verso Books, 1995.

"Disability Language Style Guide." National Center on Disability and Journalism. Accessed January 15, 2023. https://ncdj.org/style-guide/.

"Disability." American Psychological Association APA Style. Accessed December 16, 2022. https://apastyle.apa.org/style-grammar-guidelines/bias-free-language/disability.

Dror, Stephanie, and Bittner, Robert. "On Kenneth Oppel: An Interview." *Canadian Children's Book News* 40, no. 2 (2017), 12–14. Accessed January 14, 2023.

Dunn, Dana S., and Erin E. Andrews. "Person-First and Identity-First Language: Developing Psychologists' Cultural Competence Using Disability Language." *American Psychologist* 70, no. 3 (2015), 255–64. Accessed January 14, 2023. doi:10.1037/a0038636.

Duyvis, C. *On the Edge of Gone*. Waterville: Thorndike Press, 2019.

Eberly, Susan S. "Fairies and the Folklore of Disability: Changelings, Hybrids and the Solitary Fairy." *Folklore* 99, no. 1 (1988), 58–77. Accessed January 15, 2023. doi:10.1080/0015587x.1988.9716425.

Flynn, Richard. "What Are We Talking about When We Talk About Agency?" *Jeunesse: Young People, Texts, Cultures* 8, no. 1 (2016), 254–65. Accessed January 15, 2023. doi:10.1353/jeu.2016.0012.

Frisch, Sarah. "Book Review: Neurodiversity Meets the Apocalypse: *On the Edge of Gone* by Corinne Duyvis." *Ought: The Journal of Autistic Culture* 1, no. 1 (2019), 113–16. Accessed January 15, 2023. doi:10.9707/2833-1508.1023.

Goodey, C. F., and Tim Stainton. "Intellectual Disability and the Myth of the Changeling Myth." *Journal of the History of the Behavioral Sciences* 37, no. 3 (2001), 223–40. Accessed January 15, 2023. doi:10.1002/jhbs.1032.

Gubar, Marah. "Risky Business: Talking About Children in Children's Literature Criticism." *Children's Literature Association Quarterly* 38, no. 4 (2013), 450–57. Accessed January 15, 2023. doi:10.1353/chq.2013.0048.

Haffter, Carl. "The Changeling: History and Psychodynamics of Attitudes to Handicapped Children in European Folklore." *Journal of the History of the Behavioral Sciences* 4, no. 1 (1968), 55–61. Accessed January 15, 2023. doi:10.1002/1520-6696(196801)4:1<55::aid-jhbs2300040106>3.0.co;2-0.

Harrill, Juanita Lynn, et al. Portrayal of Handicapped/Disabled Individuals in Children's Literature: Before and After Public Law 94–142. ERIC, 1993. Accessed January 15, 2023. https://eric.ed.gov/?id=ED357557.

Herzog, D. *Unlearning Eugenics: Sexuality, Reproduction, and Disability in Post-Nazi Europe*. Wisconsin: University of Wisconsin Press, 2018.

Hollander, Amanda. "Liberty in the Age of Eugenics: Non-Normative Bodies in Fabian Socialist Children's Fiction." In *The Embodied Child: Readings in Children's Literature and Culture*, edited by Roxanne Harde and Lydia Kokkola, 127–39. London: Routledge, 2019.

Kavanagh-Ryan, Kit. "Who Gets to Survive the Apocalypse? Disability Hierarchy in Post-Disaster Fiction in Australian YA." *Australian Literary Studies* 37, no. 1 (2022). Accessed January 15, 2023. doi:10.20314/als.4801bfd4aa.

Kokkola, Lydia. *Representing the Holocaust in Children's Literature*. London: Routledge, 2013.

Kokkola, Lydia. "The Embodied Child: An Introduction." In *The Embodied Child: Readings in Children's Literature and Culture*, edited by Roxanne Harde and Lydia Kokkola, 1–20. London: Routledge, 2019.

Lenny Letter. "I Don't Have Autism. I'm Autistic." www.lennyletter.com. Last modified June 7, 2018. Accessed January 15, 2023. https://www.lennyletter.com/story/i-dont-have -autism-im-autistic.

Martin, Theodore. "Survival: Work and Plague: Genre, Historicism, and the Problem of the Present." In *Contemporary Drift: Genre, Historicism, and the Problem of the Present*, edited by Theodore Martin, 161–94. New York: Columbia University Press, 2017.

McGee, Micki. "Neurodiversity." *Contexts* 11, no. 3 (2012), 12–13. doi:10.1177/1536504212456175.

Meyer, A. E. *From Wallflowers to Bulletproof Families: The Power of Disability in Young Adult Narratives*. Mississippi: University Press of Mississippi, 2022.

Mitchell, D. T., and S.L. Snyder. *Narrative Prosthesis: Disability and the Dependencies of Discourse*. Michigan: University of Michigan Press, 2014.

Oppel, Kenneth. *The Nest*. New York: Harper Trophy, 2015.

Popescu, Diana, and Tanja Schult. "Performative Holocaust Commemoration in the 21st Century." *Holocaust Studies* 26, no. 2 (2019), 135–51. Accessed January 15, 2023. doi:10.10 80/17504902.2019.1578452.

Quayson, Ato. "A Typology of Disability Representation." In *Aesthetic Nervousness: Disability and the Crisis of Representation*, edited by Ato Quayson, 32–53. New York: Columbia University Press, 2007.

Radford, John P. "Sterilization Versus Segregation: Control of the 'Feebleminded,' 1900–1938." *Social Science & Medicine* 33, no. 4 (1991), 449–58. doi:10.1016/0277-9536(91)90327-9.

Renner, K. J. *Evil Children in the Popular Imagination*. New York: Palgrave Macmillan, 2016.

Russell, E. *Reading Embodied Citizenship Disability, Narrative, and the Body Politic*. New Jersey: Rutgers University Press, 2011.

Sawyer, R. A. "Changeling Stories: The Child Substitution Motif in the Chester Mystery Cycle." In *Literary Cultures and Medieval and Early Modern Childhoods*, edited by Naomi J. Miller and Diane Purkiss, 65–72. Basingstoke: Springer, 2019.

Sinclair, Jim. "Why I Dislike 'Person First' Language." Autism Mythbusters. Last modified 1999. https://autismmythbusters.com/general-public/autistic-vs-people-with-autism/ jim-sinclair-why-i-dislike-person-first-language/.

Smith, A. *Hideous Progeny: Disability, Eugenics, and Classic Horror Cinema*. New York: Columbia University Press, 2012.

"Symptoms—Obsessive Compulsive Disorder (OCD)." NHS. Last modified February 16, 2021. https://www.nhs.uk/mental-health/conditions/obsessive-compulsive-disorder-ocd/symptoms/.

Walker, N. *Neuroqueer Heresies: Notes on the Neurodiversity Paradigm, Autistic Empowerment, and Postnormal Possibilities*. Texas: Autonomous Press, 2021.

Wheeler, Elizabeth A. *HandiLand: The Crippest Place on Earth*. Michigan: University of Michigan Press, 2019.

Chapter 6

FROM AGEISM TO AGENCY

Generation Z Authors as Inevitable Activists

JILL COSTE

In the September 1944 inaugural issue of *Seventeen* magazine, a periodical aimed at the growing teenage market in mid-twentieth-century United States, editor-in-chief Helen Valentine addressed her teen readers as future citizens of the world: "You're going to have to run this show, so the sooner you start thinking about it, the better" (1944: 33). Her edict appears in a column that welcomes readers and invites them to share their interests, their perspectives, their voices. Indeed, *Seventeen* magazine was an early proponent of teenage citizenship, seemingly recognizing the importance of civic engagement, expecting agency of its readers, and even acknowledging the failings of adults. Another editorial in April 1945, in fact, outright condemned the state of the world: "We expect you to run this world a lot more sensibly than we have. No group of adults who have created a civilization which is blackened by a world war can claim to have done a good job" (Valentine 1945).

These examples from an early piece of teenage-focused media show the troubled relationship between adults and adolescents wherein adults recognize where they've fallen short and yet still expect teens to follow their instructions. But we can also look at that troubled relationship another way because the editorial's acknowledgment is an interesting reversal of Maria Nikolajeva's theory of aetonormativity, where the child is othered, protected (presumably) for their own good until they traverse normative development into being an adult. If the adult is the norm and the adult is admitting that the norm is bad, then the adult is acknowledging that young people's agency to create change is worthy and powerful. This tension between wanting control over adolescents and wanting them to change our world for the better is an important conversation in children's and young adult literature studies, especially as young adult literature increasingly shows young readers the potential for a better world. Indeed, such literature also evokes Clementine Beauvais's theory of "the mighty child," the child who is powerful because of what they *might* do, whose relationship with the authoritative adult is complicated by the way that very adult is "necessarily aware of, and deferential to, an assumed child power that the adult obviously lacks" (2015: 4). While Beauvais's study focuses on childhood and not adolescence, which she sees as "belonging to a different kind of temporal otherness" (2015: 9), her ideas are especially resonant for YA literature when we think about how frequently this genre represents youth navigating their agency—or their ability to have an impact on the world. Like Elizabeth Leach Leung in part II of this volume, I view citizenship as an essential human right to participate in one's society. However, I extend my definition of "teenage citizenship" here to include an engagement with political matters and a growing understanding of the governmental processes that affect individual rights and societal norms.

Young adult literature is a powerful space for studying the way young people can resist and change the world adults have made for adolescents. In her April 2022 keynote talk for the Young Adult Studies Association Seminar Series on YA Studies Around the World, Kelly Gardiner boldly claimed that "young people can change the world, or perhaps even save it." Gardiner's keynote addressed the way YA literature is "full of those who will refuse and resist," "magnificent monsters" who challenge the status quo (2022). And while not all YA is radical in the sense of fomenting revolution, it's often full of radical possibilities, and it raises the question of what "radical" even is—perhaps, as Gardiner notes, reading about someone who is just like you (and not usually represented on the page) is a radical act, as such identification can create spaces of community that can agitate for social change.

Young adult literature has not always been such a place for radicalism, though. Power dynamics and teenage agency have long been central to the scholarship of young adult literature. When Roberta Seelinger Trites argued that "the YA novel teaches adolescents how to exist within the (capitalistically bound) institutions that necessarily define teenagers' existence" (2000: 19) in *Disturbing the Universe: Power and Repression in Adolescent Literature*, she defined an approach to studying power in young adult novels that allows readers to find and critique the institutional power that shapes adolescents' lives. Scholarship since then has continued to point out where adolescents gain power and where they lose it, sharing similar themes across genres.

Recently, Malin Alkestrand demonstrated how much power fluctuates in her study of contemporary American and Swedish dystopian young adult literature, using motifs of adolescent killers and adolescent mothers to show how adult control of young people is exaggerated in dystopian literature in ways that reflect realistic concerns. Jeremy Johnston has shown how YA literature provides "insights into how neoliberal capitalism shapes society, individuals, and the expectations placed upon adolescents as people preparing for both the labor market and a world generally governed by neoliberal ideology," illustrating the way that YA literature cannot help but be enmeshed with capitalist structures even when it resists them (2022). And numerous scholars—such as Jacqueline Rose (1984), Trites (2000), Beverly Lyon Clark (2003), Perry Nodelman (2008), Nikolajeva (2010), and Vanessa Joosen (2018), among others—have examined the presence and influence of adult norms in children's and YA literature. How much can teen protagonists fight the system when the system is designed to keep them in it?

That said, contemporary young adult texts frequently offer overt acknowledgments of the unjust and oppressive systems that deserve interrogation, and this narrative move can have a profound effect on Generation Z readers (those born between 1997 and 2012), a cohort who are coming of age in a digital world that readily exposes them to cultural and ideological conversations and demands literacy within those conversations. During a time where conservative calls for banned books increase at a disturbing pace in the United States, Generation Z readers are growing up in a world where vociferous conversations about progress *are* happening and where the texts that represent them can support radical thoughts and, ideally, incite radical change. And when it is Generation Z writers—those who were recently teenagers themselves—integrating these discussions into their books, they offer even more of a challenge to adult normativity.

Indeed, in this essay, I argue that Generation Z writers and their approach to young adult literature are one example of how YA literature can move away from reinforcing systems of power. By looking at writers who began their work as teens and whose novels address social concerns that push back on hegemonic norms, I will show how these young writers challenge aetonormativity and prove their might by prioritizing and amplifying the conversations that can help change our world for the better. Looking at texts by Generation Z writers reveals examples of social justice, agency, and diverse cultural representation, speaking to contemporary young audiences who are increasingly aware of these conversations about identity and the systems that shape our lives and norms.

Young adult literature, of course, has a history of addressing social issues that matter to young people—teenager S. E. Hinton, for example, wrote *The Outsiders* (1967) because she "wanted something realistic to be written about teenagers . . . something that dealt with what [she] saw kids really doing" (2012: 186). But while *The Outsiders* was an early precursor to what would become known as "the problem novel" in young adult literature, more con-temporary texts clamor for social justice and draw attention to larger sys-temic problems, not just an individual's journey through personal distress. Indeed, today's Generation Z readers grew up alongside an explosion of dystopian literature that showed them the trauma of oppression. In a study of Generation Z readers who grew up with dystopian literature, Aysha Jerald—herself a college student—found that many of the participants in her study were thinking about social justice as a result of their exposure to dystopian literature. More importantly, these readers were thinking about their own roles as society's next generation. "I feel like it's my responsibility to try and fight for better circumstances for other people," one participant said. "And I feel like, as a younger generation, we can't just accept that the older genera-tion knows everything, or that they know what's best. We have to accept that they've made mistakes, and we might have to fix them" (in Jerald 2020: 87). And as Hannah Testa, a teenage climate justice activist who founded a nonprofit called Hannah 4 Change when she was fifteen, explains, "Our generation is a fresh set of eyes on the societal standards and normalities that previous generations are accustomed to. Our generation can ask, 'Why do we do this that way?' We can find intersectionalities and use our creativity to lead an interdisciplinary movement" (Jensen 2022: 56). Thus, members of Generation Z have been primed for revolutionary perspectives because of the state of the world in which they've grown up; they know the social ills that define us, and they want to see change in the systems that have long prevailed.

Several recent debut Generation Z authors show these efforts in their nov-els across genres and countries, and many of them were writing to their peers and securing book deals before they had even graduated from university. Moreover, these writers frequently offer books that feature diverse characters and normalize cultural representation that counters the historically white YA landscape. Some of these authors include Christina Li, a middle-grade author who published her first book while an economics major at Stanford University; Tashie Bhuiyan, a recent college grad whose YA romances feature Bangladeshi American characters; Ananya Devarajan, who wrote a novel highlighting her South Asian heritage while an undergraduate at University of California, Irvine; and Racquel Marie, whose YA fiction prioritizes queer-ness and mixed-race identity. Other authors, like Chloe Gong, a Chinese New Zealander whose debut novel explored political power struggles in 1920s Shanghai, and Faridah Àbíké-Íyímídé, a British Nigerian writer whose work critiques white privilege, add to this cadre of culturally rich and thoughtful authors who are tackling race, imperialism, and oppressive power structures in their work.

Moreover, Gong and Àbíké-Íyímídé have publicly addressed the age discrimination they've faced as young writers in the publishing industry and Anglophone culture at large that says young people are too inexperienced to present anything of worth. In a podcast where Àbíké-Íyímídé interviews Gong, Gong points out that people are generally respectful of older people but feel completely comfortable proclaiming, "[Y]eah, teenagers suck!" (Àbíké-Íyímídé 2020: 23:51).[1] Gong has been thorough in critiquing the assumptions that shroud her success, writing lengthy posts on her personal blog, addressing ageism in interviews, and speaking with Àbíké-Íyímídé candidly about her experience.

Gong posits an interesting theory in a blog post about people's tendencies to want to diminish the accomplishments of young writers. She says, "From what I've observed . . . it's a gut-reaction, a very human protective mechanism. 'If this person is finishing a book at 20, what the hell was I doing? Shit, that feels bad. Oh, that feels weird. No—there must be something wrong here'" (2022). Gong's idea makes sense: certainly, it's human nature (or maybe capitalist nature, where we're measured by our productivity) to evaluate the successes of someone younger and wonder whether our own accomplishments measure up. But it also reflects the ever-present urge to consider children and young adults as *other*, as less-than, because "they can't possibly know as much as adults." Indeed, Gong's comments bring to mind the notion of "childism" as Joosen explores it in her book *Adulthood in Children's Literature*. With psychotherapist Elisabeth Young-Bruehl's definition of childism as her basis, Joosen demonstrates "the disdainful adult" in children's literature. Joosen explains, though, that childism is more than just disdain and that "[c]hildist adults, in Young-Bruehl's view, put their own well-being first, rather than the child's best interest, often because they are *on some level immature or frustrated themselves*" (2018: 125, emphasis mine). This idea of frustration connects back to Gong's observation of an adult "feeling bad," suggesting that the tendency Gong has encountered of older adults to dismiss her work has some roots in a childist impulse.

Joosen brings "childism" as defined this way into the children's literature scholarship that has long addressed the inclination of adults to disregard young people. As Clark points out in *Kiddie Lit*, adults should "think about what it means when we use metaphors of immaturity to devalue something," pushing us to question our cultural tendency to infantilize childhood (2003: 4). This tendency to minimize the contributions of youth is accompanied by an inherent adult power—financial, legal, and cultural—that is reflected in children's literature's ability to "educate, socialize and oppress a particular social group" (Nikolajeva 2010: 8). As Nikolajeva and others have theorized, this imbalance between adults and children is evident in literature for young people, which has historically aimed to acculturate young people into adult norms. Aetonormativity, or normalization of the adult and otherization of the child, exemplifies adult power.

As Beauvais notes, the child's "might" can disrupt this aetonormativity, but it's also part of an inherent "tension of powers . . . between the authoritative adult and its desired addressee, the mighty child" (2015: 3). When the author and addressee are closer in age, however, that adult-child dynamic is disrupted further. Texts written by Generation Z authors for Generation Z readers become ways for young people to communicate with each other, and the texts are shadowed not by a hidden adult à la Nodelman (2008) with acculturation aims but perhaps by a disdainful adult who wants to minimize the accomplishments of these young authors. Indeed, in America especially, it may be fair to say there is a contingent of adults who do not *want* a nineteen-year-old debut author to have anything of substance to say because what she says might be damning. She might call out the rusty and antiquated modes of thinking that continue to exalt oppressive power structures, white supremacy, capitalism, and settler colonialism. A Generation Z writer's story might use allegory to illuminate the very real racism that undergirds everyday American life—and that story might become a bestseller.

This is, in fact, the case with both Gong and Àbíké-Íyímídé's work. Both are writers whose debut novels have received a great deal of attention and spent many weeks on the *New York Times* bestseller list. Gong's *These Violent Delights*, a *Romeo and Juliet* retelling, envisions rival gangs in 1926 Shanghai. By integrating the systemic injustices of colonialism with the retelling of a classic, Gong demonstrates the power and potential of young adult literature to speak to cultural issues. Similarly, Àbíké-Íyímídé's novel, *Ace of Spades*, critiques the privilege of whiteness and wealth at private schools in America, presenting a thriller that offers chilling commentary on racial power dynamics.

Both Gong and Àbíké-Íyímídé wrote the drafts of their debut novels when they were nineteen, and each received publishing deals from major New York houses while attending university. Through crafting provocative YA texts that offer fictional entrées into social (in)justice, Gong and Àbíké-Íyímídé engage in their own sort of activism. As teenage writers who were not far removed from their target audience when they wrote their debuts, Gong and Àbíké-Íyímídé can speak directly to the needs and interests of modern teenagers. Generation Z writers such as these are possibly *best* poised to address contemporary cultural issues. If "the child and adult are symbolically set apart by their belonging to different temporalities" (Beauvais 2015:

4), then the shared temporality of Generation Z writers and readers shows a shared possibility for agency and brings to mind the kind of relational agency that Nina Christensen outlines in her chapter in this essay collection. YA literature itself becomes a space of agency, and the relationships that authors and adolescents have with it, and with each other, shape their own understanding of how to participate in social change. In these YA texts, gone is the adult wish for a better future that they're deferring to the child who might change the world, and in its place is a peer-to-peer call to action, or at least acknowledgment. Moreover, the very success of these authors both repudiates those who would say teenage writers shouldn't get published and shows how much conversations about social justice resonate with young readers. While this essay focuses largely on Gong and Àbíké-Íyímídé's novels as case studies, it also addresses another Gen Z writer whose work shows how readers may interact with these texts, bringing their own understandings of diverse perspectives to the conversation. These stories openly criticize systemic injustice and invite readers to identify with characters who work to dismantle it, and they also create space for cultural conversations about how to do so.

Àbíké-Íyímídé's *Ace of Spades*, in particular, is a brutal critique of power and privilege. *Ace of Spades* is not subtle—and that's the point. As a college student in Scotland, Àbíké-Íyímídé was inspired to write her novel based on her own experiences with microaggressions and being a person of color in a sea of white faces. Having grown up in South London, Àbíké-Íyímídé says she "never really understood what it meant to be the only Black face in a white space and what that comes with" (2022). But in her college town, she would "go days without seeing people of colour" (2022). She started watching the TV show *Gossip Girl* and was inspired to write something that combined the hierarchies and backstabbings of the show with the "microaggressions and the institutional racism [she] was constantly facing at university" (2022).

The result is *Ace of Spades*, a book that follows two students, Chiamaka and Devon, at Niveus Private Academy as they navigate the beginning of their senior year and their plans and hopes for the future. It's not a coincidence that the school's name is the Latin form of "niveous," meaning "resembling snow (as in whiteness)" (Merriam-Webster)—Devon and Chiamaka are the only Black students in their school. Chiamaka is a quintessential mean girl who has become the queen bee of her school by treating others like they're beneath her. As a wealthy student, she has monetary privilege. But her Blackness diminishes her privilege, and she tries to minimize her race by straightening her natural hair and dressing to fit in with white girls. Devon is far less popular than Chiamaka. A scholarship kid, Devon dabbles in drug dealing to help offset the living expenses his single mother can't meet. Devon is a musician who dreams of going to Juilliard, and he has a (seemingly) supportive white teacher who gives him leeway to practice his work. Within the system of privilege at their school, Devon and Chiamaka work to achieve the kind of success that comes quickly to their white fellow students.

Soon after the start of the school year, all students start receiving text messages from the mysterious Aces, texts that out Devon as gay and paint Chiamaka as a liar and a thief. It's clear early on that these texts are targeting only Devon and Chiamaka and are, in fact, a racially motivated attack. As students who have worked incredibly hard to stay in this private school for its cachet and presumable support of their elite college aspirations, Devon and Chiamaka are reluctant to view the insidious messages as targeting them because they're Black. Another character, Terrell, a friend of Devon's who doesn't attend Niveus, bluntly points out that it's racism, even if it seems like their white friends are open-minded:

> Racism is a spectrum and they [white people] all participate in it in some way. They don't all have white hoods or call us mean things; I know that. But racism isn't just about that—it's not about being nice or mean. Or good versus bad. It's bigger than that. We're all in this bubble being affected by the past. The moment they decided they got to be white and have all the power and we got to be Black and be at the bottom, everything changed. (Àbíké-Íyímídé 2021: 166)

Terrell's comment that "we're in this bubble being affected by the past" speaks to racism's role in the foundation of America—this is a country that is defined by its history of slavery. "In America," as Ta-Nehisi Coates writes, "it is tradition to destroy the black body—it is heritage" (2015: 103). I want to acknowledge that I'm talking about America, but Àbíké-Íyímídé purposely makes her setting vague—it could be any city in America; it could almost be any country where white privilege holds power over historically marginalized communities. As a British Nigerian author, Àbíké-Íyímídé brings a global perspective to her work, but she also creates a story that illustrates the power dynamics that are especially prevalent in the United States. She captures the seething pervasiveness of racism in white people and draws a sinister environment where Black people are not meant to succeed.

And she makes it not only overt but fully institutional. Àbíké-Íyímídé reveals that every student, every teacher, every head of administration at Niveus Private Academy is in on a scheme to ostracize, condemn, and ruin the futures of Chiamaka and Devon because they are Black. For over fifty years, the school has strategically admitted two Black students every ten years with the express purpose of ruining their lives and "putting them in their place."

In their dark moments, as Chiamaka and Devon reckon with this horrible truth, they are discouraged to the point of giving up, feeling broken by a system designed to oppress them. Chiamaka notes that "[n]o matter what I do, no matter how much I iron down the hair that springs from my scalp, or work as hard as I can, I'm always going to be *other* to them. Not good enough for this place I've tried to call home all my life" (Àbíké-Íyímídé 2021: 315). Devon thinks, "Boys like me don't get happy endings. The stories I was fed about working hard and being able to achieve anything. . . . That's all they are, stories. Lies. Dangerous dreams" (2021: 338). Their thoughts illuminate the ways that systemic oppression makes impossible the American Dream, as white supremacy always wants to marginalize and subjugate.

But Àbíké-Íyímídé injects hope into this gothic story by way of a cleansing fire: at the end of the book, the school burns down. One of the most hideous white characters dies, among others. And Chiamaka and Devon receive support from a tweet Devon posts that goes viral, demonstrating both the way that twenty-first-century activism—Generation Z activism—gains traction and the way one person's agency can be intertwined with others'. The epilogue of the novel sees Devon and Chiamaka successful in the future, now the founders of the Ruby Bridges Academy, which actively seeks out students of color and offers them a private school experience built on a desire to "tackle the systemic inequality in schools across the country" (2021: 410). The school's name evokes the story of a well-known mighty child, Ruby Bridges, who became the first Black student to attend the newly desegregated William Frantz Elementary School in Louisiana in 1960. Such a reference underscores the realized potential of Devon and Chiamaka to fight against systemic racism and Àbíké-Íyímídé's belief in that potential.

Àbíké-Íyímídé further articulates her hope for the power of YA literature in her author's note at the end of the book. She shares that "[w]riting this book was like a form of self-therapy, and I hope that it is the same for Black people that pick this book up" (2021: 419). As a bestselling novel, *Ace of Spades* reflects a young audience's desire not only for therapeutic experiences but also for work that prompts readers to think deeply about intersectional privileges and oppression.

Chloe Gong's *These Violent Delights* is very different in tone, setting, and writing style from *Ace of Spades*, but it's equally condemning of systemic injustice. Unlike *Ace of Spades*' purposefully vague setting, *These Violent Delights* very specifically situates its story in 1920s Shanghai, a setting where a Chinese city was roiling and grasping for autonomy under French, British, and American influences and grappling with gangster rule. Gong has explained that she was especially drawn to this setting for her *Romeo and Juliet* retelling not only because her own family is from Shanghai but also because of the way the gangsters' presence invited the same kind of blood feud that permeates Shakespeare's famous play. Gong describes 1920s Shanghai as a "lawless city on the brink of civil war and revolution having undergone so much imperialism and [experiencing] colonialism's effects" (2022), making it an unstable place saturated with hybrid identities.

Exploring that hybrid identity in *These Violent Delights* is Juliette, who is Chinese by birth and American by education. Her explanation of being of two worlds illustrates the contradictions inherent in both her life and her culture. Early in her education in America, "[s]he would have rather been an outcast than admit the blood in her veins was a product of the East" (Gong 2020: 234). But as she grew older, she saw "the darkness behind the glamour of the West. It was no longer so great to be a child constructed with Western parts" (2020: 234). She sees that darkness in Shanghai, too, with commentary that echoes Àbíké-Íyímídé's condemnation of systems of white privilege and power. Juliette "thought it preposterous that her father had to ask permission to run business on land their ancestors had lived and died on from men who had simply docked their boat here and decided they would like to be in charge now" (2020: 165). She sees British and American men as those "who assumed they had the right to go wherever they wished because the world had been built to favor their *civilized* etiquette" (2020: 23). The author's emphasis on "civilized," of course, draws attention to the irony of colonialism: barbaric behavior is allowed when the perpetrator is white.

Juliette's love interest, Roma, who is the heir to a Russian gang and thus an outsider in his own way, echoes these notions of colonialism. "These days, Juliette," he tells her, "the most dangerous people are the powerful white men who feel as if they have been slighted" (2020: 166). This language, of course, echoes the contemporary rhetoric surrounding so-called men's rights groups, and savvy readers will recognize Gong's critique. Indeed, Gong expects her readers to be familiar with societal issues. When Roma posits running away and says, "They have started calling America *the land of dreams*," the narrative response is sardonic:

> A snort floats up into the clouds. . . . It is the only sound that epitomizes the land in question, somehow both charming and terrible, both dismissive and weighted down. *The land of dreams*. Where men and women in white hoods roam the streets to murder Black folks. Where

written laws prohibit the Chinese from stepping upon its shores. Where immigrant children are separated from immigrant mothers on Ellis Island, never to be seen again. Even the land of dreams needs to wake up sometimes. (2020: 392)

This litany of unjust behavior serves as a reminder to readers that the American Dream is, in fact, a fiction. Moreover, that this narration occurs in a work of historical fiction illustrates how contemporary Generation Z authors are acutely aware of systemic injustice and are attempting to reframe history to show this injustice more clearly.

Even the romance between Roma and Juliette demonstrates societal problems. When the two were younger, they "believed that this divided city could be sewn back together. She believed it when they sat under the velvet night and looked out at the haze of lights in the distance, when Roma said he would defy everything, everything, even the stars, to change their fate in this city" (2020: 360). That Gong links a hope for a better city with Juliette and Roma's young love underscores the difficulty of big, sweeping societal change. It links young love—an innocent and hopeful one—with believing in structural change, underlining the naivete of such a belief.

As the characters grow out of their naivete, now rivals who must work together several years later, Roma and Juliette encounter darkness and mystery in Shanghai that further illuminate systemic problems. The horror of *These Violent Delights* is made manifest through a monster that has been unleashed on Shanghai, infesting its residents with tiny, burrowing bugs that seize control of a human's mind and force the person to tear out their own throat. The resolution to this storyline offers a critique of classism and oppression: a British merchant discovered in England the bug that would mutate into the monster, and he brought it to Shanghai in order to kill Communists so that capitalists could thrive. Earlier in the novel, when Roma's father suggests that the Communists may be behind the monster and its madness, Roma wonders if it could "be a motive as simple as politics? Kill the gangsters so there was no opposition. Infect the workers so they were angry and desperate enough to buy into any revolutionary screaming in their ear" (2020: 121). While it turns out that the reason is the reverse—that the monster was meant to kill Communists—both reasons speak to the power dynamics that are roiling in Shanghai's culture, drawing readers' attention to the systems that shape a civilization. While Roma and Juliette cannot easily fight the corruption within these systems, their attention to what they wish Shanghai could be and their condemnation of destructive political tactics reflects what Generation Z authors bring to their writing and to their readers:

an awareness of and hope for a better world and an agency to engage with social structures in a way that demands change.

Such engagement is not always overtly political, and the reception of these YA texts can show us other ways that young readers are using their agency. Because these Generation Z writers engage with social issues in their writing, their work also draws attention to the way readers receive the depiction of these social issues and bring to bear their own socially aware critiques. I turn now, briefly, to Tashie Bhuiyan's *Counting Down with You* as an example of the way a text circulates among critical readers. Bhuiyan's novel is another text that centers on cultural representation from a Generation Z writer. *Counting Down with You* follows Karina, a Bangladeshi American whose tensions with her overbearing parents are lessened when those parents go to Bangladesh for a month. During that time, Karina can more comfortably be who she wants to be—a future English major, not a future pre-med student—and she falls for the school bad boy, Ace, whom she is tutoring. Karina has an anxiety disorder that she manages by counting down numbers, and her anxiety is heightened by her parents' expectations of her. I'll focus less on the text itself for *Counting Down with You* and more on the circulation and reviews of this text and Bhuiyan's response.

While Bhuiyan's novel received positive reviews from publishing media outlets and many rave reviews from readers on Goodreads, a popular book-reviewing website, the novel—and by extension, Bhuiyan—has been critiqued for its representation of the Muslim religion and Bangladeshi culture. One reviewer on Goodreads, for example, notes they "really liked the anxiety rep. but as a muslim, i was just too frustrated with the representation of islam. a lot of times it felt like the lines between toxic cultural ideals and religion were blurred" (razan 2021). Another reviewer points out that the book's being so heavily marketed as Bangladeshi Muslim representation was unfortunate because "the book did nothing short of attacking both of those identities" (Hamna 2022). Some responses critiqued the representation but were more measured, such as this one that says, "I appreciate how it got me to think about Muslim narratives in the diaspora as a whole" (Faatima 2022).

Bhuiyan is, in fact, a Bangladeshi American Muslim, and she tweeted in response to some of this criticism. In a tweet on January 19, 2021,[2] Bhuiyan wrote, "if someone is writing based on their lived experiences, then you don't get to tell them that their experience is wrong, even if it doesn't reflect your experience or your understanding of that marginalizination [sic]. we are not a monolith" ("Muslim"). She followed that tweet with several more in a thread that addresses the problem of policing own voices. If, as Bhuiyan writes, "I'm a Muslim woman writing my experience as a Muslim woman, then that is not falling into a stereotype. I can only ever write my truth. do I think all Muslim stories should get told? absolutely. should I have to censor my own? no. it's not my job to represent everyone" ("PSA").

The response to Bhuiyan's text shows the way Generation Z authors' work will be put under the microscope of social media, and responses from readers are part of a larger cultural conversation about how young adults function in a world where social justice conversations are easily accessible. These authors, of course, are not perfect—they are humans navigating the publishing world and social media and all their responsibilities as professional writers. Chloe Gong has also been at the center of social media controversies, particularly when she blurbed and gave a five-star Goodreads review to *The Ones We Burn* by Rebecca Mix, which was critiqued for racism.[3] While social media isn't known for its nuance, it *does* serve as a way to record and assess contemporary cultural conversations. These writers and their books, then, evince the powerful voices of young people to make themselves heard and present issues of representation, hierarchy, and power in their work, but the cultural conversations surrounding their novels also show that real readers will hold them accountable for the influence their voices have. That these authors have enough popularity to be critiqued on TikTok and Goodreads shows their reach and influence, and by having agency as young writers telling stories to young people, they can contribute to cultural shifts in publishing as well as demonstrate the kinds of cultural conversations that show the depth of thinking about social justice that contemporary young readers engage in.

Interestingly, though, the anger of these readers reflects the outrage that simmers under the surface of Gong's and Àbíké-Íyímídé's novels and even Bhuiyan's. I wonder if sensing the frustration with systemic injustice that informs these novels may even heighten readers' sense of the personal connection each author had to her novel, if it reflects their own understanding of a broken world. Gong has shared that in her research for *These Violent Delights*, she immersed herself in imperialism and colonialism and felt a personal connection to, and frustration about, the story of her heritage. "It's strange to research your own ancestral history," Gong says, "and then feel a century-old anger come to life" (2021). Àbíké-Íyímídé notes that before she started her novel, she started understanding more clearly that "the circumstances I grew up in were no accident, but a system that was created to work against me" (2021: 416).

And these young women channeled their knowledge into writing—more specifically, into writing for young readers. They speak out about the ageism they've faced in publishing, about their own feeling that, as women of color, they had to work twice as hard for their unexpected success and the responsibility that comes along with that. Foundational to their success are the heavy issues that they are tackling in their work. Their books are twenty-first-century takes on the longstanding notion that children's literature's purpose is "to amuse and instruct"—indeed, their work is didactic. Again, it's not a subtle critique of the power dynamics that leave others dead in their wake. And when that didacticism is coming from a young writer herself, she's harnessing the power of literature to make young people literate in vitally important cultural conversations that ultimately demand radical change.

Will that radical change come to fruition? I don't know. Every time there's an attack on young people—whether a violent one of war or gun worshippers or a noxious but unphysical attack like banning books with queer and other marginalized perspectives—my faith is shaken. I wonder how anything will be enough to change the tide. I wonder why adults have left young people to fend for themselves, even as they purport to "protect them." But my faith in literature—children's literature, young adult literature—is still there. Like Meg Rosoff and Justyna Deszcz-Tryhubczak in part I of this volume, I want to continue to believe that "care-full activism" will matter and that the stories young people tell have the power to change us, and with us, the world.

NOTES

1. Between the time I started writing this essay and when I finished it, Àbíké-Íyímídé's blog no longer has her podcasts available. It is still accessible via the Wayback Machine at https://web.archive.org/web/20201004044612/https://www.faridahabikeiyimide.com /the-write-type/2020/3/11/s2-e10-deadlines-while-on-deadline-navigating-publishing -and-book-deals-as-an-undergrad-with-chloe-gong-author-of-these-violent-delights.

2. I'm not entirely clear on the timeline as many of the reviews on Goodreads calling out the representation are from a later date than Bhuiyan's tweets. It's clear she was getting pushback on ARC reviews and other early reviews.

3. Having not read the book myself, I can't speak to its representation, but it stirred up a lot of negative reviews as well as strong defenses.

REFERENCES

Àbíké-Íyímídé, Faridah. *Ace of Spades*. New York: Feiwel & Friends, 2021.
Àbíké-Íyímídé, Faridah. "Deadlines While on Deadline: Navigating Publishing and Book Deals as an Undergrad (with Chloe Gong, Author of *These Violent Delights*)." March 12, 2020. https://web.archive.org/web/20201004044612/https://www.faridahabikeiyimide .com/the-write-type/2020/3/11/s2-e10-deadlines-while-on-deadline-navigating -publishing-and-book-deals-as-an-undergrad-with-chloe-gong-author-of-these -violent-delights. Accessed May 10, 2022.

Àbíké-Íyímídé, Faridah. "Meet-the-Author Recording for *Ace of Spades*." www.Teaching
  Books.net. Accessed May 10, 2022.
Alkestrand, Malin. *Mothers and Murderers: Adults' Oppression of Children and Adolescents
  in Young Adult Dystopian Literature*. Göteberg & Stockholm: Makadam Publishers,
  2021.
Beauvais, Clémentine. *The Mighty Child: Time and Power in Children's Literature*.
  Amsterdam and Philadelphia: John Benjamins Publishing Company, 2015.
Bhuiyan, Tashie. *Counting Down with You*. New York: Inkyard Press, 2021.
Bhuiyan, Tashie. "Muslim." X (formerly Twitter). Last modified January 19, 2021. https://
  twitter.com/tashiebhuiyan/status/1351588747561869313.
Bhuiyan, Tashie. "PSA." X (formerly Twitter). Last modified January 19, 2021. https://twitter
  .com/tashiebhuiyan/status/1351588031388647427.
Coates, Ta-Nehisi. *Between the World and Me*. New York: Spiegel & Grau, 2015.
Clark, Beverly L. *Kiddie Lit: The Cultural Construction of Children's Literature in America*.
  Baltimore: Johns Hopkins University Press, 2003.
Dimock, Michael. "Defining Generations: Where Millennials End and Generation Z
  Begins." Pew Research Center. Last modified January 17, 2019. https://www.pewresearch
  .org/short-reads/2019/01/17/where-millennials-end-and-generation-z-begins.
Faatima. Review, *Counting Down with You*. Goodreads. Last modified January 12, 2022.
  https://www.goodreads.com/review/show/3832000525.
Gardiner, Kelly. "A World of YA." Keynote lecture, YA Studies Association Seminar Series,
  April 28, 2022.
Gong, Chloe. "A Letter from Chloe Gong, Author of *These Violent Delights*." Bookshop.org
  Newsletter. Accessed September 22, 2021. Cache.
Gong, Chloe. "Meet-the-Author Recording for *These Violent Delights*." www.Teaching
  Books.net. Accessed November 12, 2023. Cache.
Gong, Chloe. "The Truth About Being a Youth™ in Publishing, Part 2." Last modified May
  8, 2022. https://thechloegong.com/2022/05/08/the-truth-about-being-a-youth
  %ef%b8%8f-in-publishing-part-2/.
Gong, Chloe. *These Violent Delights*. New York: Margaret K. McElderry Books, 2020.
Hamna. Review, *Counting Down with You*. Goodreads. Last modified January 31, 2021.
  https://www.goodreads.com/review/show/3800226364.
Hinton, S. E. *The Outsiders*. New York: Speak, 2012.
Jensen, Kelly. "Climate Justice for All." *School Library Journal*, December 2022, 56–59.
Jerald, Aysha. "Exploring the Relationship Between Dystopian Literature and the Activism
  of Generation Z Young Adults." *American Journal of Undergraduate Research* 16, no. 4
  (2020), 81–93. doi:10.33697/ajur.2020.009.
Johnston, Jeremy. "Economic Conservatism & the Neoliberal Commitments of Young
  Adult Literature." Lecture, YA Studies Association Seminar Series, July 13, 2022.
Joosen, Vanessa. *Adulthood in Children's Literature*. London: Bloomsbury Publishing,
  2018. Merriam-Webster: America's Most Trusted Dictionary. "Niveous." Accessed
  February 28, 2024. https://www.merriam-webster.com/dictionary/niveous#:~:text=niv
  ·%E2%80%8Be·%E2%80%8Bous,(as%20in%20whiteness)%20%3A%20snowy.

Nikolajeva, Maria. *Power, Voice and Subjectivity in Literature for Young Readers*. New York: Routledge, 2010.

Nodelman, Perry. *The Hidden Adult: Defining Children's Literature*. Baltimore: Johns Hopkins University Press, 2008.

Razan. Review, *Counting Down with You*. Goodreads. Last modified May 22, 2021. https://www.goodreads.com/review/show/3985129050.

Rose, Jacqueline. *The Case of Peter Pan or The Impossibility of Children's Fiction*. London: Palgrave Macmillan, 1984.

Seelinger Trites, Roberta. *Disturbing the Universe: Power and Repression in Adolescent Literature*. Iowa City: University of Iowa Press, 2000.

Valentine, Helen. "Seventeen Says Hello." *Seventeen*, September 1944.

"The World is Yours." *Seventeen*. April 1945.

Part III

Childhood Ecologies and the Agency to Act and Heal

Chapter 7

SHIFTING BOUNDARIES

Objects, Narratives, and Nonhuman Entities as a Means Toward Agency in Narratives on Child Abuse and Neglect

DANIELA BROCKDORFF AND KATRIN DAUTEL

Trauma, narrated in its raw form through stories of abuse and neglect, challenges agentic paradigms of the child as powerful. As established throughout this volume, citizenship does not exist in a vacuum but requires relational conditions in order to thrive. When children are victims of abuse, can they also be active citizens and, if so, what is the process they need to go through to act against violence? In this chapter, we argue that family ecologies play a crucial role in the empowerment or disempowerment of children as actively contributing citizens in the wider sphere of society. Moreover, we continue building on the argument that literature provides for engaging and powerful examples of negotiations of agency serving as a tool, both for adults and children, to explore different ways of asserting children's rights in a community.

Domestic violence and abuse can have many forms: it can be physical, psychological, or sexual, directed toward children and parents, or even consisting of toxic relationships between partners or siblings. Not surprisingly, however, classic examples of abuse in literature of the past centuries more frequently deal with violence against women. One could mention, among others, Anne Brontë's *The Tenant of Wildfell Hall* (1848) or Theodor Fontane's *Effi Briest* (1895). The most seminal example depicting domestic violence toward children, however—the topic of this chapter—may be Euripides's play about the child murderess *Medea*, widely adapted in world literature and theater even in contemporary times. Equally paradigmatic but not less disturbing is Vladimir Nabokov's *Lolita* (1955), in which Humbert, an English teacher, marries a woman for the sole reason of staying closer to her daughter. In Mark Twain's *Adventures of Huckleberry Finn* (1884), thirteen-year-old

Finn escapes his abusive alcoholic father, whose violence initiates the boy's famous adventures.

Despite the many examples of domestic violence in Western literature, scholars have noted that for a long time there has been a "critical silence" on the abuse of children in literary criticism, which, in Ursula Mahlendorf's opinion, reflects "society's denial of the abuse of children within the family" (Mahlendorf 2000: 10). In fact, she further states that "the large critical literature about abuse in schools proves that it is not abuse itself which is psychologically intolerable for most of us but rather the abuse in the family, the first and last secure haven of bourgeois ideology" (10). However, one must acknowledge that in recent years, there has been considerable growth in children's literature studies, or literature focused on a child's perspective, which has given more prominence to trauma in childhood (e.g., Lejkowski 2012; Markland 2013; Schönfelder 2013; Roy 2017; Ross 2020; Kertzer 2022). Nevertheless, age-appropriate literature on domestic violence and its subsequent trauma, together with literary criticism on it, remains somewhat limited. While acknowledging the challenge of tackling this highly sensitive topic, it is therefore of utmost importance that child abuse in literature is given more attention, acknowledging children's multifarious perspectives on the matter and their traumatic experiences, which considerably impact their contribution to society and their role as citizens.

Reviewing German and English literature since the end of World War II and, more prominently, since the turn of the millennium, shows a seemingly increasing amount of literary and filmic representations of domestic violence against children. Andreas Zielcke writes that these narratives often have very little in common, but they make the commonly known even more obvious, that is "the mockery of any childhood idyll or adolescent harmony. Childhood is a murderous-difficult trial" (Zielcke 2010). While every narrative about child abuse, both in children's literature and in literature for adults, has to be seen in its own sociopolitical and historical context, tying in with the topic of this volume we will analyze two examples of contemporary British and German literature dealing with child abuse, specifically focusing on the aspect of agency within these narratives. Carrying out a close reading of the novels *The Bone Dragon* (2013) by British writer Alexia Casale and *Ich freue mich, dass ich geboren bin* (2016) by German author Birgit Vanderbeke, we adopt a relational approach to argue that agency is a collective phenomenon, negotiated in a complex assemblage of sociomaterial and corporeal aspects embedded in the environment of the child (on corporeal aspects of citizenship and adolescents' relationship to their environment, see also Klomberg in part III of this volume). In both literary works, the contact with objects, narratives, and nonhuman entities prompts an increased radius of move-ment, affecting the children's relationship with their setting. This is also done through the imagination, transforming ordinary objects into tools of power. Furthermore, it invites spatial and temporal journeys, both in the imagined as well as in physical time and space. Therefore, in the narratives to be discussed, it is evident that the place of trauma is one that needs to be confronted or escaped from. Even though evasion and escape might be associated with a lack of agency, the interaction with artifacts and, for example, fantastical creatures and fictional characters prompting the relocation to other places, can form an important part of children's agentic complexes and their inter-actions with their surroundings. Expanding the space available to them is a crucial aspect of their journey toward empowerment and a more active role in society. As Klomberg states, "[S]pace is often not self-evidently available to adolescents and so, the way they experience their environment can impact on their emerging sense of citizenship."

The ability to creatively interact with objects and nonhuman entities is an elemental part of the process that enables children and young adults to negotiate their sense of self toward a means of empowerment and agency. As Lambros Malafouris declares in "Creative *Thinging: The Feeling of* and *for* Clay" (2014: 140), "Humans are organisms of a creative sort. We make new things that scaffold the ecology of our minds, shape the boundaries of our thinking and form new ways to engage and make sense of the world. That is, we are creative 'thingers.'" Indeed, as will be discussed, we consider both protagonists to be resourceful "creative 'thingers,'" moving across this fragile territory as victims of abuse, equipping themselves with their own imagina-tion to expand the confines of their thinking and thus to experiment with different perspectives on their world in which they can be active citizens.

SOCIOMATERIAL ASPECTS OF AGENCY

Critics such as Marah Gubar (2016) and Richard Flynn (2016) have acknowl-edged that attempting to clearly and objectively define "agency" and, espe-cially, "child agency" often proves to be problematic. This is especially true given that the ones attempting to define "child agency" are not children, or more accurately, no longer children. One has to bear in mind, therefore, that literary accounts of child agency are not only fictional but also based on what adults believe or remember a child's perspective could be. In her entry on the topic in *Keywords for Children's Literature* (2021), Nina Christensen summarizes important aspects of the concept of child agency. As she states, only recently have sociologists shifted their focus onto the active participation of children in creating and shaping their own reality. Key factors in the definition of agency comprise the children's autonomy in their way of acting, the capability to make their own choices, and the way they express and voice ideas. The child's historical, social, and cultural background, however, is crucial in the analysis of agency, as the construction of "the child" as such can lead to oversimplifications. In the context of literature, Christensen suggests that a focus on child agency "provides an alternative to viewing the child as vulnerable and dependent on adult power and protection" (13).

Furthermore, in *Reimagining Childhood Studies* (2018), Spyros Spyrou, Rachel Rosen, and Daniel Thomas Cook foreground the need to reconceptualize and reconsider the idea of the child to allow for "alternative ways of knowing" in parallel to the concept of agency with its key role in childhood studies (4). What is needed is a repositioning of "relationality as the core focus of writing, conception, and research . . . to push past conceptualizing children in essentially monadic terms—i.e., as beings which have . . . agency—and into realms where children and childhood can only fruitfully be located by way of linkages with other human and non-human aspects of the world" (6).

This relationality, therefore, goes beyond the mere relationship with other persons but also comprises "objects, technologies, systems, epistemes, and historical eras" (6). It requires reflections not only on what children are "but how they affect and are affected in the event assemblages they find themselves in" (8). Similarly, in his important article "Extending Agency, The Merit of Relational Approaches for Childhood Studies" (2016), Eberhard Raithelhuber discusses new directions in the context of research on children's agency. He advocates an extension toward an "understanding of agency as social and collective" (90), referring to a selection of recent contributions (e.g., Sax 2006 and 2013; Schatzki 2010; Latour 2005; Holland et al. 1998), suggesting and renegotiating a more relational concept. Since the "new childhood paradigm" (James and Prout 1990) in the 1980s, approaches to agency have conceptualized the paradigm within the agency/structure binary, proceeding from the idea that childhood and children's agency are socially constructed and heavily influenced by their sociocultural context (Raithelhuber 2016: 90–91). This can have both enabling and detrimental effects on the agency of children since "structural and socio-cultural conditions of childhood in modern society block, handicap or distort this fundamental capacity" (91). According to Raithelhuber, this conventional understanding of agency "joins the line of dualisms that characterize Western, Eurocentric perceptions of the world and about the world. It rests on fundamental divisions and oppositions, such as mind and body, individual and society, micro and macro, human and non-human, and so on" (91) that have to be overcome. Moreover, the conventional understanding is based on an individualistic, capacity-centered approach to agency that was increasingly criticized by scholars during the past decade, highlighting its simplistic view since it ignores relational and collective aspects of agency as a result of a negotiation process with various agents (91–92). Concepts of agency extending beyond the conventional refer to the important aspect of relational complexity, which is a result of the child's environment and its various agents in an interplay of relationships with humans and nonhuman entities.

Therefore, not only do peers and family contribute to the negotiation of agency, but objects or spiritual experiences can also have mediating effects. With reference to Alfred Gell's seminal work on *Art and Agency* (1998), Raithelhuber especially hints at the important role of unanimated things in the complex network of "everyday practices and discourses in which humans attribute agency" (96). In this context, the work of Tara Woodyer is also significant. In her article on corporeal aspects in children's everyday human geographies (2008), she discusses the long-ignored sociomaterial component and heterogeneous assemblages of links children are embedded in, especially the physical, bodily experience of everyday life that forms an important part of the composition of relational geographies. According to Woodyer, the "haptic emerges at the interface between the subject and object, the human and the non-human, offering an explicit account of relational configurations at this primary juncture" (350). Thus, children's play and physical contact with nonhuman objects can have an impact on everyday life practices and movements in social contexts. This, yet again, ties in with Malafouris and his observations on "creative *thinging*," providing a fruitful and multilayered perspective from which to observe a child in literature. This aspect will be referred back to in the context of our analysis of the works by Casale and Vanderbeke in the next part of this chapter.

This theoretical framework of agency calls for discussions on the relational complexity between the figure of the child in literature and their peers, adults and the material world, the author creating the child on the page, and the child or even adult reader. To further elaborate on the concept, children's agency as depicted in fiction about children is often influenced by external forces in parallel with an innate impulse toward self-definition. Children are, as Káren Sanchez-Eppler (2005) claims, individuals "inhabiting and negotiating" (xv) discourses of agency, or else as Gubar conceptualizes it, as "actors who are simultaneously scripted and scripting" (Gubar 2016: 297). Yet keeping relationality in mind, one must not only reflect on the abused child in literature and their quest toward agency but also the scripting of the abused child by the writer and reader of contemporary trauma literature, a reflection that "demands of us decisions as to the theoretical and conceptual resources we mobilize: *What kind of child do we choose to bring into light? What kinds of inclusions and what kinds of exclusions result from our choice?*" (Spyrou, Rosen, and Cook 2018: 6). Thus, when one considers children and young adults who are victims of abuse, their path toward such "inhabiting and negotiating" is, inevitably, a more complex one, and their journey toward agency and a more active citizenship is often fraught with internal battles they must negotiate. Their agency is constantly being tied down and subjected to a power seemingly more forceful than their own. In this context, parents, grandparents, and guardians play a crucial role. Therefore, a difficult journey toward manifesting and voicing agency must be embarked upon, often requiring a disassociation from the traumatic scene either literally, but especially metaphorically, through the imagination. Yet this does not mean that they can be considered less of an active citizen than other children. They are active citizens in their own right, remolding their immediate setting as part of their quest for agency, with ramifications in their wider sphere—the outside world.

The need to distance oneself from the place of trauma is an understandable one. This is especially true since, as Paula Reavey (2010) explains, "abuse not only places a mark on the spaces that children and adults inhabit, the spaces themselves can actively shape the experience itself" (323). She even goes as far as stating that agency—here in a more conventional understanding as the catalyst of change—"can then only be realized when a person is able to physically relocate and remove themselves from the rule bound shared spaces of home" (324). Yet most often, in spite of such physical relocation, the memory of trauma still lingers, so both the time and place of the trauma tend to remain present nonetheless. Even with the passing of time, Reavey explains how, for victims of abuse, the past cannot simply be "refashioned at will. . . . Many survivors continue to experience the intrusion of the past into the present in powerful and sometimes overwhelming ways" (319). Therefore, perhaps a means of gaining independence is a literal spatial shift coupled with a more metaphorical one through the imagination, allowing a protagonist to attempt to rise above the entanglement of place, space, memory, and time to consider their complex relationship from a new position of agency and power. Indeed, spatial shifts are a common trope in literature, allowing a protagonist to gain a different perspective on their relationship with the world. Venturing beyond boundaries, both in a literal and metaphorical manner, is often the first step toward self-definition and, thus, arguably, toward renegotiating agency and an active citizenship, particularly when one's narrative involves trauma. This is the perspective from which the following two narratives will be explored.

ALEXIA CASALE: *THE BONE DRAGON* (2013)

Alexia Casale's *The Bone Dragon* is a novel aimed at young adults, narrated in the first person through Evie's point of view. The girl, a fourteen-year-old, is now living in Cambridge with her adoptive parents, Amy and Paul, a few miles from the home in which she was abused by her grandparents. She has just had an operation to remove a piece of broken rib that she gets to keep. She carves a dragon out of her rib that comes to life on certain nights, enabling her to journey toward healing and self-discovery.

Evie's relationship with the rib in a specimen pot, and eventually her carving it into a bone dragon, is interesting when considering a child's negotiation of agency through inanimate objects, specifically in relation to "creative *thing-ing*" and what Woodyer calls "the interface between the subject and object, the human and the non-human" (2008: 350). Reflecting on this when reading, one is probably drawn toward attempting to define the demarcation where reality ends and Evie's imagination takes over, imposing symbolic significance on the bone and the dragon, consciously and relationally informing who Evie is, as a child or young adult. It seems that the rib becomes a symbol of loss, a lack of agency, that she turns into its opposite. She opens herself up to different possibilities to establish her relationship with that part of her that can still be carved, once again literally into a dragon, but especially metaphorically. Therefore, she embarks on a project with her uncle to form a dragon out of her rib—with Casale establishing an interesting parallel with the creation tale in the Bible—and all she wishes is that it breathes fire: danger, life, warmth, power.

It becomes evident that what Evie desires is empowerment through revenge. In fact, one of the many literary allusions present within the text is that of Shakespeare's *Hamlet*, which Evie describes as "sand under my skin" and admits that "[s]omething about it bothers me" (45), mostly what she considers as Hamlet's inability to act. It is a narrative that she constantly refers back to and reflects upon in relation to her own situation. The dragon comes to life at night and allows Evie to roam freely in the Cambridgeshire Fens, and these passages in the novel are rich in symbolic suggestions, brought to life by the beautifully written nightscapes, creating a magically realistic space for the protagonist to discover herself and her agency anew. Such descriptions create the possibility of an interesting and poignant parallel with Evie's inner world.

The protagonist's interactions with the dragon are equally of interest. For Evie, the dragon's remarks are frustratingly cryptic. What is stylistically noteworthy is that the dragon's voice is not marked in quotation marks as the rest of the dialogue within the narrative. Instead, it is italicized. This allows for interesting ruminations on temporal and spatial shifts that go beyond dualisms, opening a space where binaries are no longer valid. The dragon's voice, very much like the bone out of which it has been carved, is both external to Evie and yet inherently hers. The novel thus follows her trajectory as she negotiates these spaces until she achieves what she needs to heal and carve her own identity.

Indeed, a shift from her place of trauma was initially imposed upon Evie after her mother, having been diagnosed with terminal cancer, abandons her at Social Services. Evie was still too young within the narrative to be able to relocate herself; however, this change of place enabled her to start realizing her agency within a safe space with her new adoptive parents, who allowed her to do so. Yet relocation does not necessarily mean that the trauma is left behind, particularly because the space of trauma often becomes the one a victim inhabits within memory. In fact, Evie exclaims to herself, "How *do* you tell the difference between *then* and *now* when feelings and smells and sounds are creeping in too? When *then* is suddenly flaring into your senses again, no longer dim and distant but clear and sharp and *present*" (87). She resists recounting painful memories from her past, but when she is being pressed by her teacher to voice her trauma with the intention to propel the girl toward healing, some overwhelming memories come flooding in. She anxiously attempts to cling to the present, "[f]ighting to remember *when* I am" (204). However, she cannot entirely restrain it, "[a]nd just like that *then* starts to become *now*, rushing like floodwater into the present" (205), revealing some very dark aspects of her past.

Thus, a spatial shift to a new home and temporal shifts to her past to face her memories, although necessary, are seemingly not enough for the young protagonist to be able to voice her own self-defined agency. Instead, what is needed is Evie's direct engagement with objects, narratives, and nonhuman entities that have shaped her and with which she interacts to shape herself. In fact, the adults in her life, despite their genuine good intentions, cannot share in Evie's own distinct journey, and thus, they try to impose their own perspective onto hers, assuming, as adults sometimes tend to do, that a child's agency is somewhat deficient and needs guidance from a more informed perspective. This is the evidence one expects to find in a novel about child abuse, of how a child's agency is relationally affected. As a reader, in fact, there are moments when one might feel that Evie is not being cooperative or is not appreciative enough of the space and relationships that her teacher and adoptive family are, with all their love, carving for her. As readers, we expect Evie to trust the adults around her to ensure a better future for her. Similarly, there are moments when one morally questions Evie's statements, such as when she blatantly declares that she "celebrate[s]" (187) her biological mother's death even though her adoptive parents make her visit her mother's grave as is socially expected.

Yet Evie is fully aware that her experience of abuse has inevitably scripted her agency to a certain extent, knowing that others will never be able to understand. In spite of her tender age, her trauma has exposed her to the knowledge of darkness in the world, something that is not granted automatically when one comes of age, she explains. In fact, she believes that her adoptive parents are still rather innocent and thus states:

> It's not fair, not fair, not fair that this is what they think, still, at *their* age and I can't even *remember* what it is not to know: I can't remember what that sort of innocence feels like. And right now I can barely remember that I love them because I hate them for not knowing when I've never had a time when I *didn't* and I want that, oh how I want that. (243)

Thus, most of the time, Evie's complex emotions translate into either anger or silence with those around her. To further elaborate on this, in an interview at the end of the book, Casale states that capturing Evie's voice entailed a whole process, prompting yet again reflections on the problematic dualism of adult voices as opposed to children's voices. Casale explains:

> Evie as a character is all about silence—and apparent inconsistencies: the trauma in her life has made her developmentally stunted in some ways and wise beyond her years in others. The difficulty was finding a way to convince the reader that what seemed like inconsistency is actually completely consistent with Evie's personality and history. For me, these are the things that make Evie real and complex. (2013)

To distance herself from the present time and place that are entangled with her traumatic past memories, one could say that Evie resorts to the imagination, specifically, the dragon as a fantastical creature that she has carved out of her own bone. This enables her to take control of her own narrative that is persistently in conflict with all the narratives being imposed upon her. Her journeys along the streets of Cambridge with the dragon by her side allow her to find herself as she is encouraged to patiently wait and immerse herself in a journey of healing. It is ambiguous from the start as to whether these nighttime imaginary travels are indeed imaginary, as there is plenty of evidence within the narrative indicating otherwise, yet the fine line between what is real and what is imagined is left purposefully blurred throughout. However, when the police turn up at her adoptive parents' house to let her know that her abusive grandparents have died in a fire, there is very strong proof to suggest that Evie has burned down their home during her last journey with the dragon. This is perhaps why the ending comes as quite a shock.

This is not the ending that most would anticipate, not the ending that fits neatly within a positive conceptualization of healing and agency. Yet Evie has been, to use Gubar's metaphor, "scripted" and is now indeed "scripting" her own agency. Moreover, this fictional narrative perhaps tries to capture a child's agency, as Christensen claims, providing "an alternative to view-ing the child as vulnerable and dependent on adult power and protection" (Christensen 2021: 13). Thus, very much as it is essential for Evie to experience embodied agency through relocation and roaming around with the dragon, as adults, we must equally engage in imaginary journeys of our own through reading such fiction, to explore a perspective, a different knowledge of the world, which is perhaps dissimilar to ours.

Therefore, on a metafictional level, through theories of relational agency, further thought could be given to the idea of Evie having been scripted not only within her fictional world but also as a fictional character meant to reflect real issues of trauma and abuse. She is a product of a literary culture that seeks to give voice to such children, albeit through fiction, and to fos-ter a society that propels discussions on how such a child is perceived and expected to behave in the circumstances. She is, therefore, seemingly being constructed in a way that does not depict her as a victim needing to be saved. Furthermore, she is not only being assigned agency because the context that produces her wants to award her with agency, but she is also a character that resists such oversimplifications. The agency that she asserts is, to some extent, inevitably relationally affected by sociocultural expectations on a plot level, but significantly, it is one that somehow defies the expectations of society and its value system that is creating the child protagonist and, at the same time, reading or interpreting her.

Indeed, Evie's choices and actions at the end of the novel hark back to what Meg Rosoff states in part I of this volume. Active citizenship, in its more obvious form of public protest and social action, is, of course, more than necessary and valuable, "but engagement with the inside of your head is the most important part of being human. It's subversive and dangerous and it's where the really deep ideas are born." She calls for children to "question authority, to understand the power that resides in their own heads," to be "anarchists," and that, we feel, is precisely what Evie embodies.

BIRGIT VANDERBEKE: *ICH FREUE MICH, DASS ICH GEBOREN BIN* (2016)

The second literary text to be discussed is Vanderbeke's German-language novel *Ich freue mich, dass ich geboren bin* (2016), translated into English by Jamie Bulloch in 2019 with the title *You Would Have Missed Me*. It is the first part of a trilogy of novels published between 2016 and 2020, which is said to be partly autobiographical. Vanderbeke was one of the most widely read German novelists since her acclaimed debut, *The Mussel Feast*, in 1990, written from the perspective of an eighteen-year-old girl with an overly authoritarian father. Nearly thirty years later, in *Ich freue mich, dass ich geboren bin* (*You Would Have Missed Me*), she resumes a similar child perspective and family situation. The title of the novel is an adaptation of the traditional German birthday song *We Are Happy That You Are Born* (in German: *Wir freuen uns, dass du geboren bist*). It alludes to the main temporal setting of the novel: it is the protagonist's seventh birthday, during which the girl precociously reflects and remembers the past years of her childhood, constantly being faced with her parents' disappointment about her way of being. The birthday song, sung by her mother in a very high and squeaky voice, verging on the sound of crying, ironically twists the parents' unhappiness about their daughter and, at the same time, re-affirms the girl's presence in her discouraging environment. The girl is highly suspicious of her parents' happiness about her existence.

The protagonist's family situation is closely linked to the historical context of the 1960s in Germany. After fleeing from the GDR, the family spent some time in a refugee camp in West Germany before being able to afford their own flat, thanks to the father's stellar career. The girl remembers her time in the refugee camp as the most beautiful in her life due to her friendship with other adult refugees from the East, who, in contrast to her parents, offered an affectionate space she could always refer to. Once relocated to the new flat, she is deprived of any contact with her friends and feels the parents' rejection even more physically. Her parents, each in their own way, are frantically trying to adapt to their new reality in West Germany. Finally, having the chance to "live their dream" and being able to afford a more comfortable lifestyle, they try to leave their past as refugees behind and keep up with the expectations of a capitalist society with all its emphasis on appearance and status. For them, their daughter instead seems to impede their image as a happy family, and they act out their tension and ambition at her expense. When she does not behave as expected, the irascible father physically abuses her. In the girl's memory of earlier years, he turns into a monster who came to take her from her baby bed with enormous paws and threw her against the wall. Afterward, nothing in her body was as it was supposed to be; every bone felt misplaced. When approached by the doctor about the girl's bone deformation, the mother denies any knowledge of the causes or wrongdoing. But for the girl, the biggest problem is that she is deprived of her voice, that she has no one to talk to, and that her parents do not listen. As she states, "[U]ltimately it would have been better for everyone if I hadn't existed at all. I would have needed someone to talk about it" (17).

On her seventh birthday, she remembers her dear friends from the refugee camp telling her about the three monkeys. Having its origin in a Japanese proverb, the three monkeys, who cover their ears, mouth, and eyes, represent the ability to wisely ignore all evil happening around you; instead, in Western culture, it was turned into its opposite, that is, the denial of it. Therefore, the three monkeys are used as a symbol of the lack of agency in voicing one's own opinion or the lack of civil courage. Even if the girl does not understand everything her friend tells her, this allegory becomes her negative role model. She declares, "[I] decided to never in my life look away or to not listen when something evil is happening, because that would be cowardly. Look very closely, Uncle Winkelmann said when he had explained to me that the three monkeys were cowards. Look very closely, do you hear? It doesn't matter what they tell you: Listen closely and open your mouth. The world would have been spared something" (57).

This passage illustrates the crucial role of interaction and exchange in a shared social space for a more active, engaging citizenship. By talking to her friends, the girl is exposed to important ideas about a person's role in society and possible valuable contributions. Eventually, bearing the three monkeys in mind, it is a book, a broken globe, and a snow globe that serve as configurators of her ability to act and speak up against her parents. She receives a long-awaited gift from her friends at the refugee camp, the book *The Time Machine*, in which a man travels to the future to flee his dull present. After having been beaten up by her father again, the decisive moment has finally come. Having the book next to her and pressing the snow globe as hard as she can, she manages to catapult herself into the future in order to ask for help:

> This all just happened because I wanted it, and I wanted to get farther and farther away, the window in my room broke since the globe gathered speed, my room was too small for the speed, in my snow globe the changes also gathered speed, everything became electric and was flashing, I continued shaking, but no matter how much snow fell, it didn't manage to cover the world, it didn't even look white, rather grey, like ash. The globe shot cracking through the burst windowpane with me and my snow globe into the black sky, into the night, into the black. (112–13)[1]

In the future, she asks for someone to talk to and manages to meet herself forty years later. As of this moment, back in the present, she is accompanied by her own, older voice that gives her advice and helps her stand her ground at school and with her parents. Together with this voice, she undertakes imaginary voyages and has a continuous conversation partner to talk to who helps her negotiate a sense of self and her behavior with her parents. The change this situation brings about, having someone to talk to, reaches its peak when she throws a glass of water into her father's face and tells him off.

Objects as well as stories prove to be essential in the complex assemblage of involved agents in the girl's emancipation process from the parents. Reading, in particular, mobilizes the protagonist's imagination to travel to another time and place, "'If you can read,' she thinks, 'one can perform magic and go to all countries of the world or change into an animal or suddenly be in another time'" (77). The book *The Time Machine*, in particular, contributes to her ability to transcend her reality and imagine other periods and places, transporting her into an imagined future. Interestingly, this intertextual reference seems to be a recurring motif in literature about children in traumatic environments. As Irene Barbara Kalla points out in part III of this volume, the protagonist of Marcin Szczygielski's novel *The Ark of Time* (2013) reads a book with the same title. This helps the boy—even if in completely different ways—come to terms with his harsh reality during World War II. This commonality between the two narratives further emphasizes the important role of stories as well as (imagined) mobility in time and space as a contributor to agency, allowing children to take a critical stance toward their realities. In the case of Vanderbeke's novel, the change, triggered by the narrative, is realized in connection with the two globes, referring to other, remote places, by means of which she manages to undertake an imaginary time travel; that way, she overcomes the boundaries of her difficult domestic environment. Most importantly, in dialogue with her older self, she finds her voice, which in turn gives her the courage to speak up to her parents. Being deprived of her friends and the lack of a trusted person forces the girl to disassociate from herself and become her own imaginary conversation partner. The girl's story emphasizes the importance of being integrated into a network of verbal exchange, even if only an imagined one, in order to negotiate one's own role and position within the family and society. Interestingly, in the case of Vanderbeke's protagonist, it is not a peer the girl desires to talk to, but it is her alter ego that she seeks advice from. She imagines her older, wiser self taking the role of an experienced guide, similar to her friends from the refugee camp, who is able to direct her in her discouraging everyday life. Her other self, however, also becomes a substitute for the guidance the girl is missing from her parents.

Vanderbeke's depiction of the girl's empowerment highlights the variety of agents involved in the process leading to change, ranging from narratives and objects to—even if imagined—mentors and peers. Stories and artifacts are indispensable mobilizers for her imaginary travels that expose her to different times and places. As mentioned in relation to Woodyer, the haptic experience in the context of agency, in the girl's case, touching and shaking the globes becomes crucial in her attempt at transporting herself to the future. There, she is exposed to a more supportive environment, providing her with the necessary tools to face her harsh reality upon return. Her way of engaging with the material world exemplifies the concept of "creative *thinging*" coined by Malafouris as outlined above, which is not only the "thinking and feeling *with, through* and *about* things" (Malafouris 2014: 143) but also creating things, or rather, in the girl's case, creating a specific *constellation* of artifacts as a condition for her transposition to another reality. This, as Malafouris states, is due to humans' "capacity for inventiveness that is inseparable from the capacity to affect and be affected through movement and sensation from the phenomenal qualities of the materials that surrounds [*sic*] us" (144). The girl's inventiveness, engaging with the objects available to her, allows her to overcome the boundaries of her human body and create an assemblage of relations between herself and the nonhuman world, bringing everything into movement to gain momentum for an essential change. This, as can be said in Malafouris's terms, "brings things to life," reconfigures her mind, and leads to a reinvention of herself (144), eventually paving the way for a more embodied type of activism against her father.

As in the novel by Casale, the threshold between the material and the human world is blurred, giving way to new forms of existence at the juncture of reality and imagination. Vanderbeke's novel, therefore, is a good example of the representation of a child who is continuously deprived of a space of expression but who, by means of repositioning herself in a sociomaterial network of linkages and resourcefulness, manages to change her life by traveling into an imaginary future, where she finds the support and the space to voice the ideas she is constantly deprived of. As her alter ego states, "It's very simple . . . you just have to remember the future" (Vanderbeke 2017: 149).

CONCLUSION

Exploring the two novels within the framework of agency, and especially more recent relational approaches, shows the crucial role of the interplay between objects and humans on a child's journey toward empowerment and emancipation. Both protagonists are victims of trauma and are attempting to construct their own selves while interacting with the world around them. This consists of human relationships, but more prominently, playful engagements with objects within their physical sphere, propelling them toward temporal and spatial shifts. Such shifts enable the necessary distancing from the place and/or space of trauma where the child's self can carve, script, and create themselves anew as a person who has been informed by those around them, specifically their abusers, with all their sociocultural baggage, and will continue to be formed by those who are now providing them with the possibility of a healthier interaction with society. This does not only mean that the child is depicted entirely as being a victim who needs to be led toward a better self and experience of the self. Rather, this negotiating of agency relies equally on the child's relationship with themselves. In Casale's novel, Evie navigates a surreal nightscape along with her dragon, and in Vanderbeke's work, the girl converses with her older self through time-traveling. It is significant that both children create imaginary alter egos in order to voice their concerns, seek advice, and find comfort. This further foregrounds the necessity of having *another* beyond the self to negotiate agency with, even if it is an imagined friend or companion, setting in process change within their immediate sphere, however with significant implications on their wider environment, transforming them into active citizens, nonetheless.

The two novels belong to different genres. Casale's is a fictional tale written for children and young adults; Vanderbeke's novel is rather intended for adult readers. It is intriguing how the child is brought to life in these two novels, which have as many similarities as they have differences. In both cases, it is significant that the child is being scripted by a voice that is not a child's yet is akin to it. Equally, both texts urge thoughts on the power adults can have on a child's experience of themselves and the world and the relational agency intrinsic to the reading process, urging necessary conversations and writings that explore an ideational and, even more, a political, space, where an adult's power stands alongside that of the equally powerful child, the young citizen of the world. Through this, the relational interplay between these seeming binaries can be explored with the texts discussed, providing opportunities for young and adult readers alike to be part of the multiplier effect of conscious collective citizenship.

In fact, at the end of Casale's novel, the author includes a set of Reading Group Questions. Indeed, if these novels were to be read with children or young adults discussing such questions, this would allow for what Spyrou, Rosen, and Cook, referring to Cheney's article in the same volume (2018), defined as the coconstructing of knowledge on children together with children, heralding a "disruptive intervention which might lead to other, and potentially more ethical, ways of knowing" (Spyrou, Rosen, and Cook 2018: 9). If we acknowledge the inevitability of sociocultural negotiations as part of the coconstruction of childhood agency, then the role and the voice of the child in the matter is crucial and indispensable for a world that has increasingly acknowledged the centrality of the child citizen. Having such discussions with children and young adults would encourage shifts in perspectives among various age groups, allowing for a complex yet interesting interplay between fact and fiction, imagination and reality, younger and older. Yet it is perhaps also necessary to go beyond class or reading group discussions. Such instrumental conversations should be documented and formally recognized as part of the collective body of work that goes into researching children, their citizenship, and their agency.

NOTE

1. All quotations from Vanderbeke's novel *Ich freue mich, dass ich geboren bin* are the authors' own translation from German.

REFERENCES

Casale, Alexia. *The Bone Dragon*. London: Faber & Faber, 2013.
Christensen, Nina. "Agency." In *Keywords for Children's Literature*, edited by Philip Nell, Lissa Paul, and Nina Christensen, 2nd ed., 10–13. New York: New York University Press, 2021.

Flynn, Richard. "What Are We Talking About When We Talk about Agency?" *Jeunesse: Young People, Texts, Cultures* 8, no. 1 (2016), 254–65. Accessed January 3, 2024. doi:10.1353/jeu.2016.0012.

Gell, Alfred. *Art and Agency: An Anthropological Theory*. New York: Oxford University Press, 1998.

Gubar, Marah. "The Hermeneutics of Recuperation: What a Kinship-Model Approach to Children's Agency Could Do for Children's Literature and Childhood Studies." *Jeunesse: Young People, Texts, Cultures* 8, no. 1 (2016), 291–310. Accessed January 3, 2024. doi:10.1353/jeu.2016.0015.

Holland, Dorothy, William Lachicotte Jr., Debra Skinner, and Cain Carole. *Identity and Agency in Cultural Worlds*. Cambridge: Harvard University Press, 1998.

James, Allison, and Alan Prout. *Constructing and Reconstructing Childhood: Contemporary Issues in the Sociological Study of Childhood*. London: Routledge, 1990.

Kertzer, Adrienne. "Trauma Studies." In *A Companion to Children's Literature*, edited by Karen Coats, Deborah Stevenson, and Vivian Yenika-Agbaw. New Jersey: John Wiley & Sons Ltd., 2022.

Latour, Bruno. *Reassembling the Social: An Introduction to Actor-Network-Theory*. Oxford: Oxford University Press, 2005.

Lejkowski, Richard. "Childhood Trauma and the Imagination in American Literature." Master's thesis, Rutgers, 2012. Accessed January 5, 2024. https://rucore.libraries.rutgers .edu/rutgers-lib/37285/PDF/1/play/.

Mahlendorf, Ursula. "Medea Darning Socks: German Child Abuse Fiction as Cultural Critique." *Pacific Coast Philology* 36 (2001), 10–31. Accessed April 18, 2023. doi:10.2307/3595467.

Malafouris, Lambros. "Creative *Thinging*: The *Feeling of* and *for* Clay." *Creativity, Cognition and Material Culture* 22, no. 1 (2014), 140–58. Accessed January 5, 2024. doi:10.1075 /pc.22.1.08mal.

Markland, Anah-Jayne. "Representations of Trauma in Contemporary Children's and Young Adult Fiction." Master's thesis, University of Calgary, 2013. Accessed January 5, 2024. https://prism.ucalgary.ca/bitstream/handle/11023/940/ucalgary_2013_Markland _Anah.pdf?sequence=4&isAllowed=y.

Nagel, Barbara Natalie. "Ambige Aggression: Häusliche Gewalt im Realismus." *Weimarer Beiträge: Zeitschrift für Literaturwissenschaft, Ästhetik und Kulturwissenschaften* 61, no. 2 (2015), 181–201. Accessed January 8, 2024. https://publikationen.ub.uni-frankfurt .de/opus4/frontdoor/index/index/year/2019/docId/49031.

Raithelhuber, Eberhard. "Extending Agency: The Merit of Relational Approaches for Childhood Studies." In *Reconceptualising Agency and Childhood: New Perspectives in Childhood Studies*, edited by Florian Esser, Meike S. Baader, Tanja Betz, and Beatrice Hungerland, 89–101. London: Routledge, 2016.

Reavey, Paula. "Spatial Markings: Memory, Agency and Child Sexual Abuse." *Memory Studies* 3, no. 4 (2010), 314–29. Accessed April 18, 2023. doi:10.1177/1750698010370035.

Ross, Kyra. "Trauma in Children's Literature." Graduate research paper, University of Northern Iowa, 2020. Accessed April 18, 2023. https://scholarworks.uni.edu/grp/1558.

Roy, Aurélie. *Surviving Childhood: Trauma and Maturation in J. D. Salinger's "The Catcher in the Rye," S. E. Hinton's "The Outsiders," and Stephen Chbosky's "The Perks of Being a Wallflower."* Quebec: Laval University, 2017.

Sánchez-Eppler, Karen. *Dependent States: The Child's Part in Nineteenth-Century American Culture.* Chicago: University of Chicago Press, 2005.

Sax, William S. "Agency." In *Theorizing Rituals, Volume 1: Issues, Topics, Approaches, Concepts,* edited by Jens Kreinath, J. A. M. Snoek, and Michael Stausberg, 473–81. Leiden: Brill, 2018.

Sax, William S. "Agency." In *Ritual und Ritualdynamik: Schlüsselbegriffe, Theorien, Diskussionen,* edited by Christiane Brosius, Axel Michaels, and Paula Schrode, 25–31. Göttingen: Vandenhoeck & Ruprecht, 2013.

Schatzki, Theodore. "Materiality and Social Life." *Nature and Culture* 5, no. 2 (2010), 123–49. Accessed January 3, 2024. doi:10.3167/nc.2010.050202.

Schönfelder, Christa. *Wounds and Words: Childhood and Family Trauma in Romantic and Postmodern Fiction.* Bielefeld: Transcript Verlag, 2014.

Spyrou, Spyros, Rachel Rosen, and Daniel Thomas Cook. "Reimagining Childhood Studies: Connectivities . . . Relationalities . . . Linkages. . . ." In *Reimagining Childhood Studies,* edited by Spyros Spyrou and Rachel Rosen, 1–20. London: Bloomsbury Publishing, 2018.

Vanderbeke, Birgit. *Ich freue mich, dass ich geboren bin.* München: Piper, 2017.

Vanderbeke, Birgit. *You Would Have Missed Me.* Translated into English by Jamie Bulloch. London: Peirene Press, 2019.

Woodyer, Tara. "The Body as Research Tool: Embodied Practice and Children's Geographies." *Children's Geographies* 6, no. 4 (2008), 349–62. Accessed January 5, 2024. doi:10.1080/14733280802338056.

Zielcke, Andreas. "Die Hölle, das ist das Zuhause." *Süddeutsche Zeitung,* March 19, 2010. Accessed February 15, 2024. https://www.sueddeutsche.de/kultur/kindesmissbrauch -und-literatur-die-hoelle-das-ist-das-zuhause-1.16992.

Chapter 8

ECOLOGICAL EDUCATION IN TWENTY-FIRST-CENTURY CHILDREN'S LITERATURE ABOUT THE HOLOCAUST

A Comparative Ecocritical Reading

IRENA BARBARA KALLA

TRANSLATED BY PATRYCJA PONIATOWSKA

Books on the Second World War and the Holocaust foster readers' critical engagement with environmental themes and issues. As observed by Aleksandra Ubertowska, a Polish researcher of representations of the Holocaust in fiction, "[T]he search for affinities between . . . the histories of extermination of human communities and the devastation of nature is probably fueled by the belief that traditionally compartmentalized fields in fact make up one ecosystem which eludes depictions underpinned by anthropocentric research concepts" (2013: 36).[1] Postcatastrophic literature and ecocriticism are interconnected and complementary in this respect. This correlation deserves a detailed examination in recent children's literature, particularly in works that encourage young readers to think critically and take action. Such books do not focus exclusively on environmental topics, thus avoiding the pitfall that, as Suzanne van der Beek and Charlotte Lehmann state, "lies in [the] tendency to simplify the complex issue of climate change and to offer potential ways for fighting climate change which are not accessible to all young readers" (2022). I argue that, in some contemporary children's and young adult literature about the Holocaust, the educational function of teaching about the *Shoah* (the Hebrew term for the Holocaust) and keeping the memory of it alive is intertwined with the function of spreading ecological education and increasing youth activism. Through this combination, these books become part of environmental justice children's literature, which Kamala Platt defines as "stories for children that examine how human rights and social justice issues are linked to ecological issues, how environmental degradation affects human communities, and how some human communities have long sustained symbiotic relations with their earth habitats" (2004: 186). As such, they can play an important role as appropriate material in ecopedagogy for civic engagement (Gaard 2009: 324).

In today's world, ravaged by a global climate crisis as it is, the urgency of acknowledging all human beings' responsibility for the planet is a pivotal challenge. This crisis and this challenge are intertwined with other exigencies of the twenty-first century, such as poverty, hunger, migration, and human rights issues. Multiple organizations, such as UNESCO, recognize these interlacements and launch local and global projects to further the goal of disseminating global citizenship education (GCE). As put by Sobhi Tawil, GCE "highlights essential functions of education related to the formation of citizenship [in relation] with globalization" and is involved "in preparing children and young people to deal with the challenges of today's increasingly interconnected and interdependent world" (Tawil in UNESCO 2014: 15). It is in this context that I have comparatively explored two books: *The Ark of Time* by Polish author Marcin Szczygielski and *Fing's War* by Dutch author Benny Lindelauf. My comparative framework for addressing the themes of the Holocaust and the environment is founded on deep ecology and the environmental history of the Holocaust. I seek to establish the ways in which nondidactic environmental children's literature pursues the mission of ecological education while at the same time engaging with the Holocaust. My special focus is on the network of interdependencies among humans, animals, and the environment, as portrayed in Szczygielski's and Lindelauf's texts, in order to show how they can be higher-lever activators of child agency and social engagement.

CHALLENGES FOR CITIZENSHIP EDUCATION: ECOCIDE AND GENOCIDE

My argument draws on ecocriticism as a theoretical perspective for textual analysis. Specifically, I rely on ecocentric theories, such as ecophilosophy and holistic ecology, "which view the human and the natural environment as interdependent and having an equal value" (Yarova 2021: 66). One of the most influential environmental philosophies, deep ecology, which was developed by Arne Naess in the 1970s, promotes a relational view of humans and the planet:

As a counter to egoism at both the individual and species level, Næss proposes the adoption of an alternative relational "total-field image" of the world. According to this relationalism, organisms (human or otherwise) are best understood as "knots" in the biospherical net.... If people conceptualise themselves and the world in relational terms, the deep ecologists argue, then people will take better care of nature and the world in general. (Brennan and Norva, *Environmental Ethics*, 2022)

Deep ecology boasts a pedagogical dimension, which nurtures responsibility toward and for the environment along with the acknowledgment of the interdependence of humans and nonhumans (for various types of relationships between humans and nonhumans, see Brockdorff and Dautel in this volume). This pedagogical investment of deep ecology dovetails with the educational commitment of children's and young adult literature, which is particularly pronounced in its environmental subgenres geared to enhancing readers' empathy with nature and inculcating responsibility for the environment in the face of climate catastrophe (O'Brien and Stoner 1987; Sigler 1994; Jaques 2015; Yarova 2021). Because the two books I discuss deal with the Holocaust, I also avail myself of the environmental history of the Holocaust, which emphasizes the relationship between "violence that humans commit against each other and their attitudes to nature" (Małczyński et al. 2020: 184) and posits that the notion of domination is a common denominator of both genocide and ecocide (Małczyński et al. 2020: 185). Recognizing the entanglements of human beings and the environment, the subdiscipline investigates "the agency of non-human (f)actors" (Małczyński et al. 2020: 186) with a view to remodeling public awareness and promoting "an ecological democracy" (Małczyński et al. 2020: 185). Crucial for my argument, the study of strategies that artworks revolving around the Holocaust adopt in representing nature is among the major pursuits of the environmental history of the Holocaust (Małczyński et al. 2020: 188).

The recommendations of GCE underscore three central aspects of sustainability: environment, society, and economy. In terms of practice, GCE emphasizes the "use of curriculum and learning materials that challenge bias, stereotypes, exclusion and marginalization" and encourages critical and creative thinking. However, a common complaint is that educational resources for the development of GCE competencies are limited (UNESCO 2014: 26–27). While contemporary children's literature incorporates all these crucial themes, it remains an underappreciated repository of materials that might support GCE both at school (in classroom settings) and outside it (in individual reading experiences). Such potential of children's literature with elements of magic realism is analyzed by Aliona Yarova in *Narrating Humanity: Children's Literature and Global Citizenship Education* (2021). Yarova mainly attends to two educational fields: human rights and the environment. Two of her four case studies are books about the Second World War: Sonya Hartnett's *The Midnight Zoo* (2011) and Marcus Zusak's *The Book Thief* (2005). This thematic selection is no surprise in the context of human rights education, but Yarova also examines these narratives as a valuable resource for environmental education.

While Yarova's research mainly looks into magical realism, which she believes may be a vehicle for GCE, the opulent presence of nature in fiction about the Shoah is neither out of the ordinary nor random. It was in the woods that the Jewish fugitives from ghettos and deportation trains hid, trying to survive individually, as families, in small communities, and also as bigger, structured guerrilla groups. This experience is examined by Tim Cole in *"Nature Was Helping Us": Forests, Trees, and Environmental Histories of the Holocaust* (2014). Cole analyzes published and unpublished memories of the survivors who escaped death by hiding in forests and argues that "these sites as both material and memory landscapes should play a far more significant role within the historiography, given the role that forests and trees—and nature more broadly—played both in survival and its retellings" (Cole 2014: 680). Cole's declared purposes indicate that nature as an agent of and in history has been underexamined in Holocaust studies so far. By exploring the materiality of nature in the narratives of survivors who "told stories of 'nature' acting on their behalf" (2014: 666), Cole asks new questions and seeks new answers regarding the agency of nature in the history of the Holocaust.

A similar gap is discernible in research on the Holocaust since the representations of nature and its functions in literature about the Holocaust have only recently begun to be explored from the ecocritical perspective. Ubertowska observes that the conspicuous neglect of this aspect in research projects is attributable to the prevalence of the anthropocentric paradigm in the humanities, which has thwarted the recognition of the historical agency of nature (2015: 94). Ubertowska argues that the active role of nature has always been an axial, albeit ignored, component of artworks about the Holocaust. Despite its salience, the role of nature in children's Holocaust-themed literature has been particularly neglected in research. Anne Frank's horse chestnut tree is one of the few widely known elements of nature associated with the Holocaust. Eric Katz makes the relationship between Anne and the tree into "a new starting point for an examination of post-Enlightenment ideas about nature, domination, autonomy, technology, and human evil" (2015: 1). Anne's contact with nature was limited to a view of the sky, the stars, the moon, clouds, the sun, snow, birds, and the chestnut tree behind her window. Represented in this manner, nature is associated with the concept of domination, as the Nazi terror and constraints imposed on the Jews precluded their free interaction with nature. Interaction with nature in childhood (and in adolescence; for this issue, see Klomberg in this volume) is one of the basic conditions for later commitment to nature and social issues, which is founded on environmental awareness, and, as Asah, Bengston, Westphal, and Gowan state, pays off in adulthood: "Childhood-nature experiences have lifelong effects on environmental citizenship and commitment to nature-based activities" (2018: 807). Katz deciphers Anne's tree as a symbol of her protest against the evil that surrounded her: "In nature—in this tree—she found a touchstone to resist the continual human project of the domination of nature and humanity" (2015: 4). In 2010, Anne Frank's chestnut tree was struck down by a storm, but before that happened, its chestnuts had been collected and germinated, and the saplings had been planted in various locations across the world to commemorate the Holocaust. Anne Frank's tree and the sapling project it sparked invite rethinking the nature-technology connections in terms of domination and autonomy. Katz's insights are precious and, like Cole's research, they inspire a closer scrutiny of the functions and roles of nature in literature about the Holocaust, including books for a young readership.

ECOLOGICAL EDUCATION IN HOLOCAUST BOOKS BY MARCIN SZCZYGIELSKI AND BENNY LINDELAUF

The plotlines and motifs of *The Ark of Time* and *Fing's War* are aligned with the concepts propounded by environmentalists such as Mark Levene (2013) and David Christian (2011; 2018), who seek to redefine history. They insist that rather than being an attribute of human communities, history is a property of the entire globe and the universe. As Levene argues, this is what we should be especially dedicated to realizing now "as we hurtle towards our renewed encounter with extinction" (2013: 152). The children in both Holocaust books seem to perfectly sense, if not understand, these interrelationships and react accordingly and actively, undertaking various interventions toward the environment. My investigation of environmental issues in these two books was directly triggered by a crucial episode in Szczygielski's *The Ark of Time*. In this episode, the protagonist, a nine-year-old Jewish boy named Rafe, who lives in the Warsaw ghetto, travels in time from 1942 to 2013. Time travel is employed here as an opportunity for confrontation (compare the similar function of the time travel motif in Brockdorff and Dautel in this volume). While surprised by several things he sees, Rafe finds himself utterly petrified by one particular event:

> Ahead of us, where the lanes cross the park, I see three boys. . . . They're talking loudly, laughing and kicking a football back and forth. Two of them are trying to stop the third getting hold of the ball. It's a strange game. Suddenly I stop, stunned, looking at the ball . . . impossible. That's not a ball . . . it's a loaf of bread! All covered in muck, but I can see it is real.
>
> "What are you doing?!" I shout, running towards them.
>
> I run in between the boys, kneel and pick up the bread. Trying to clean it of dirt, I feel like crying.
>
> "Oi, you," says one of the lads. "You gone mad or something?"
>
> "How can you . . ." I mumble under my breath.
>
> The bread isn't even very stale, with no mould anywhere.
>
> "Leave that," the second boy tells me. "Else you'll get some!"
>
> I stand up, pressing the loaf to my chest. The third lad hits me in the back. (Szczygielski 2015: 117–18)[2]

This passage perfectly encapsulates the concerns of environmental ethics, which is one of the thematic foci of Szczygielski's book. Specifically, Rafe is horror-stricken at the fundamental disrespect for food, selfishness, impertinence, and aggression unashamedly displayed by the teenagers. Nevertheless, rather than standing by, he actively tries to oppose the boys, which is in and of itself a lesson in citizenship. It is by no means a coincidence that the episode is situated exactly in the middle of the narrative and serves as its axis, around which the themes of human-animal and human-environment relationships revolve.

The action of *The Ark of Time* commences in the ghetto, where green places are few and far between, which may be the reason why nine-year-old Rafe, who is the first-person narrator in the book, pays considerable attention to all manifestations of nature, no matter how modest they might be. Some ghetto inhabitants arrange kitchen gardens in the courtyards, and the boy helps them in their efforts (Szczygielski 2015: 46). In April 1942, the Toporol (Society for the Support of Farming) establishes a garden for children in Chłodna Street, and the protagonist is very impatient to have it finished. He also looks after onions planted in boxes on the windowsill in his flat, and when sneaking out of the ghetto, he worries that he will no longer be able to tend to them. In the deserted zoo, where Rafe hides for some time, Warsaw residents have arranged allotments and patches to grow vegetables, which Rafe, Emek, and Lidka pick to feed on and alleviate their gnawing hunger.

Animals are also few and far between in the ghetto. When dwelling in the zoo, Rafe only lists them because he barely had any opportunity to interact with them within the ghetto walls. These included Mrs. Bela Gelbart's dog, a few cats in the basements, and one purebred. Besides, there were horses that pulled carts and carriages. Rafe also mentions birds: pigeons, crows, rooks, magpies, and sparrows. The boy notes the gradual proliferation of rats and mice in the ghetto. The animals mentioned in the part that depicts Rafe hiding in the zoo mainly include beasts that are actually not there because they were either transported away to German zoos or killed in warfare. A raccoon and a jackal, two animals that have sneaked out of their cages, ramble across the zoo and share the lot of the hiding children who take care of them. These beasts will have a role of their own to play in the text. Rafe only knows the other creatures from books. Accordingly, they are fantastic "great crabs on the shore of the sea" (Szczygielski 2015: 32) and dinosaurs that appear in *The Time Machine*. Whether the animals are real or from the pages of a book, Rafe consciously deliberates on his relationship with them and, consequently, on his place in the world and its history. Being himself a part of this world, he realizes that it is interconnected and interdependent. This awareness then has consequences for the further actions the boy undertakes.

Lindelauf's novel recounts the painful maturation experienced by Fing, who lives with her sisters, father, and grandma (Oma) Mei in a house called Nine Open Arms in a fictitious village in Nazi-occupied Europe. A clever and ambitious girl, Fing has her aspirations and plans for life thwarted by wartime upheavals. Instead of pursuing education, she works as a maid at the home of a wealthy industrialist and must look after wayward Liesl without knowing that she is, in fact, a Jewish child in hiding. The action of Lindelauf's book takes place in a small town in the province of Limburg, where the natural environment is simply taken for granted. Given this, Fing does not pay any special attention to it as the first-person narrator. Similarly, the kitchen garden appears in the text as a self-evident thing. Only a handful of the components of the natural environment are somewhat more consequential in the book: a huge old linden tree at the graveyard and a meadow bordering the road. The latter is called Sjlammbams Sahara, a name that conveys its human-caused degradation, as the meadow is covered in dust from coal, transported to needy farmers to help them heat their homes. *Fing's War* predominantly features farm and domestic animals. Animals most frequently appear in conjunction with children's daily lives, their dreams, and the war, which poses the gravest threat to those most vulnerable and deprived of agency by circumstances—the beasts and the children. The dream of a stable and ordered life cherished by adolescent Fing is wrecked by the war, just as are the lives of all the characters of the novel, children and animals alike, ruptured, destroyed, or annihilated by the war.

However, Fing and Rafe, the main child protagonists in these books, have an agency that manifests itself in their relationship with their natural environment. While Fing is, as a rule, indifferent to the natural world around her, she becomes interested in a huge linden tree at the graveyard when she watches Bèr Daams take care of it. The linden tree has been hurt in the war, and the boy tries to heal it by wrapping a bandage around it as if it were human:

> Even the lanky arms of the Idiot weren't long enough to embrace this gigantic tree. Under the skin of his bony face, I could see muscle spasms twitch like the jags of lightning bolts. I resisted the urge to walk away.
> "Need help?"
> In reply, all he did was pass the bandage around the tree to me.
> We bandaged the tree together as if it were the most normal thing to do. (Lindelauf 2019: 215–16)

Attempts to revive the tree are undertaken by an individual who is regarded as a lunatic in his community and abusively called "the Idiot." However, the naturalness of his behavior sways over skeptical Fing, who, though not particularly empathetic toward nature, joins in his efforts. Fing's act of openness can be read as a reckoning with the bias against and marginalization of people like Bèr Daams, which corresponds to the goals of the GCE. Admittedly, Fing and Bèr Daams fail to save the tree, but their remedial endeavors delay its death, which, inevitable as it is, eventually comes at the best possible moment. In fact, the linden tree falls over because its roots have had to veer from their natural growth trajectory from the very beginning in order to bypass a hoard of flint objects buried in the ground thousands of years before. Fing renders this story in a polyvalent sentence, observing that "[i]n order to survive, the tree made its roots change direction" (Lindelauf 2019: 408).

In the context of Holocaust literature, the statement invites a metaphorical reading as implying that, in their struggle for survival, Jews must adopt various roles and identities, often at odds with their original beliefs, religion, and original choices. This strategy is adopted by young Liesl, who pretends to be a doll in a toy shop on the Night of Broken Glass and, in this way, is the only one of her family to make it through the night. Later, when she hides in the Cigar Emperor's house, she is further compelled to adjust to the circumstances time and again. Thus, the Jewish girl Liesel has no real agency in the book, which is more often the rule than the exception for Jewish protagonists in Dutch children's literature (Kalla 2022) but causes Fing to try to regain control of her life to the extent that is possible under these wartime circumstances. Fing's observation expresses what Liesel's story has made her understand and what she now sees reasserted as a mechanism that operates as a ubiquitous natural law valid across the scales of existence. Her insight prompts readers to realize that there are principles at work in the world that concern life as such, rather than only human life. This enmeshment is substantiated by the further course of events since, paradoxically, by crushing down onto and ruining the house and thus driving its dwellers away, the tree saves their lives, as the very next moment, the wrecked house is hit by a bomb.

The story of the linden tree vividly encapsulates the interdependence of all the elements of the environment—trees, rocks, and people alike—and this interconnectedness is shown to span millennia. At the same time, the narrative makes one realize that the activity of prehistoric humans (the production and accumulation of objects) affects the lives of people who inhabit the earth thousands of years later. How complex, multilayered, and ambivalent such contingencies and connectivities may be is embodied in Sjlammbams Sahara, which, itself devastated by human activity, is the only place where the Jews can still enjoy communion with nature. In Lindelauf's book, the desolate meadow is not coincidentally associated with the fate of the Jews as its ashen image anticipates the Holocaust.

The connections forged between children and nature take up more space and are told more literally in *The Ark of Time*, where all the young protagonists have a distinctive attitude toward the environment. Children secretly harvest vegetables from the allotments arranged in the zoo and cultivated by the Warsaw residents. Although the vegetables picked from the patches are often the children's only available food supply, they make efforts toward sustainability. Despite their dismal situation, they do not practice "overharvesting" and implement compensatory measures (bring water, weed the patches, remove snails, etc.) out of respect for other people. Respect for humans and nonhumans and respect for nature prove intrinsically intertwined and mutually complementary. Rafe's bond with the jackal is also an intriguing motif.[3] Sharing some kind of understanding with the animal, the boy treats the jackal as an equal being and manages to persuade him to board the ark. His friend Lidka is skeptical, as she believes that "Amber is an animal, and they don't think like us at all" (Szczygielski 2015: 196). When Rafe disagrees and points out that, after all, we cannot know that, Lidka calls him "odd." Rafe addresses Amber, convinced that the jackal understands him, knows what will happen, and will respond to the verbally articulated invitation. The boy is also prepared to share his very modest food provisions with the beast. Notably, Rafe himself is marginalized as a Jewish boy in Nazi-occupied Poland. His actions against the marginalization of nonhumans, even in the face of a threat to his own life, can be understood as meeting, and indeed exceeding, the GCE guidelines on exclusion and marginalization. His dedication to equal treatment sparks his abhorrence of the thought of violence, such as laying snares for the jackal or locking him up in a cage. No such detestable measures are necessary, though, since the jackal responds to the invitation and boards the ark of his own accord, which casts into relief the value of interspecies alliances in the face of common danger.

In *Fing's War*, animals play a similar role, but the relationships between animals and humans concern not only children. Heyvish is a huge Belgian draft horse. He worked in a mine, but having developed a fear of darkness, he began to suffer from panic attacks, which made him unpredictable and dangerous. Hermes, a blacksmith, took him then to work at his smithy and thus saved him from slaughter:

> The very first evening that Heyvish stood in his stall, the animal began getting restless when it started getting dark. Now, "Nose" Hermes had enough gear in his house to control any uncooperative horse. But instead, he fetched candles, which he stuck down on the anvil with their own wax. Not just one, but twenty or more. He kept doing this until the corner where Heyvish stood was no longer dark. Everyone who heard about this declared him crazy, but Hermes took no notice. "The only thing that horse needs," he'd said, "is a heaven to look up to." (Lindelauf 2019: 290–91)

The smith's treatment of the horse is kind and considerate; the man not only recognizes and fulfills the material needs of the animal but also ascribes higher-order needs to him. This attitude does Hermes no favors, exposing him to disrespect and derision. When the smithy proves a compromised hideaway, Heyvish has another fit of panic and sets it on fire, frantically trying to get out of the dark. In yet another narrative twist, the apparent mishap breeds beneficial outcomes, as the fire helps Fing and Liesl escape. The titular *De hemel van Heivisj* (*Heyvish's Heaven*), literally denoting light amid the darkness, evokes security that both children and animals need. Remarkably, the original title of the book channels attention toward the world of nature, insisting that not only humans need a heaven. A whole community is constructed around Heyvish, consisting not only of children who care about nature and who, in many environmental children's books, are granted the unrealistic agency of the "eco-hero" (van der Beek & Lehmann 2022). This community also incorporates adults, such as the smith Hermes. The inclusion of this character not only makes the (eco)system conjured up in the novel complete and interconnected but also highlights that responsibility for the world does not rest solely on the agency of children.

The plot also appoints a role of some importance to a rat that plunders the cellar where provisions are kept. At the beginning of Lindelauf's novel, a rat steals the food stored in the cellar of Nine Open Arms. All measures launched to get rid of the rat fail. When the war breaks out and Oma Mei decides to let a Jewish girl hide in the basement, keeping this fact secret from all the other lodgers, the dwindling of food supplies and the noises heard from there can conveniently be blamed on the rat. In this way, Lindelauf projects a parallel between the rat and the Jewish girl, which is as functional to the plot of the novel as it is ambivalent, since comparing the Jews to rats was a stock device of the Göbbelsian propaganda during the war (see Sax 2000; Neumann 2012) and has since been used by sundry postwar antisemites as well (Avraham 2021). However, this narrative device may also be construed as an attempt to dismantle the rat stereotype, which has already been practiced in Dutch children's literature. For example, in *Frog and the Stranger*, a picture book by Max Velthuijs, the rat represents the Other against whom everybody is prejudiced because of rampant stereotypes. Ultimately, however, the rat proves helpful and friendly. The overcoming of stereotypes appears to be a possible avenue for becoming closer to other human beings and nature alike, which corresponds to the GCE's goals of stereotype-challenging educational materials.

Both books reverberate with the pressing question of how much time we still have and whether there is any ark that can save humans from humans themselves. Szczygielski's novel alludes to the biblical ark of Noah, but it eventually deconstructs this traditional narrative. If the title of the novel is an explicit allusion to the biblical story of Noah's ark, Noah himself is replaced by Time in the book, and the text addresses the theme of animal-human relations as they transform over time. This preoccupation is vividly rendered in the following passage:

I like the bit where Doctor Flycatcher and Professor Antediluvian meet dinosaurs. Dinosaurs are creatures that lived on the Earth a long time ago, massive beasts that roamed in herds—many times bigger than any human being. But actually there were no people on the Earth back then, dinosaurs ruling the world for a very long time. Still, a

time came when they all started to die out—perhaps because of some
ginormous catastrophe, an earthquake or something like that. I feel
sorry for the dinosaurs and think a lot about what they were thinking as their era was extinguished, animal by animal. They must have
been very afraid, that much is certain. Will we, humans, go the same
way? In *The Time Machine*, there was no trace of human beings in
the distant future, and so this is inevitable, I think. The end of people
must come, sooner or later, and this is something we have to accept.
It will probably be hardest on those who will have to go first, when
the end comes. I would like it to start with the Morlocks, but that's
not going to happen—I know that. It's enough to look outside our
window. (Szczygielski 2015: 44)

Rafe reflects on the respective periods of animal and human rule on the
Earth, sympathizes with the dinosaurs facing extinction, and perceives them
as thinking and sentient creatures. Having read *The Time Machine*, he comes
to believe that the era of human reign is bound to end and links this insight
to his own times. The boy inscribes these times in the history of the planet
and in the natural course of things, which helps him accept the reality he
inhabits. At the same time, he is acutely aware that humans are the first to be
eradicated and that the annihilation of the human species as a whole is immi-
nent. The passage stands out as voicing the notion of total disaster, which
informs the mode of thinking embraced by the adherents of ecocriticism and
historians of the Holocaust. In Szczygielski's novel, the ark stands also, more
literally, for a boat constructed by Emek. Like Noah's ark, the boat is supposed
to be the children's getaway from disaster, forestalling a confrontation with
the Nazis. Boarding their ark, the fugitives take with them the raccoon and
the jackal, which roam the deserted zoo and are as vulnerable as the Jewish
children hiding there. The ark of time has another incarnation in a vehicle
that transports Rafe into our own times, where the relations between humans
and nature prove to be disturbed, as bread is thrown into mud and kicked
like a football. While there is no war in the future, humans seem to have only
become more selfish toward other people and toward nature. Tellingly, *The
Time Machine* does not inspire Rafe to admire the vast potential of future
human beings powered by technological advancements; rather, it makes
him envisage a looming extinction of the human species. Time travel gives
him an opportunity to see for himself the dismal consequences of technological progress: while the war did not end in ultimate disaster, this disaster
is being generated by people themselves amid the alleged time of peace as
humans are, in fact, involved in an ongoing suicidal war against nature and

the environment, which is metaphorically pictured in the episode of the "match" the boys play using a loaf of bread.

If the motif of Noah's ark in Lindelauf's book is not as central or multi-layered, it is explicitly evoked and deserves some attention. In *Fing's War*, Oma Mei says, "We aren't Noah's ark" (Lindelauf 2019: 145) when Liesl visits Fing, bringing her dog along with her. Thus, the dog must go back. Oma Mei's reaction stems from a traditional vision of the world with the binary opposition of nature and culture, in which houses are solely inhabited by humans, with animals relegated outside. Nonetheless, it is Oma Mei's intervention that makes the Nine Open Arms house an asylum that helps a Jewish girl survive the war. The motif of Noah's ark is knitted into the book's texture of biblical references that surface in situations involving animals and contemplate ethical issues, such as the instrumental use of animals in conflicts between people. In one of such poignant and unsettling episodes, the white Persian show cat, Poor Little One, owned by Mrs. Vroon, who explicitly sympathizes with the occupiers, disappears one week before a show, only to be dropped at the threshold of the house in a bag with a note containing a biblical wisdom: "He that toucheth pitch. . . . You've been warned!" (221).[4] Poor Little One is smeared all over with tar, including over the eyes, as a result of which he stops eating and drinking and dies after a few days of torment. For the perpetrators, the animal is entirely irrelevant as a living creature; it only represents its owner. It does not really matter on which side of the conflict the tormentors actually are. Fing comprehends this perfectly, and she blames the war, but at the same time, she neither accepts the motivation of the perpetrators nor is disposed to understand them. By making the supporters of the right cause torturers of innocent creatures, Lindelauf invites critical reflection on the asymmetries in human-environment relationships, which cannot be easily explained away, and even less so, justified by scriptural wisdoms.

CONCLUSION

Szczygielski's *The Ark of Time* and Lindelauf's *Fing's War* epitomize the kind of environmental children's literature that can have a stimulating impact on youngsters' environmental consciousness instead of only providing ready-made guidelines on how to act vis-à-vis the natural environment. Since, at the same time, they represent literature about the Holocaust, the two novels spotlight the links between ecocide and genocide. The books extensively rely on literary devices that breed empathetic attitudes in young readers. Rafe attempts to establish a rapport with animals and believes that it is indeed possible to reach an understanding between and across divisions. Consequently, he bridges the gap between the world of humans and the world of animals or at least reduces this gap. Rafe and his friends have an unconventional approach to nature, and similarly, some adults embrace attitudes toward animals and/or the environment that differ from the generally endorsed ones. Such adults are called "crazy" (e.g., Hermes the smith) or "the Idiot" (e.g., adolescent Bèr Daams, who swathes a sick tree). Likewise, nine-year-old Rafe is considered "odd" by Lidka because he believes that animals are capable of responses that are, as a rule, thought of as exclusively human. However, the small acts performed by these marginalized "oddballs," both children and adults, trigger cause-and-effect reactions that ultimately produce positive changes in other people and in the environment. In this understated way, both books not only celebrate the value of otherness but also call for developing an understanding of the long-standing historical interrelatedness of the various elements of the world around us. This awareness is the cornerstone of civic education, especially for a future threatened by the climate crisis in which the agency of all the elements of the system, human and nonhuman alike, is central to all manifestations of life. They also spotlight the advantages that a remodeling of the ways in which we think and act may produce for the environment and, consequently, for humans as well. Notably, such consciousness-raising is among the preeminent aims of global citizenship education. Given this, mobilizing nondidactic environmental children's literature—in particular, its subgenre that addresses the Holocaust and portrays the dire effects caused by a despicable mistreatment of life regarded as inferior—for educational purposes can contribute to the achievement of GCE goals.

The biblical motifs, such as Noah's ark, are harnessed to convey the traditional and instrumental perception of animals and their role in the world. At the same time, however, the very title of *The Ark of Time* engages in a critical discussion with the scriptural topos by foregrounding not a human agent (Noah) but the Time that the human is given on earth, both in the past and today. The original title of Lindelauf's book, *De hemel van Heivisj* (*Heyvish's Heaven*), similarly recasts the anthropocentric perspective, and the Holocaust as annihilation is inscribed in a broader context of sequential changes unfolding across the history of the Earth: the extinction of the human species and the extinction of other species. In this way, the two books about the Holocaust are vehicles for ecopedagogy focused on civic engagement in which the child's agency is an important and natural possibility but not an imposed obligation.

NOTES

1. Although Ubertowska's article has been published in English as "Nature at Its Limits (Ecocide): Subjectivity After the Catastrophe" (*Teksty Drugie 1*, 2015: 173–85), this version has been deemed unsuitable for quoting here, and the passage is given in the translation by the translator of this paper.

2. The quotations from Szczygielski's *The Ark of Time* in this paper come from an unpublished translation by Marek Kazimierski, which was made available to me under the project *Twenty-First Century Literature and the Holocaust: A Comparative and Multilingual Perspective*. The page numbers in parenthetical citations refer to the second Polish edition of the novel (see Reference List). On a handful of occasions, very minor adjustments have been made in Kazimierski's translation.

3. The choice of the animal species with which Rafe can communicate so comfortably is by no means random. The jackal has traditionally and derogatorily represented the Jews in literary writings (see Hanssen 2012), as exemplified by Franz Kafka's short story "Schakale und Araber" ("Jackals and Arabs").

4. Sir 13.1: He that toucheth pitch shall be defiled therewith; and he that hath fellowship with a proud man shall be like unto him.

REFERENCES

Asah, Stanley T., David N. Bengston, Lynne M. Westphal, and Catherine H. Gowan. "Mechanisms of Children's Exposure to Nature: Predicting Adulthood Environmental Citizenship and Commitment to Nature-Based Activities." *Environment and Behavior* 50, no. 7 (2018), 807–36.

Avraham, Rachel. "Why Does Western Media Ignore Jews Being Compared to Rats?" *Israel Hayom*, April 3, 2021. Accessed January 5, 2023. https://www.israelhayom.com/opinions/why-does-western-media-ignore-jews-being-compared-to-rats/.

Brennan, Andrew, and Norva Y. L. Yeuk. "Environmental Ethics." In *The Stanford Encyclopedia of Philosophy*, edited by Edward N. Zalta. Summer 2022. Accessed January 8, 2023. https://plato.stanford.edu/archives/sum2022/entries/ethics-environmental/.

Christian, David. *Origin Story: A Big History of Everything*. New York: Little, Brown and Company, 2018.

Christian, David. "World Environmental History." In *The Oxford Handbook of World History*, edited by Jerry H. Bentley, 124–42. Oxford: Oxford University Press, 2011.

Cole, Tim. "'Nature Was Helping Us': Forests, Trees, and Environmental Histories of the Holocaust." *Environmental History* 19, no. 4 (2014), 665–86. Accessed January 10, 2023. doi:10.1093/envhis/emu068.

Creany, Anne Drolett. "Environmental Literature: Books That Preach and Books That Teach." *Journal of Children's Literature* 20, no. 1 (1994), 16–22.

Gaard, Greta. "Children's Environmental Literature: From Ecocriticism to Ecopedagogy."
    Neohelicon 36 (2009), 321–34. Accessed January 8, 2023. doi:10.1007/s11059-009-0003-7.

Hanssen, Jens. "Kafka and Arabs." *Critical Inquiry* 39, no. 1 (2012), 167–97. Accessed January
    15, 2023. doi:10.1086/668054.

Jaques, Zoe. *Children's Literature and the Posthuman: Animal, Environment, Cyborg.* New
    York: Routledge, 2015.

Kalla, Irena B. "Holocaust als non-fictie in de hedendaagse Nederlandse en Vlaamse jeug-
    dliteratuur." *Neerlandica Wratislaviensia* 33 (2022), 27–38. Accessed January 15, 2023.
    doi:10.19195/0860-0716.33.3.

Katz, Eric. *Anne Frank's Tree. Nature's Confrontation with Technology, Domination, and the
    Holocaust.* Winwick: White Horse Press, 2015.

Levene, Mark. "Climate Blues: Or How Awareness of the Human End Might Re-Instil
    Ethical Purpose to the Writing of History." *Environmental Humanities* 2, no. 1 (2013),
    147–67. Accessed December 30, 2022. doi:10.1215/22011919-3610387.

Lindelauf, Benny. *Fing's War.* Translated by John Nieuwenhuizen. New York: Enchanted
    Lion Books, 2019.

Małczyński, Jacek, Ewa Domańska, Mikołaj Smykowski, and Agnieszka Kłos. "The
    Environmental History of the Holocaust." *Journal of Genocide Research* 22, no. 2
    (2020), 183–96. Accessed June 20, 2022. doi:10.1080/14623528.2020.1715533.

Neumann, Boaz. "National Socialism, Holocaust, and Ecology." In *The Holocaust and
    Historical Methodology,* edited by Dan Stone, 101–24. New York: Berghahn Books, 2012.
    Accessed January 15, 2023. doi:10.1515/9780857454935-007.

O'Brien, Kathy, and Darleen K. Stoner. "Increasing Environmental Awareness through
    Children's Literature." *The Reading Teacher* 41, no. 1 (1987), 14–19. Accessed January 10,
    2023. www.jstor.org/stable/20199688.

Pelgrom, Els. *The Winter When Time Was Frozen.* Translated by Maryka Rudnik and
    Raphael Rudnik. New York: William Morrow, 1980.

Platt, Kamala. "Environmental Justice Children's Literature: Depicting, Defending, and
    Celebrating Trees and Birds, Colors and People." In *Wild Things: Children's Culture and
    Ecocriticism,* edited by Sidney I. Dobrin and Kenneth B. Kidd, 183–97. Detroit: Wayne
    State University Press, 2004.

Sax, Boria. *Animals in the Third Reich.* New York: Continuum, 2000.

Sigler, Carolyn. "Wonderland to Wasteland: Toward Historicizing Environmental Activism
    in Children's Literature." *Children's Literature Association Quarterly* 19, no. 4 (1994),
    148–53. Accessed January 10, 2023. doi:10.1353/chq.0.1011.

Szczygielski, Marcin. *Arka czasu czyli wielka ucieczka Rafała od kiedyś przez wtedy do
    teraz i wstecz,* 2nd ed. Warszawa: Instytut Wydawniczy Latarnik, 2015.

Ubertowska, Aleksandra. "Natura u Kresu (Ekocyd). Podmiotowość po Katastrofie." *Teksty
    Drugie* 139/140, no. 1/2 (2013), 33–44.

Ubertowska, Aleksandra. "'Kamienie niepokoją się i stają się agresywne.' Holokaust w
    Świetle Ekokrytyki." *Poznańskie Studia Polonistyczne, Seria Literacka,* no. 25 (2015),
    93–111. Accessed December 16, 2022. doi:10.14746/pspsl.2015.25.4.

UNESCO. *Global Citizenship Education: Preparing Learners for the Challenges of the 21st Century*. Paris: UNESCO, 2014. Accessed January 15, 2023. https://unesdoc.unesco.org /ark:/48223/pf0000227729.

Van der Beek, Suzanne, and Charlotte Lehmann. "What Can You Do as an Eco-Hero? A Study on the Ecopedagogical Potential of Dutch Non-Fictional Environmental Texts for Children." *Children's Literature in Education* 55, no. 2 (2022), 141–61. Accessed April 22, 2023. doi:10.1007/s10583-022-09482-z.

Wójcik-Dudek, Małgorzata. *Reading (in) the Holocaust: Practices of Postmemory in Recent Polish Literature for Children and Young Adults*. Translated by Patrycja Poniatowska. Berlin: Peter Lang, 2020.

Yarova, Aliona. *Narrating Humanity: Children's Literature and Global Citizenship Education*. Holmbergs: Tryck, 2021.

Chapter 9

ROOTS OF REBELLION

An Ecofeminist Reading of Citizenship
and Climate Activism in Adolescent Fiction

ANNE KLOMBERG

In the past few years, Swedish climate activist Greta Thunberg has regularly demonstrated the power of adolescent activism in public and political spaces. At sixteen years old, she addressed the United Nations during the Climate Action Summit (2019) in New York City. In her now well-known speech, she accuses the attending world leaders of neglect and blames them for taking insufficient measures to tackle the climate crisis. As a young girl, Thunberg claims a position for herself and on behalf of her peers in an adult-governed and mostly male political context that is usually inaccessible to adolescents. Moreover, she uses that position to openly question adult politicians' actions and maturity in the process as she asserts, "We are in the beginning of a mass extinction and all you can talk about is money and fairy tales of eternal economic growth. . . . And you are still not mature enough to tell it like it is" (Thunberg 2019: n.p.).

In turn, Thunberg's international performances have elicited some rather severe responses, which I believe are the result of a perceived discrepancy between her adolescent subject position and the rather adult role she has assumed within the political arena. Her presence at the UN Summit essentially defies traditional power dynamics between adults and adolescents. Accordingly, some of the backlash she received expressly highlights her age as a reason to discredit her. British television host Jeremy Clarkson, for instance, advises Thunberg that "banging your fists on the table won't change a thing. You'll learn that when you've got a few more years under your belt" (Clarkson 2019: n.p.). He implicitly links adulthood to reason and wisdom while portraying adolescence as a state of being emotionally out of control. Clarkson seems to suggest that only when Thunberg is effectively considered an adult herself may she be deemed fit to concern herself calmly and rationally with matters of global importance, such as the climate debate. His implication is further underscored by his remark that Thunberg's parents should have ignored their daughter's demands to change their lifestyle in aid of the environment. Instead, Clarkson claims, Thunberg should "be a good girl [and] shut up" (Clarkson 2019: n.p.). Following his line of reasoning, adolescents have little to contribute until they are actually perceived and treated as adults themselves.

Clarkson's criticism is one of many that specifically focus on Thunberg's embodiment. As critics emphasize not only her age but also her gender and neurodivergence (referring to her Asperger's diagnosis), they tacitly reveal a privileging of another kind of body instead—one that is not-adolescent, not-female, and not-neurodivergent. The normative body against which Thunberg's embodiment is judged (and found wanting) is adult, male, and neurotypical. It is the kind of body that blends in on global political stages, whereas Thunberg's, by comparison, is deemed divergent. Her body is recognized as a "body out of place" (Ahmed 2000: 39), meaning that it is perceived as not belonging in this particular environment as opposed to particular, other bodies.

In this chapter, I argue that adolescent bodies are always, already, somewhat out of place as a result of aetonormativity. That is, in short, a societal privileging of adulthood over other life phases (Nikolajeva 2010). Taking my cue from Thunberg's example, I observe a possible conflict between young adults wanting to participate in society, developing their own citizenship, and their being considered outsiders to this same society based on the normative position of adulthood. One of the ways in which adolescents have recently engaged in such matters of citizenship is through climate activism, as Thunberg's case aptly exemplifies. Many youngsters from across the world have rallied behind her in protest, joining her in school strikes, climate marches, and other kinds of demonstrations to express their disapproval of the current (political) course of events.

Adolescent activism adds an interesting dimension to youngsters' assumed outsider position, which I will later characterize as *outsiderhood*. As Thunberg's example shows, it potentially complicates normative ideas about the relationship between adults and adolescents in terms of power as well as the latter's accepted role and place in society. Taking their assumed outsiderhood as a starting point, I explore how young adults develop and enact their emerging citizenship through climate activism and how they might counter aetonormative views regarding their subject position and desired forms of citizenship in the process. I do so through an analysis of Lauren James's young adult novel *Green Rising* (2021), which centers on a very embodied form of adolescent climate activism. Before I turn to my analysis, I first offer a more extensive explanation of my concept of outsiderhood.

ADOLESCENT OUTSIDERHOOD

As previously stated, aetonormativity denotes a positioning of adulthood as the norm (Nikolajeva 2010), a phenomenon illustrated quite vigorously by Clarkson's reaction to Thunberg cited above. Adulthood as a subject position holds the most power through its associations with knowledge and authority. Roberta Seelinger Trites (2000) notes how this positive evaluation of knowledge essentially renders adolescents *outsiders* in young adult literature so that "the only way teenagers can obtain that goal [wisdom] is to grow, to quit being adolescents themselves, to become more like the insiders, the adults" (79). She concludes that youngsters can only achieve real empowerment by becoming adults (Seelinger Trites 2014).

Even so, this does not mean that adolescents are necessarily disempowered. In fact, adolescents constantly grapple with questions of power as they navigate their coming of age, alternately acquiring power and losing it again as they go. With specific regard to children, Clémentine Beauvais (2015) recognizes how aetonormativity tends to tip the scales of power toward adulthood yet maintains that this does not automatically rob children of power. She argues that children and adults both possess particular forms of power that are regulated by their "temporal otherness," by which she means "the fact that child and adult are symbolically set apart by their belonging to different temporalities" (4). Their differences are grounded in time, which grants each party specific time-bound powers. Beauvais theorizes that children have "might," which refers to the time they (hopefully) have left to spend. It describes their future potential. Adults, by contrast, have "authority" as a result of their time already lived. As adolescence typically occupies a liminal position between childhood and adulthood, I agree with Beauvais when she states that their unique subject position theoretically warrants their own kind of temporal otherness (2015: 9), the parameters of which I begin to explore here.

Specifically, I propose that adolescents' temporal otherness is informed by what I call their *outsiderhood*—that is, a state of being (perceived as) outside of society's norms, age-related and otherwise. This concept is very much embodied. Briefly put, embodiment theory holds that our subjectivity and identity are shaped by our experience of living as bodies that see, feel, and think (see Bradford et al. 2008). Adolescents are recognized as outsiders based on an evaluation of their bodies relative to other (adult) bodies. In *Strange Encounters* (2000), Sara Ahmed explains how "the human body . . . is marked by privilege; it is, for example, a white, male, middle-class, heterosexual body" (46). She points out that such privileged bodies determine the demarcation of social spaces, as they reinforce their own normativity by expelling others who are deemed "stranger" than them from their comfortable zones of living. These bodies are presented as "in-place," whereas those that deviate from the expectations of so-called normative bodies are, in comparison, perceived as out of place.

Given the advantaged position of adulthood within aetonormativity, I suggest we can also add *adult* to Ahmed's enumeration quoted above. Aetonormativity privileges adulthood in ways that might disempower other age groups through acts of ageism. Originally, Robert Butler coined the term *ageism* to describe "prejudice by one age group against another" (Avalon and Tesch-Römer 2018: 3, see also Butler 1969). Though Vanessa Joosen (2022) observes that the term is currently "often reserved for old age only" (4), Butler understands it to include "discrimination by the middle-age group against the younger and older groups in society" (Avalon and Tesch-Römer 2018: 2). Comparable to mechanisms of racism and sexism, ageism thus marginalizes those that deviate from a presupposed norm, in this case, adulthood.

As such, aetonormativity and ensuing acts of ageism impact adolescents' experience of social space. Nancy Lesko (2012) notes how the presence of adolescents in public areas is often met with a sense of discomfort: "Teenagers are so obvious and omnipresent that we seem hardly to notice them unless their peals of laughter cause us to *nervously* look their way, or they interfere with the expected movement or pace of a common task such as standing in line or shopping for groceries, or they walk *too close* on the street or in the mall" (1, my italics).

Once they come too close and/or display unforeseen behavior by disrupting the "expected movement or pace," adolescents stand out and apparently cause unrest in adults around them. Alison Waller (2009) confirms this feeling of unease that groups of teenagers may inspire, as she remarks that "to meet on the streets, in a park or in other public spaces as a group sends out certain messages of threatening behaviour to a society nervous of collectives of young people" (148). Consequently, theirs are the bodies that are being watched cautiously and apprehensively, especially in numbers. Not only do they attract attention, but they are even perceived as potentially dangerous.

Nevertheless, as also discussed in this volume by Jill Coste in part II and Daniela Brockdorff and Katrin Dautel in part III, engaging with their sociocultural and material environment is imperative to young adults' development of self. Seelinger Trites (2000) asserts that much of young adult fiction is "dedicated to depicting how potentially out-of-control adolescents can learn to exist within institutional structures" (7). In effect, the ability to negotiate their place in society is one of the parameters of adolescent characters' growth in many young adult novels. Essentially, they are not just growing up, but they are developing themselves as citizens. Definitions of citizenship may vary across contexts and countries, but in broad terms, citizenship practices are "those activities that citizens are obliged to engage in so as to maintain the well being [sic] of the collective" (Gabrielson and Parady 2010: 383). With regard to adolescents, who are actively developing their identity and subjectivity during this particular life phase (McCallum 1999, Waller 2009), citizenship may be primarily about finding their place within society in relation to others, including coming to terms with society's existing power dynamics.

Of special importance to adolescence is the premise that citizenship is not limited to relationships with other members of the state and with the more general notion of the state itself but that it also extends to the natural world one finds oneself in. As mentioned, space is often not self-evidently available to adolescents, so the way they experience their environment can impact on their emerging sense of citizenship. Especially in light of the ongoing climate crisis, the dire situation of the natural world puts adolescents' futures under strain. Teena Gabrielson and Katelyn Parady (2010) foreground the centrality of nature in matters of citizenship with their concept of "corporeal citizenship." They maintain that "[h]uman subjectivity and citizenship practices emerge from the individual's socioecological positioning" and that "those environments, in turn, shape our understandings of ourselves" (381). This means that humans are situated "within both natural and social contexts" (381) that concurrently influence how we organize society and position ourselves within it. Our environment informs our being in ways that may go unnoticed most of the time yet prove to be profound when they are accentuated. This becomes especially apparent in climate activism, where the impact of the natural world on our well-being (and perhaps even survival) is emphasized. As a means through which adolescents can claim some power for themselves in a society that does not fully recognize their input (yet), climate activism entwines matters of citizenship, adolescent embodiment, and the environment.

In the following analysis of *Green Rising* (2021), I demonstrate how young adult characters find power in their relationship with the natural world, which enables them to (partly) counter the hegemony of adult-governed corporations and develop their own sense of corporeal citizenship, one that explicitly foregrounds the values of care and community and constitutes a form of care-full activism.

PLANT POWER: CONSTRUCTING CITIZENSHIP THROUGH CLIMATE ACTIVISM

Embodiment and the Environment

Green Rising is set in the near future, where climate disasters (like floods, storms, and droughts) happen regularly and all over the world. The novel centers on a group of young adults—the so-called Greenfingers—who suddenly manifest the ability to grow actual living plants using their own bodies as a kind of vessel. They are subsequently employed by a major oil company called Dalex in a project that investigates their powers' potential for creating biofuels. Through a series of training sessions, the Greenfingers gradually come to understand the full extent and implications of their powers while simultaneously trying to find more immediate ways of reversing climate change. However, when they learn that Dalex actually intends to use their powers to melt the Arctic ice caps for their own gain, the Greenfingers hatch a plan to save Earth and bring the company down in the process.

Green Rising features three main characters, all Greenfingers themselves: seventeen-year-old Gabrielle and Theo and eighteen-year-old Hester. Hester is the daughter of Dalex director Anthony Daleport, and she leads the research project on biofuels. It is her first time managing a team of her own. Theo is one of her recruits, while Gabrielle is not part of their research group but joins Hester and Theo later in their attempt to destroy Dalex. Gabrielle is the fiercest climate activist in the story, with some of her actions bordering on illegal offenses. She is also the first one to display her powers in the novel's opening chapter, illustrating the embodied connection between nature and adolescents.

In this chapter, Gabrielle—yet unaware of her Greenfingers power—joins a small group of students protesting an annual Fuel Summit, where large oil companies have convened to discuss further oil extractions and opening new power plants. Carrying signs and chanting slogans like "*Climate change is not a lie, do not let our planet die*" and "Save our future" (James 2021: 8, italics in original), the young activists reveal their displeasure about the continued oil drillings and lack of restrictive legislation. The use of the possessive pronoun "our" in their slogans suggests a close alignment between the fate of the Earth and the young adults' own future; the (inhabitable) continuation of the Earth is a necessary precondition for their own existence.

As such, the students demonstrate a tentative awareness of their corporeal citizenship, meaning that they recognize how their own lived experiences are inevitably tied up with their environment. This link between adolescents and nature becomes explicitly embodied when Gabrielle unintentionally manifests her Greenfingers power: without much warning, vines start to grow from underneath her fingernails. Gabrielle's initial panic is short-lived and quickly turns to acceptance and fascination. The vines grow larger and surround her, and Gabrielle is described to be "in the centre of the pulsating layer of green leaves" (11). Gabrielle, being physically surrounded by plant growth and comfortably so, hints at her understanding that human life is not separate from but embedded in the natural world.

This embodied connection between adolescents and nature, as represented in *Green Rising*, is telling in light of ecofeminist perspectives on the position of particular groups in relation to each other and to the environment. Ecofeminist theory maintains that "there are important connections between how one treats women, people of colour, and the underclass on one hand and how one treats the nonhuman natural world on the other" (Seelinger Trites 2018: 59). What underpins this premise is a belief that dualistic notions of human and nonhuman tend to privilege the first over the latter, rendering the natural world secondary to human experience. Moreover, ecofeminism recognizes how this human experience is differentiated based on various embodiments. Some embodiments—like those of women, people of color, and the underclass—are marginalized in contrast to white, male, middle-class bodies (Ahmed 2000). Aetonormativity and ageism produce comparable connections between adolescents, adults, and the environment as they tend to construct adolescents as outsiders compared to the more privileged adult subject position. Therefore, I understand ecofeminism to also encompass the shared experience of young adults and the environment as marginalized parties in relation to human adulthood.

Ecofeminism often structures such connections in negative terms, such as oppression (Bradford et al. 2008: 84). In *Green Rising*, young people's and nature's shared connection also resides in a form of oppression, that is, the experience of not being heard properly. Gabrielle notes how "[h]er planet needed Gabrielle's voice, because even though it was crying out for help, nobody was listening" (9). It is implied that the collective of young activists is, in fact, attuned to hear Earth's call, only they seem almost equally powerless; Gabrielle adds how many of her fellow protesters are "too young to vote or to make any political difference" (James 2021: 9). They can only try to make themselves heard through demonstrations and other forms of climate activism, but that proves to be not at all straightforward: at the start of the aforementioned student protest, for instance, all the executives are inside and oblivious to the students' grievances. It seems they can quite easily evade dissonant voices. Adolescents' age thus tends to render them quite powerless and voiceless in terms of established, adult-governed modes of democratic power. This is not to say that their climate activism is necessarily doomed to be ineffective but merely that there is a matter of dependency involved in adults actually listening.

However, with the emergence of the Greenfingers' power, this dependency is significantly reduced. In spite of the young characters' lack of political clout, the Greenfingers' ability offers them a means to make a direct impact on the environment. For example, one Greenfingers is described as single-handedly regrowing a forest near her village that prevents their crops from being washed away by monsoons. Everything the Greenfingers grow, grows fast and can thus immediately play its role in the ecosystem, restoring almost at once the balance that was lost because of humanity's exploitation of the Earth.

Nature vs. Technology

The Greenfingers' embodied link with nature inspires in them a sincere desire to care for the environment. This desire to be the one caring is stimulated by a strong sense of empathy, as Hester explains how it "was impossible not to *care* for the plants around her when she could *feel* their drowsy, contented vibrations as they soaked up the sunlight and fresh rainwater" (193, my italics). She feels the environment being alive and is even able to interpret the plants' moods as "drowsy" and "contented." Such empathy is a precondition for an ethics of care. Seelinger Trites (2018) asserts that "empathy is required in an ethics of care, and that empathy is based, in part, on our perceptions of the cared-for's physical and cognitive world" (157). Greenfingers are sensitive to nature in ways that make them susceptible to the plants' inner experiences, forging an especially strong and even emotional bond between them.

Their empathic connection to the earth stands in rather stark contrast to the adults' lack of care as perceived by the Greenfingers. In fact, Gabrielle's climate activism is predominantly motivated by her feeling neglected. She encourages her online followers to convince their parents and guardians (so adults, generally) that they are "failing to care for [youngsters'] welfare if they don't engage with the climate crisis" (James 2021: 34). For Gabrielle, adults neglecting to adequately take care of the natural world equates to disregarding younger generations' futures. This sentiment is repeated several times throughout the narrative, with Theo, at one point, claiming that "energy companies were all the same. They were only interested in profit. They didn't actually *care* about the planet at all" (62, my italics). The novel suggests that big (energy) companies bear the greatest responsibility in slowing climate change and finding sustainable solutions instead of choosing the easy and/or profitable route.

The plot of *Green Rising* culminates in Hester and her peers filing a lawsuit against her father's company after she learns the full extent of its destructive impact. Not only has her father willingly ignored scientists' warnings for years, but he and his business associate, Edgar Warren, have made plans to abandon Earth altogether and go live on Mars instead. For that to happen, though, they need to melt the Arctic ice caps in order to obtain enough oil to fuel their rockets and power their outer space establishment, with disastrous consequences for the Earth. Notably, Hester's father's motives are driven by his intention to keep his daughter safe—to *care* for her—as he tries to assure his daughter: "[T]hink about how much safer [living on Mars] will be, for all of us! No pollution to make us sick. No smog in our lungs or pesticides and mercury in our food. This place is ruined, Hester" (156). However, Hester does not accept the role of being the one cared-for if it means giving up on Earth and its inhabitants. She recognizes the importance of keeping Earth inhabitable for *all* people, especially given how her father's plans for Mars will only truly accommodate the wealthy. Her understanding of corporeal citizenship and care thus extends a lot further than her father's as she accepts the necessity for an ethics of care that encompasses all life on Earth.

The implied differences between the young adult Greenfingers and the adult characters of Anthony Daleport and Warren are further reinforced by pitting them against one another in a presupposed binary between nature and culture/technology, respectively. Daleport is the main representative of Dalex, and he maintains a rather capitalist and profit-minded outlook. Also, as the above citation insinuates, he distances himself as much as possible from life on Earth, wanting to leave the planet sooner rather than later but still making plans to keep on exploiting its resources from the assumed safety of Mars. He symbolizes a capitalist, economic model that is antagonistic to the natural environment, as it deliberately aims to take advantage of the latter. Hester concludes: "Corporate greed has destroyed the planet" (334). In addition, the other leading adult character, Warren, exhibits a strong preoccupation with electronics that sharply contrasts the Greenfingers' compassionate relationship with nature. Warren is a space magnate and loves to flaunt his fascination with brand-new gadgets. He is described as casually carrying around a laptop, "an iPad, a second laptop, a console, a tablet and three other gadgets that Theo couldn't even identify" (163). Theo's failure to recognize some of these items adds to his and Warren's apparent (socioeconomic) differences and serves to further alienate them.

According to Clare Bradford, Kerry Mallan, John Stephens, and Robyn McCallum (2008), disproving the nature/culture binary is one of the main concerns of ecofeminism, for it opens up possibilities to expose other binaries—like mind over body, reason over emotion, and male over female—as false as well, which presumably benefits society as a whole: "The *eco* element of ecofeminism demands an interrogation of the nature/culture binary as a step towards dismantling the other binarisms and for creating an environmentally aware society in which often discounted values (friendship, nurturance, love, trust) shape human subjectivity" (85, italics in original).

In *Green Rising*, Hester's character development illustrates a gradual coming together of nature and culture, negating its assumed dualistic relationship. Standing on the threshold of adulthood, she expressly occupies a liminal position that interweaves her embodied experience as a Greenfingers (affiliated with nature) and as a prospective adult (associated with culture and technology). In the beginning of the novel, Hester tends to lean toward the cultural/technological side of the binary, and it is here that the impact of aetonormativity on her embodied experiences becomes especially salient. From a very early age, she has been prepared to one day succeed her father as director of Dalex. Much in her life has been in service of that goal, like her receiving speech training at the age of two to get rid of a stutter and her extensive public speaking training afterward. Even her appearance "had been adjusted until she received the best possible responses from their test audiences" (James 2021: 24). Her looks and behavior have been modified in service of her prospective role in the company. Adulthood, and specifically her father's version of it, has always been presented to Hester as the ultimate goal.

As an apparent consequence of her public speaking training, Hester is repeatedly described as talking like a robot in the beginning of the novel, reinforcing her affiliation with technology as opposed to nature. In their first meeting, Theo notices how "[t]here was something grating about her voice: stiff and formal, like she was reciting a memorized speech. It was robotic" (59–60). Later, when he asks Hester why she talks like "a business robot or something" (79), Hester is taken aback by his comment and challenges this image of her, thinking to herself: "Everything she said was perfectly sensible. Most of it was memorized from press documents" (79). Hester remains unaware of how she exactly proves Theo's point in this instance. She appears unable to think for herself, relying heavily on the stream of information provided to her by Dalex. Only after Theo calls her out for being oblivious to the dire state of the climate does she discover that everything she knows about climate change has been a lie deliberately fed to her by her father's company.

Another element that adds to the presupposed binary between nature and culture is Hester's initially sheltered life. Her socioeconomic position enables her to reside in places where the direct consequences of climate change—in this case, the persistent heat—are hardly noticeable: "She tried to avoid the unbearable summer heat as much as possible, moving from house to car to office in a perfectly cool haze of air-conditioning. There were even tunnels connecting the city high-rises, so she could go shopping without sweating through her clothes, or coming into contact with the year-round spate of mosquitos" (27).

Her advantaged situation almost allows her to ignore climate change completely, as she lives her life in a kind of bubble that limits climate nuisances like heat. The description of her environment excludes any hint of a natural environment (apart from the mosquitoes, which she successfully avoids). Her surroundings are thus structured mainly in terms of culture and technology and not much nature.

However, after the discovery of her Greenfingers power, Hester is made acutely aware of the world she has (unconsciously) been overlooking. As she gradually understands and appreciates both her own and humanity's close relationship with the environment, Hester acknowledges nature and culture as equal elements of her embodied experience. Combining her training as a Dalex executive with her awareness of humanity's intricate bond with nature puts her in a suitable position to consider both in harmony with each other instead of as a dualism. At the end of *Green Rising*, Hester has gained influence within Dalex after her father was asked to step down. Even though aetonormative discourses still judge her as being "too young" to act as CEO (despite Hester being legally of age), she has been given the lead on the "environmental recovery process" (366). As such, she is adequately positioned to bridge the gap between nature and culture previously advanced by her father's management.

Bradford et al. (2008) contend that disproving the idea of nature and culture as opposites creates an opportunity to dismantle other purported binarisms as well. In the next section, I examine how Hester's awareness of her own corporeal citizenship leads her to challenge her father's privileging of ratio over emotion (and, coincidentally, mind over body). An apparent prerequisite of that process is Hester's sense of community and a desire to care—for the environment, for others, and for herself.

Caring Citizens

As suggested in the beginning of the previous section, the Greenfingers' embodied connection with nature engenders an ethics of care, and both of these, in turn, strongly inform their construction of citizenship. This becomes apparent in the Greenfingers' responsibility for the environment, their relationships with peers, and their agency. In part I of this volume, Justyna Deszcz-Tryhubczak asserts the significance of care as an essential component of citizenship and agency. She discusses the concept of *response-ability* in caring relationships, which ties together notions of responsibility and accountability with a willingness and an ability to act. In their assumed role as the one-caring, Greenfingers demonstrate such response-ability as they use their powers to try and counter climate change, particularly when dealing with some unforeseen consequences of their actions.

For instance, when one of their training sessions goes wrong, the recruits accidentally create a huge excess of toxic algae that endangers all other sea life. A "dead zone" (James 2021: 131), authorities call it. Afterward, Hester asks her father for a chance to make it right: "Dad—this is really important to me. I feel responsible for what happened. I want to fix my mistake" (150). The idea that they have actually damaged the ecosystem when all they wanted to do was help is unbearable to her. As she acknowledges her fault and wishes to make amends, she expresses a desire to enact her citizenship in ways that recognize humanity's relationship to the natural world and ensure the welfare of the collective (Gabrielson and Parady 2010)—humans and nature alike. Hester clearly accepts her own accountability and shows a willingness to work toward improvement for all parties involved. However, her father denies her request, dismissing it as a minor issue that he has already solved by making a huge donation to Greenpeace. His solution suggests how the environment, for him, can only be defined in terms of money and further magnifies his alienation. As her father, he fails to understand the significance of Hester owning her mistake and fixing it herself for her development as a responsible, caring citizen. Moreover, he gives her lead on the project away to Warren, claiming that she has proven herself not yet fit for management. Hester's opportunity to meaningfully engage her own citizenship is thus denied and her agency curbed.

Nevertheless, Hester and the other Greenfingers do, in fact, take responsibility for the environment, and this is in part because of their strong sense of community—not only with the environment itself but also with their peers. All Greenfingers can connect with each other through the mycorrhizal network, an underground system of fungi that stretches all over the world. Being part of such a worldwide community physically strengthens their power; Greenfingers experience an actual surge in their abilities when they link up with one another, symbolizing the power of community in a very material manner. Notably, this sense of community encompasses non-Greenfingers as well, as Gabrielle explicitly invites them to join their rebellion. In addition, being part of a group fills Greenfingers with a sense of belonging, as Theo explains: "He'd never felt like part of a team before. It calmed an anxious, insecure part of his brain that he hadn't even realized existed. He wasn't an *outsider* here like he'd always been when he was working on Dad's boat. He was part of this" (James 2021: 115, my italics). The quote illustrates the importance of interactions with peers, as Theo notes how being surrounded by the adult workers on the boat makes him feel "useless" (15) and out of place. Finding his place within a community makes him feel better physically. Conversely, Theo feels "cold and lonely" (116) when his material connection to the other Greenfingers is broken. The embodied effects of being included or excluded, of being connected to each other, signal the importance of community to society's well-being as a whole.

Furthermore, an ethics of care involves recognizing how "our relationships are part of what constitutes our identity" (Held 2006: 14). The Greenfingers' interpersonal relationships affect their own sense of self as well as their agency. Hester illustrates this point, as her interactions with the others encourage a process of self-reflection that makes her understand the limitations of her epistemology. As a corollary of her sheltered life and the strong focus on her prospective job at Dalex, Hester has not had much opportunity to interact with people her own age, so she has been easily manipulated by false information as she has had little reason to doubt its truthfulness. That changes when she ventures outside her bubble and gets to know her trainees. Their stories and experiences expand her horizon. Through her conversations with Theo especially, Hester learns the full implications of climate change and discovers her father's betrayal. As a result, everything she thinks she knows becomes uncertain. Hester starts to wonder: "How much of her life had been made up of people telling her where to go, what to do and say? She's never even noticed until now. Yet [Theo] Carthew somehow called her on it within minutes of meeting her" (James 2021: 102). This is a pivotal moment as she realizes the extent of adult influence on her life and how her future has, effectively, been a lie. It sets in motion her defiance of her father and his ideology.

One telling way in which Hester stands up to her father is through accepting her own emotionality. As a side effect of her Greenfingers power, Hester is unable to stop small plants from growing on her body when she feels emotional. She is thus physically unable to hide her feelings. At first, this greatly annoys her as she does not want to disappoint her father, who considers this unintentional plant growth a sign of a lack of control, which he despises: "He hated anything unsanitary or disordered. Her wild plants didn't fit into his world" (23). Her father's take on adulthood seemingly does not allow for spontaneity or chaos. In fact, there is not much room for emotions, either. When Hester emotionally confronts her father about his failure to trust her, he responds to her outburst, mortified: "Lower your voice, you sound hysterical" (248). Her emotions are not acknowledged but rejected. However, as Hester distances herself from him, she begins to value this particular aspect of her inner Greenfingers in the process. Specifically, she appreciates how the plants keep her honest, perhaps in response to her father having lied to her so profoundly: "The plants made her actually pay attention to all the feelings she usually suppressed. Well, she wasn't doing that any more. She deserved better than a life of hiding how she really felt, of having a stray flower be the only sign that she was a real person and not a corporation" (250).

Hester's father clearly values reason over emotion, while Hester does, in fact, recognize the significance of expressing her emotions for her own well-being. From an ecofeminist perspective, this can be understood as a dismantling of dualistic thinking that privileges reason over emotion. In this respect, it simultaneously involves subverting a mind-over-body dualism, for Hester's emotionality is very much embodied and accentuates the centrality of her body in these matters. As the narrative foregrounds the adolescent subject position, it advocates for emotion to be reestablished as valuable, in addition to rational thought, and for the body to be in harmony with the mind.

CONCLUSION

In the past few years, adolescent climate activists have often faced adversity when trying to actively engage in matters of citizenship, as the case of Thunberg exemplifies. I contend that this is a probable effect of aetonormativity. The societal privileging of adulthood over adolescence, coupled with ageist perspectives on their agency and experience of space, virtually renders adolescents outsiders. Yet, through climate activism, adolescents demonstrate their desire and ability to participate in ways more meaningful than aetonormativity often allows them to. Because of their outsiderhood, I believe that adolescents are especially suited to recognize their own embeddedness in the natural world precisely because those spaces are not always self-evidently available to them yet are of central importance to their development as citizens. By affirming adolescents as responsible, caring citizens, novels like *Green Rising* show the risks of adults not acknowledging adolescents as full members of society, thereby dismissing their potential and maintaining their alleged outsiderhood.

With my analysis of James's *Green Rising* (2021), I have tried to illustrate how an awareness of the ways in which the natural world and human embodied experiences are intertwined can foster a greater ethics of care and an enhanced sense of community that may ultimately benefit society as a whole. On a personal level, Hester starts to care for herself more deeply as she recognizes her own emotionality—accepting her embodiment in full—and allows herself to be "a real person." Rejecting her father's views on appropriate adult behavior, she reclaims her emotions as a form of strength, not as a weakness, and, nonetheless, takes them as a sign of her humanity. Her (self-)care is advanced through forging meaningful relationships and becoming part of a community that acts toward improvement for humans and nature alike.

In her book *The Ethics of Care* (2006), Virginia Held advocates for the implementation of care in social, political, and economic spheres and extending relationships of care outside private domains to society and citizenship in general. She states, "The ethics of care as it has developed is most certainly not limited to the sphere of family and personal relations. When its social and political implications are understood, it is a radical ethic calling for a profound restructuring of society" (19). For Greenfingers, this involves an equal consideration of nature and culture not as opposites that exclude or harm one another but as mutual components of embodied experience. Their climate activism, including their material connection to the Earth and the ethics of care this relationship incites and propels, shows how an understanding of the significance of care to corporeal citizenship envisions the improvement of life on Earth in general.

REFERENCES

Ahmed, Sara. *Strange Encounters: Embodied Others in Post-Coloniality*. London: Routledge, 2000.

Ayalon, Liat, and Clemens Tesch-Römer. "Introduction to the Section: Ageism—Concept and Origins." In *Contemporary Perspectives on Ageism*, edited by Liat Ayalon and Clemens Tesch-Römer, 1–10. Basingstoke: Springer, 2018.

Beauvais, Clémentine. *The Mighty Child: Time and Power in Children's Literature.* Amsterdam: John Benjamins Publishing Company, 2015.

Bradford, Clare, Kerry Mallan, John Stephens, and Robyn McCallum. "Reweaving Nature and Culture: Reading Ecocritically." In *New World Orders in Contemporary Children's Literature: Utopian Transformations*, edited by Clare Bradford, Kerry Mallan, John Stephens, and Robyn McCallum, 79–104. Basingstoke: Palgrave Macmillan, 2008.

Butler, R. N. "Age-Ism: Another Form of Bigotry." *The Gerontologist* 9, no. 4 (1969), 243–46.

Clarkson, Jeremy. "The World May Be Getting Hotter, Greta Thunberg . . . But Having a Meltdown Isn't Going to Help." *The Sun*, September 27, 2019.

Curry, A. *Environmental Crisis in Young Adult Fiction: A Poetics of Earth.* Basingstoke: Springer, 2013.

Gabrielson, Teena, and Katelyn Parady. "Corporeal Citizenship: Rethinking Green Citizenship Through the Body." *Environmental Politics* 19, no. 3 (2010), 374–91. Accessed January 15, 2024. doi:10.1080/09644011003690799.

Held, Virginia. *The Ethics of Care: Personal, Political, and Global.* Oxford: Oxford University Press, 2006.

James, Lauren. *Green Rising.* London: Walker Books, 2021.

Joosen, Vanessa. "Connecting Childhood Studies, Age Studies, and Children's Literature Studies." *Barnboken* 45 (December 2022). Accessed January 15, 2024. doi:10.14811 /clr.v45.745.

Lesko, Nancy. *Act Your Age!: A Cultural Construction of Adolescence.* London: Routledge, 2012.

Milman, Oliver. "Greta Thunberg Condemns World Leaders in Emotional Speech at UN." *The Guardian*, September 23, 2019.

Nikolajeva, Maria. *Power, Voice and Subjectivity in Literature for Young Readers.* London: Routledge, 2008.

Seelinger Trites, Roberta. *Disturbing the Universe: Power and Repression in Adolescent Literature.* Iowa City: University of Iowa Press, 2000.

Seelinger Trites, Roberta. *Literary Conceptualizations of Growth: Metaphors and Cognition in Adolescent Literature.* Amsterdam: John Benjamins Publishing Company, 2014.

Seelinger Trites, Roberta. *Twenty-First-Century Feminisms in Children's and Adolescent Literature.* Jackson: University Press of Mississippi, 2018.

Waller, Alison. *Constructing Adolescence in Fantastic Realism.* London: Routledge, 2009.

Part IV

Systemic Agency and Sites of Recognition and Engagement

Chapter 10

READING OF WHAT IS YET TO COME

Anthropocentric Children's Literature and Childhood Agency

FARRIBA SCHULZ

While environmental protection, conservation, and climate change are not new buzzwords, what has changed is the extent to which the rapidly expanding global movement, *Fridays for Future* (FFF), started protesting for the government to keep its promises about climate policy. The protest movement has received strong support from international networks such as Extinction Rebellion and Letzte Generation (Declare Emergency, US). The participants of the demonstrations and protest activities partake in the discourse by putting the topic on the agenda and making the scientifically abstract topic accessible to the mainstream (see Haunns and Moritz 2020). Interestingly, from an educational perspective, a European survey of the emergence and prospects of FFF conducted by the Institute for Protest and Social Movement Studies (Institut für Protest und Bewegungsforschung) shows that the political commitment to environmental and climate protection in this protest movement was initially primarily motivated by children and young adults and is, compared to other protest movements, on average more likely to be supported by young people (see Sommer, Rucht, Haunss, and Zajak 2019). As part of the study, protesters in nine European countries were asked who was to blame, and the young participants shared two perspectives: one group cited individual action and another group cited the economy, companies, and politics as responsible. When asked about problem-solving expertise, the students in Germany do not seem to place much confidence in corporate and political mechanisms. Against the backdrop of "how to actually win those over who cannot or do not want to connect to such issues and movements for politics and social engagement," Björn Milbradt suggests taking up the already raging climate catastrophe more systematically, drawing attention to the existence of different social and economic situations and promoting "a more reflexive,

empathic, political engagement" (2020: 4-6; translated in English).[1] If changes
are required, this would mean, in accordance with Meg Rosoff, the need for "a
better class of political leaders, entrepreneurs, scientists, parents, and social
policy-makers." Thinking about how this can be achieved, it is perhaps not
surprising that, from her perspective, she believes "at least some of it begins
with books" (see Rosoff in this volume). And, as Nicky Parker puts it in part
I of this volume, "children's literature can thus be seen as a creative candle
that lights the darkness, safely revealing the monsters and supporting young
readers to a position of greater understanding and strength."

The concept of the Anthropocene is already reflected in a widely ramified
network of discourse that focuses on the dominant relationship between
humans and nature. Current children's literature takes up this discourse in
a variety of ways and, due to its broad aesthetic range, can be viewed in the
field of tension between ecocriticism and ecopedagogy. While, according
to Greta Gaard, ecocriticism aims at providing a home for (1) the academic
discourse, (2) a cultural-ecological literature analysis, (3) the exploration of
"interconnections between nature and culture," and (4) a response to "environmental problems" (2009: 322), "[e]copedagogy articulates a commitment
to the coherence between theory and practice" and "looks at children's environmental texts for their potential to illuminate current environmental issues,"
pursuing "the goal of putting theory into action" (Gaard 2009: 332f). As simple
as this may sound, transitioning to an ecological civilization and, as Marek
Oziewicz puts it, "[h]elping young people *believe* that we can" (2022: 241) is
the hard part. Conceptions of childhood and notions of child's agency by all
those involved in the socialization of children determine whether, and in what
way, the status quo is deconstructed, norms shifted, and the "child in/with/
as nature" (Malone, Tesar, and Arndt 2020) is empowered. And, as Justyna
Deszcz-Tryhubczak puts it so beautifully in part I, these entangled relations
unfold "and may involve nonhuman materialities, agents, entities, forces, and
intensities, such as books, toys, classrooms, and institutions." This argument,
extended throughout this volume, implies that the relationality of children's
agency in society not only "begins with children's literature" but also with
"culture scholarship." Building on this, my chapter focuses on student teachers'
self-understanding as well as their understanding of the world through literature and its potential for the literary classroom. Student teachers' reviews of
children's literature in the context of the Anthropocene are regarded through
the lens of childhood agency, considering the following questions: What is
the importance of teaching literature in the light of global citizenship? What
is the role of the selection of literature, the possible readings of it, and what
Berbeli Wanning describes as the potential in a cultural-ecological perspective

"to see through the social factors and processes related to environmental problems?" (Wanning 2019: 433; translated in English).

Accordingly, this study focuses on student teachers' understanding of anthropocentric discourse through a case study that started during the pandemic, when writing assignments were a good way to move reflective aspects out of the classroom and into the digital realm. The writing task has been maintained since and is carried out in a teaching course in the primary teacher education section. The data comprises Master's university students' book reviews conveyed as book tubes, podcasts, or written texts, dealing with didactic questions about children's literature in the context of political education and historical learning. At the heart of the project lies the focus on the different constructions of the Anthropocene as articulated by the literature aimed at children between five and twelve, in addition to what university students recognize as agency and childhood, the pedagogical framing of the child and nature, and the representation of nature and culture in selected children's literature. Once all student reviews were complete, I analyzed the book reviews, using the qualitative content analysis method, by reading the corpus of students' book reviews systematically (Krippendorff 2013). Referring to the context of the climate change discourse and comparing the students' texts to professional critiques or literature award justifications, such as The German Youth Literature Award, I'm going to test the positioning of the reviewers. Are they taking a stand? In which way is the understanding of the "child in/with/as nature" (Malone, Tesar, and Arndt 2020) and its consequences for the pedagogical framing in the literary classroom reviewed through the lens of childhood agency? Evaluating reader responses to the chosen children's books, key aspects of the connections between ecocriticism and ecopedagogy (Gaard 2009) can be studied. The way in which children's literature is reviewed by university students also says something about the learning target dimensions in the literary classroom that the future teachers prioritize, with limitations, of course (see Wieser 2008). In both reading promotion and the engagement with literature, the question emerges of how the anthropocentric discourse in children's literature can be tackled in the literary classroom that has children's agency at its conceptual core.

CHILDREN'S LITERATURE IN THE CONTEXT OF THE ANTHROPOCENE

Referring to the US context, Clare Echterling states that "the most contemporary children's environmental picture books and easy readers [. . .] focus

overwhelmingly on individual environmentalist acts and lifestyle changes"
and therefore "overlook the connections between environmental degradation and systematic social problems such as class disparities, and ultimately
over-simplify environmental crisis" (2016: 283). Six years later, the current
German book market represents a variety of positions found in anthropocentric discourse. From do-it-yourself books, informative nonfiction, dystopian
fiction, and adventurous comics to exciting fantasy, books present life hacks
to change your lifestyle, illustrate biodiversity, inform about environmental
destruction and its causes, and introduce climate heroines and their ecological projects in simple explanatory stories as well as in depicting systematically different social and economic situations. Among them are "numerous
children's and young people's books that are dedicated to the subject areas
of climate, environmental and nature protection and in which the staging
of child and adolescent climate heroines is also emphasized" (Mikota and
Pecher 2020: 9; translated in English) that have become more popular since
2019, when FFF declared its first global protest on March 15. The range of
products on the book market corresponds to the changing needs of a new
generation of customers, also called Greenomics or LOHAS (Lifestyle of
Health and Sustainability)—the ethical-green consumer elite (see Mikota
and Pecher 2020: 10). In 1996, Cheryll Glotfelty formulated the hope that the
movement would differentiate into a multiethnic one if "stronger connections
are made between the environment and issues of social justice, and when
diversity of voices are encouraged to contribute to the discussion" (1996:
xxv, in Gaard 2009: 321). And much has changed since Gaard described
the trajectory from the beginnings of ecocriticism, mainly driven by one
group consisting of "primarily white, middle-class and predominantly heterosexual scholars," through the influences of feminism and the movement
and then to the beginnings of children's literature criticism in that context
(2009: 322–25). Glotfelty's hope is updated in Oziewicz and Lara Saguisag's
introduction to their *Lion and the Unicorn* issue about Children's Literature
and Climate Change as they call for an extension of the approach from the
"commitment to justice and equity" far beyond "Eurocentrism and Whiteness
of children's publishing and children's literature studies" to demand equity
in children's publishing, educational institutions, and academia" (Oziewicz
and Saguisag 2021: viii).

Addressing the concept of the Anthropocene in children's literature mirrors transformations and continuities related to pedagogy and aesthetics,
blurring the line between moral/instruction and entertainment. Children's
literature has traditionally been situated in an educational setting, which
either includes instructions for a child to be prepared for adulthood or

conveys a romantic ideal of childhood, placing hope for restoring society on children. In relation to environmental children's literature, therefore, the values and ideas associated with society and childhood shape the discourse around environmental agency and, by implication, the activist role that young people take on in their community. How is the anthropocentric discourse in children's and young adult literature shaped by the representation of nature and environmental values? Which interconnections between the binaries of nature and culture are inherent? How are childhood and its actors constructed?

ANTHROPOCENTRIC CHILDREN'S LITERATURE SELECTED FOR THE LITERARY CLASSROOM

School is an important place of education where an understanding of society and subject comes into effect (Bourdieu 1991, Althusser 2019). Since several member states of the Council of Europe adopted a charter on education for democratic citizenship and human rights education and the UN identified sustainable development goals related to global citizenship, children ought to be empowered to become proactive contributors to these goals. Still, "training for citizenship" depends on how "children's agency is considered within school setting[s]," Sheila Greene and Elizabeth Nixon emphasize, as they trace the extent to which schools as institutions struggle to enable agency between hierarchy- and student-centered models (2020: 114). Christensen describes this problem in relation to children's literature as follows: "At one end of the spectrum, the term recalls the romantic child: free, independent, divine. At another end, the child figure finds herself restricted, defined, denied by her structural predicament" (2021: 13). Considering the adult-child relationship and understanding agency as an interactive process with all actors within a society (see Marah Gubar's kinship model in Christensen 2021: 11), a practice, Paulo Freire defines as "reflection and action upon the world in order to transform it" (2000: 51) could open up the classroom to recognition and negotiation of different identity and reality concepts. Therefore, critical literacy is crucial to this goal, and texts need to be analyzed with regard to their ideological content but also be at the core of the curriculum to identify power relations, engaging in dialogues about "symbolic power" (Bourdieu 1991).

While presenting the wide range of environmental children's literature, even those texts that are oversimplifying the issue might provide an excellent platform, engaging university students and enabling them to participate in the environmental (academic) discourse by (1) analyzing the literature with a cultural-ecological perspective, (2) exploring the "interconnections between nature and culture," and (3) responding to "environmental problems" (Gaard 2009: 322) as it prepares future teachers to carefully choose the children's literature for their primary classrooms. As these teachers will be facilitators in literary classrooms and will teach their students to read, the question of what reading means is core. Reading, from a global point of view, is a very complex activity that is not limited to decoding a text but also entails children's capability to understand what they have read and integrate it into their own context and personal experiences by analyzing it in a critical way, so they are able to take a stand on what they have read. Only this kind of thorough reading education will take children toward a real, integrated literacy (see Nikolayeva 2014). In order to emancipate the reader and build citizenship, literature can contribute to a change of perspective by generating knowledge and providing insight into ethical and political dimensions (Wanning 2019: 431). Wanning notes that literature can thereby create a connection between cognitive knowledge and emotions and depict cognition (*erkenntnisvermögen*) that ensures a connection to reality.

Children's literature in anthropocentric discourse offers cultural-ecological and didactic perspectives that might enable the reader to see through the socially related environmental problems. Oziewicz and Saguisag invite literary scholars to pose "questions of what it means for a book to be about climate change. What strategies in text and mixed-media narratives are most effective to overcome representational challenges of climate change and are able to mobilize action?" (Oziewicz and Saguisag 2021: ix). Within global citizenship, which aims for a more sustainable, just, and peaceful world, Wanning defines the role of teachers as change agents who challenge the status quo and help imagine a desirable future through the literature that they bring to class and their perspective on bigger issues (Wanning 2019: 433). These would be stories offering solutions, happy endings, and "understanding that have the potential to mobilize the audience's agency" (2022: 248).

REVIEWING AND CHOOSING CHILDREN'S LITERATURE FOR THE CLASSROOM: GATEKEEPERS AND CHANGE AGENTS

The way in which literature is evaluated and selected depends on the individual's relationship to the field of children's and young people's literature. What should be heard, seen, and read by children and young adults is determined by authorities, which historically included the church but are nowadays represented in a more secularized way, including a variety of critics (e.g., parents, teachers, educators, librarians, booksellers, publishers, literary scholars, and journalists; see Ewers 2002: 4) and therefore various points of views. These, in turn, produce recommendations for books worth reading and nominations for awards. With an average of 7,500 publications in the field of children's and young adult literature per year (see *Börsenverein des Deutschen Buchhandels*: Wirtschaftszahlen/Titelproduktion 2020 and 2021), awards, recommendation lists, blogs, and bookstagrammers filter the market and thus create a preselection for readers. The German Youth Literature Award, sponsored by the Federal Ministry for Family Affairs, Senior Citizens, Women and Youth, for instance, was founded to act as an important guideline for the offered children and youth literature. With the first call in 1955, the founding association, der Arbeitskreis für Jugendliteratur e.V., intended to promote quality. It appointed jury members who were involved in children's literature or work with children. Particularly since the 2000s, a discussion about early childhood education that was reignited with the results of the PISA study has shown a pedagogical focus in relation to the picture book nominations of The German Youth Literature Award (ct. Schulz 2013: 500). Acting as "minders of make-believe" as Leonard Marcus would say, practices in which "publishers, critics, librarians, booksellers" (2008: ix) shape and reshape the children's literature industry, are also practices of gatekeeping (see Kidd and Thomas 2017, Ramdarshan Bold 2019). The group of those who recommend literature as worth reading has expanded immensely due to social networks. Book bloggers have created a voice for themselves as amateur readers and thus reach a public beyond the feuilleton. One's own reading behavior becomes shareable and communicable (Brendel-Perpina 2018: 77). It is a living community that refers to each other and locates itself socially. The community is so important for the book market that the Börsenverein des Deutschen Buchhandels founded its own award to honor the best German-language blog, podcast, or social media channel.

In a didactical context, Ina Brendel-Perpina attributes a special potential to book reviews primarily because of their subject matter and relatively open structure. The objective of the literary evaluation always depends on the critic's point of view and their role. The literary critique ranges from informing orientation, selection, and the function to convey didactically, didactic sanction, being reflective and communicative or simply entertaining (Brendel-Perpina and Stumpf 2013: 33). Based on this, Brendel-Perpina derives the following target perspectives of cultural practice "book review" for teaching:

1. Evaluative forms of writing are suitable for developing the ability to make judgments and critical expressions in relation to literary texts in one's own linguistically designed production process.
2. In the discussion of book reviews, students learn to recognize different language patterns in their dependence on function, addressee, and place of publication and can use this for writing their own reviews.
3. Reviews of new book publications enable connection and participation in contemporary literary discourses and are thus part of school reading culture. (Brendel-Perpina 2019: 224)

The university students engaged with the format of a book review and had to reflect on questions about the genre, the topic, aesthetic quality, reading requirement, and especially reflections on the didactic nature of the works and their own reasons for choosing them based on the following questions:

1. What is the importance of engaging with nature?
2. How is thinking about human beings made possible in the context of the Anthropocene?
3. Are the structural interrelationships of social factors and processes related to environmental problems presented? If so, how?

These questions link to reflect the concept of ecopedagogy and/or ecocriticism (see Gaard 2009; Wanning 2019) and the objective to read children's literature critically to understand changes of perspective, cultural-historical self-reflection, and the deconstruction of power relations (see Oomen-Welke, Rösch, and Ahrentholz 2016).

REVIEWING CHILDREN'S LITERATURE IN THE CONTEXT OF ECOPEDAGOGY AND ECOCRITICISM: CAPITALOCENE

Being asked which books focused on environmental protection, nature conservation, climate change, and climate protection, student teachers would choose for primary classrooms, one university student selected the nonfiction picture book *Auf nach Yellowstone! Was Nationalparks über die Natur verraten* (*Yellowstone! What National Parks Reveal About Nature*) (2020) by Aleksandra Mizielinska and Daniel Mizielinski. They focused their review mostly on "the beautiful colorful illustrations," which, in their point of view, supports deeper understanding:

It is fascinating how much content and topics the book contains and doing it in so much detail and with attention to accuracy in terms of content and being suitable for children at the same time. The beautiful, colorful illustrations support the comprehensibility incredibly. What I also really enjoyed were the introductory graphics of the national parks, where an incredible amount of information is hidden, but what is perfectly designed is simultaneously responsible for one having a great time looking and discovering details. This book is really fun! (Review Student A; translated in English)

Even though the book itself offers a lot of ecocritical angles, the university student's recommendation does not focus on ecocritical aspects. Surprisingly, the jury of The German Youth Literature Award does not address the sociocritical aspects of this picture book in its statement of reasons for the award either. The jury statement of 2021 explains:

In their large-format nonfiction comic, artist couple Aleksandra and Daniel Mizieliński immerse readers in the fascinating and multifaceted world of national parks. [. . .] Embedded in the adventure of Ula and Cuba [main characters] in the interplay of comic episodes, diagrams and detailed views, useful basics are conveyed as well as knowledge about animals, plants and scenic features of the national parks. (Arbeitskreis für Jugendliteratur e.V.; translated in English)

Instead of arguing toward ecocriticism, the jury of The German Youth Literature Award of 2021, as well as the university student, expresses what was proclaimed as fundamental in Friedrich Justin Bertuch's picture book for children in 1792. While Bertuch is renewing the medium in the eighteenth century with colored copper engravings, he sets new standards referring to pedagogical authorities of his time, highlighting the combination of information and entertainment. In the context of reading promotion, this combination is also to be understood as an attempt to combine reading for pleasure with information-extracting reading. According to Louise Rosenblatt (1978), competent readers take one of these two stances, namely the "efferent stance" or the "aesthetic stance" or a hybrid of them, depending on the text at hand. To be able to take a critical stance, hybrid approaches to the text must be possible and, above all, must be made possible in the literary classroom. Using critical reading (Nikolajeva 2014) in the context of global citizenship is therefore crucial to "empower learners to engage and assume active roles, both locally and globally, to face and resolve global challenges and ultimately become proactive contributors to a more just, peaceful, tolerant, inclusive, secure, and sustainable world (UNESCO 2013: 4 in Greene and Nixon 2020: 114).

But the university students, as the jury of The German Youth Literature Award of 2021, refer mainly to the potential of the picture book in the context of reading promotion in their reviews. It seems like the future teachers and the jury members of 2021 are, in this particular instance, more focused on reading promotion than on critical reading, which falls in line with the restricted literacy understanding that PISA (OECD 2010; see also Wieler 2003) is mostly concerned with. Of course, there were some other book reviews that were more focused on reading promotion, entertainment, and colorful aesthetic enjoyment, but also several university students' reviews that contained various keywords, which suggests a reflection on structural problems within the anthropocentric discourse. These book reviews highlight different aspects, "showing how sustainable consumption can work in everyday life" and "[t]hat man is an important and large factor within influencing the environment"; position "climate change deniers or climate skeptics," and depict "that there is also protest regarding the global situation" as in the "global movement of students for a better future, simply Fridays for Future" (Review Student C and D; translated in English).

In the book review of the graphic novel *Yasmina und die Kartoffelkrise* (*Chef Yasmina and the Potato Panic*) (2021) by Wauter Mannaert, for instance, one university student focused on what Björn Milbradt calls for, namely "the need to draw attention to the existence of different social and economic situations" (2020: 6; translated in English) and what Wanning describes as the potential in a cultural-ecological perspective "to see through the social factors and processes related to environmental problems" (Wanning 2019: 433; translated in English): "The subject is a capitalistically designed society, in which a hard-working person, like the father, does not earn enough to support himself [and his daughter Yasmin], as well as the pros and cons of wild gardening and purposeful cultivation of vegetables using chemical inputs, genetically modified food and convenience foods, the key question about ingredients" (Review Student B; translated in English).

The graphic novel certainly uses narrative strategies like adventure and suspense to entertain as it tells how Yasmina and her friends manage to get rid of the city's large corporation that produces genetically modified potato chips that turn everyone into monsters. Yasmina is a passionate cook who provides herself and her father, who works in a fast-food restaurant, with lovingly prepared dishes every day. Before Yasmina goes to school in the morning, she collects the ingredients for her inventive dishes from her allotment gardener friends Marco and Cyril. When a large corporation uses Marco and Cyril's land for the large-scale production of genetically modified potatoes, not only does Yasmina's vegetable spring dry up but the town is also flooded with potato chips. Between questions about gentrification and healthy eating, this comic, like the classic film *The Wing or The Thigh* with Louis de Funès (1976), criticizes the fast-food industry and celebrates slow food. Mannaert stages Yasmina's adventures in the special cast of characters, the landscape and spatial design, and the selected image details in such a way that readers can immerse themselves cinematically in the story with a multitude of details depicted in the panels. In decoding and assembling the diverse information, the narrative then expands sequentially so that the pictorial symbolism influences several narrative levels at once.

While this graphic novel hasn't received any awards, it was highly recommended on social media platforms, for example, by Julia Bousboa, who runs a well-received and, by the Börsenverein des Deutschen Buchhandels, well-awarded blog called "Juli Liest." Bousboa classifies this graphic novel as a story that "encourages further thought about vital questions like "Is food in little plastic bags really more convenient?," "What happens when we interfere with nature?," and, indeed, "How can it be that someone works all day in a snack bar and still has too little money to live a healthy life?" while "a discourse about genetic engineering, money and market power" is embedded in the story setting (Bousboa; translated in English). The university student, as well as Bousboa, thus take up the essential aspects that Wanning (2019) and also Gaard (2009) mention in the context of ecocriticism, namely, to offer cultural-ecological and didactic perspectives that might enable the reader to see through the socially related environmental problems. Taking up a sociocritical attitude that focuses on changes of perspective and the deconstruction of power relations allows experiences to be part of dialogues about "symbolic power" (Bourdieu 1991). In the light of global citizenship, this might add to an

> education, training, awareness rising, information, practices and activities which aim, by equipping learners with knowledge, skills and understanding and help with developing their attitudes and behaviour, to empower them to exercise and defend their democratic rights and responsibilities in society, to value diversity and to play an active part in democratic life, with a view to the promotion and protection of democracy and the rule of law. (Council of Europe 2010 in Greene and Nixon 2020: 114)

CONCLUSION

Children's and young adult literature addresses the concept of the Anthropocene in a variety of ways and through a broad aesthetic range. Transformations and continuities related to pedagogy and aesthetics can be traced in the depiction and also in the approach through which the university students select, evaluate, take a stand, and understand "child in/with/as nature" (Malone/Tesar/Arndt 2020). Its consequences for the pedagogical framing in the literary classroom through the lens of childhood agency are as multifaceted as the discourse is in society. Even though the books presented here all address the structural problems and try to convey their complexity, this does not guarantee that the readers will perceive these aspects as the most important ones for themselves. Personal perceptions of childhood and pedagogy, as well as personal ideological bias, all play a part in the selection of books made by student teachers. Pleasure and reading promotion are convincing arguments for the use of literature for children in the literary classroom, but in order to do justice to the role of changing agents, a special critical perspective or promotion of judgmental capability is required for children to be empowered to become proactive contributors to the sustainable development goals related to global citizenship. Blenkinsop, Morse, and Jickling especially call for "rebel teachers" within *wild pedagogies* as "agents for educational change" because they "believe that current times require responses that are imaginative, creative, courageous, and radical" (2022: 36). The university student's book reviews give reason for hope. At least some, if not all, of them have identified the "bright spots" described by Oziewicz (2022: 248). Stories such as *Yasmina und die Kartoffelkrise* (*Chef Yasmina and the Potato Panic*) (2021) offer solutions and happy endings, have the potential to mobilize, and what's more, in addition to providing insight into structural problems, are also extremely entertaining. In the context of ecocriticism and ecopedagogy, however, this needs to be reflected upon.

Using book reviews as a method of training student teachers does not only foster critical thinking but is also a possibility for university students to get an overview of the book market and participate in social discourses represented in children's and young adult literature. Exploring anthropocentric discourse through children's literature requires that university students identify relevant books, reflect on them in a critical way, and share their reading experience, which may conflict with some of their existing knowledge and that of their peers or supervisors. Ultimately, however, this method allows students to explore an alternative mode of classroom discussion. Abraham and Brendel-Perpina describe that for the development of a capacity for judgment, evaluation as a mental act, as an act of cognition, and as a linguistic expression are interrelated. The evaluation, as it were, is based on the perception of an object and can also be changed by changing or comparing perspectives on the object. Therein lies a special didactic potential (2015: 25–27). Giving students the opportunity to share their different perspectives with each other in a conversation afterward, for example through literary debates, has the potential to broaden their perspectives. With this method, (adolescent) discourse practices with their participatory, peer group–oriented patterns of use can be taken into account. The form of the book review thus becomes the object of reading culture, literary learning, the promotion of media literacy, and critical reading, which align with John Dewey's concept of learning (2009), where aesthetic experiences based on relationships with media may offer learners opportunities that draw on personal literary and life experiences to create meaning (Iser 1976 and Rosenblatt 1978) but foremost to take a stand. Using methods of postcolonial discourse in order to recognize the depiction of the child *in/with/ and nature*, to identify how thinking about human beings is made possible in the context of the Anthropocene aesthetically and engage in dialogues about the structural interrelationships of social factors and processes related to environmental problems presented in children's literature, student teachers can be empowered through critical literacy themselves. Positioning student teachers as mediators of children's literature through cognitive criticism approaches can create an environment where agency is seen as an interactive process with all actors within a society (see Gubar's kinship model in Christensen 2021: 11). It also fosters reader engagement that could empower readers "to become proactive contributors to a more just, peaceful, tolerant, inclusive and secure and sustainable world" (UNESCO 2013: 4 in Greene and Nixon 2020: 114).

NOTE

1. All translations from German, unless otherwise stated, are done by the author.

REFERENCES

Althusser, Louis. *Ideologie und ideologische Staatsapparate. Aufsätze zur marxistischen Theorie.* Hamburg: VSA, 2019.

Arbeitskreis für Jugendliteratur e.V. "Jurybegründung—Auf nach Yellowstone!" *Der Deutsche Jugendliteraturpreis*, n.d. Accessed April 23, 2025. https://www.jugendliteratur. org/buch/auf-nach-yellowstone-4236.

Arbeitskreis für Jugendliteratur e.V. *Der Deutsche Jugendliteraturpreis: eine Dokumentation*. München: Arbeitskreis für Jugendliteratur, 2000.

Bertuch, Justin. *Bilderbuch für Kinder*. Weimar: Verlag des Comptoirs, 1792.

Blenkinsop, Sean, Marcus Morse, and Bob Jickling. "Wild Pedagogies: Opportunities and Challenges for Practice." In *Pedagogy in the Anthropocene: Re-Wilding Education for a New Earth*, edited by Michael Paulsen, Jan Jagodzinski, and Shé M. Hawke, 35–51. London: Palgrave Macmillan, 2022.

Börsenverein des Deutschen Buchhandels. *Wirtschaftszahlen*. n.d. Accessed April 23, 2025. https://www.boersenverein.de/markt-daten/marktforschung/wirtschaftszahlen.

Bourdieu, Pierre. "Ökonomisches Kapital, kulturelles Kapital, soziales Kapital." In *Die verborgenen Mechanismen der Macht*, edited by Pierre Bourdieu, 49–80. Hamburg: VSA, 1992.

Bousboa, Julia. "Juliliest." Accessed April 23, 2025. https://juliliest.net.

Brendel-Perpina, Ina, and Felix Stumpf. *Leseförderung durch Teilhabe: Die Jugendjury zum Deutschen Jugendliteraturpreis*. München: Kopaed, 2013.

Brendel-Perpina, Ina. "Was (jugendliche) BuchbloggerInnen bewegt: Funktionen und Formate digitaler Anschluss-kommunikation." In *Literalität und Partizipation: Reden, Schreiben, Gestalten in und zu Medien*, edited by Petra Anders and Petra Wieler, 63–82. Tübingen: Stauffenburg, 2018.

Brendel-Perpina, Ina. *Literarische Wertung als kulturelle Praxis: Kritik, Urteilsbildung und die digitalen Medien im Deutschunterricht*. Bamberg: University of Bamberg Press, 2019. Accessed April 23, 2025. https://fis.uni-bamberg.de/handle/uniba/45592.

Christensen, Nina. "Agency." In *Keywords for Children's Literature*, edited by Philip Nell, Lissa Paul, and Nina Christensen, 2nd ed., 10–13. New York: New York University Press, 2021.

Dewey, John. *Democracy and Education: An Introduction to the Philosophy of Education*. Kentucky: Feather Trail Press, 2012.

Echterling, Clare. "How to Save the World and Other Lessons from Children's Environmental Literature." *Children's Literature in Education* 47, no. 4 (2016), 283–99.

Ewers, Hans-Heino. "Was ist Kinder- und Jugendliteratur? Ein Beitrag zu ihrer Definition und zur Terminologie ihrer wissenschaftlichen Beschreibung." In *Taschenbuch der Kinder- und Jugendliteratur*, edited by Günter Lange, 2–16. Baltmannsweiler: Schneider Hohengehren, 2002.

Freire, Paulo. *Pedagogy of the Oppressed*. New York: Continuum, 2020.

Gaard, Greta. "Children's Environmental Literature: From Ecocriticism to Ecopedagogy." *Neohelicon* 36 (2009), 321–34.

Glotfelty, Cheryll, and Harold Fromm. *The Ecocriticism Reader: Landmarks in Literary Ecology*. Athens, GA: University of Georgia Press, 1996.

Greene, Sheila, and Elizabeth Nixon. *Children as Agents in Their Worlds*. London: Routledge, 2020.

Iser, Wolfgang. *The Act of Reading: A Theory of Aesthetic Response*. London: The Johns Hopkins University Press, 1978.

Kidd, Kenneth, and Joseph Thomas Jr., editors. *Prizing Children's Literature. The Cultural Politics of Children's Book Awards*. London: Routledge, 2017.

Krippendorff, Klaus. *Content Analysis: An Introduction to Its Methodology*. Thousand Oaks, LA: SAGE, 2013.

Malone, Karen, Marek Tesar, and Sonja Arndt. *Theorising Posthuman Childhood Studies*. Basingstoke: Springer Nature, 2020.

Mannaert, Wauter. *Chef Yasmina and the Potato Panic*. New York: First Second, 2021.

Mannaert, Wauter. *Yasmina und die Kartoffelkrise*. Berlin: Reprodukt, 2021.

Marcus, Leonard S. *Minders of Make-Believe: Idealists, Entrepreneurs, and the Shaping of American Children's Literature*. Boston: Houghton Mifflin Harcourt, 2008.

Mikota, Jana, and Claudia Pecher. "Klima-, Umwelt- und Naturschutz in der Aktuellen Kinder- und Jugendliteratur." *Kjl&m Krisenmodus Oder Lifestyle? Umwelt und Naturschutz in der Kinder- und Jugendliteratur*, 2020.

Milbradt, Björn. "Jugend, Politik und Engagement. Blinde Flecken und Herausforderungen am Beispiel Fridays for Future." *kjl&m Krisenmodus Oder Lifestyle? Umwelt und Naturschutz in der Kinder- und Jugendliteratur*, 2020.

Mizielinska, Alexsandra, and Daniel Mizielinski. *Was Nationalparks über die Natur verraten*. Frankfurt am Main: Moritz, 2020.

Neuber, Michael, Piotr Kocyba, and Beth Garrity Gardner. "Die Fridays for Future-Demonstrierenden im Europäischen Vergleich." In *Fridays for Future—Die Jugend gegen den Klimawandel: Konturen der weltweiten Protestbewegung*, edited by Sebastian Haunss and Moritz Sommer, 67093. Bielefeld: Transcript Verlag, 2020.

Nikolajeva, Maria. *Reading for Learning: Cognitive Approaches to Children's Literature*. Amsterdam: John Benjamins Publishing Company, 2014.

OECD. *PISA 2009 Ergebnisse: Was Schülerinnen und Schüler wissen und können: Schülerleistungen in Lesekompetenz, Mathematik und Naturwissenschaften*. Bielefeld: Bertelsmann Verlag, 2010.

Oomen-Welke, Ingelore, Heidi Rösch, and Bernt Ahrentholz. "Deutsch." In *Orientierungsrahmen für den Lernbereich Globale Entwicklung im Rahmen einer Bildung für Nachhaltige Entwicklung*, edited by Jörg-Robert Schreiber and Hannes Siege, 129–55. Bonn: Engagement Global, 2016. Accessed April 23, 2025. https://www.kmk.org/fileadmin/veroeffentlichungen_beschluesse/2015/2015_06_00-Orientierungsrahmen-Globale-Entwicklung.pdf

Oziewicz, Marek, and Lara Saguisag. "Introduction: Children's Literature and Climate Change." *The Lion and the Unicorn* 45, no. 2 (2021), v–xiv.

Oziewicz, Marek. "Introduction: The Choice We Have in the Stories We Tell . . ." In *Fantasy and Myth in the Anthropocene: Imagining Futures and Dreaming Hope in Literature and Media*, edited by Marek Oziewicz, Brian Attebery, and Tereza Dinová, 1–12. London: Bloomsbury, 2022.

Oziewicz, Marek. "Planetarianism Now: On Anticipatory Imagination, Young People's Literature, and Hope for the Planet." In *Pedagogy in the Anthropocene: Re-Wilding Education for a New Earth*, edited by Michael Paulsen, Jan Jagodzinski, and Shé M. Hawke, 241–56. London: Palgrave Macmillan, 2022.

Ramdarshan Bold, Melanie. *Inclusive Young Adult Fiction: Authors of Colour in the United Kingdom*. Basingstoke: Springer, 2019.

Reynolds, Kimberley. *Children's Literature: From the Fin de Siecle to the New Millennium*. Liverpool: University Press, 2012.

Rosenblatt, Louise M. *The Reader, the Text, the Poem: The Transactional Theory of the Literary Work*. Carbondale IL: Southern Illinois University Press, 1978.

Schulz, Farriba. *"Spieglein, Spieglein an der Wand . . ."—Kindheit in nominierten Bildebrüchern des Deutschen Jugendliteraturpreises von 1956 bis 2009*. Hamburg: Kovač, 2013.

Sommer, Moritz, Dieter Rucht, Sebastian Haunss, and Sabrina Zajak. 2019. "Fridays for Future. Profil, Entstehung und Perspektiven der Protestbewegung in Deutschland." Ipb Working Paper 2/2019, Instituts für Protest- und Bewegungsforschung, Berlin. Accessed April 23, 2025. https://www.otto-brenner-stiftung.de/fileadmin/user_data/stiftung/02_Wissenschaftsportal/03_Publikationen/2019_ipb_FridaysForFuture.pdf.

Wanning, Berbeli. "Literaturdidaktik und Kulturökologie." In *Grundthemen der Literaturwissenschaft: Literaturdidaktik*, edited by Christiane Lütge, 430–53. Berlin: De Gruyter, 2019.

Wieler, Petra. "Varianten des Literacy-Konzepts und ihre Bedeutung für die Deutschdidaktik." In *Deutschdidaktik und ihre Themen nach PISA*, edited by Ulf Abraham, Albert Bremerich-Vos, Volker Frederking, and Petra Wieler, 47–68. Freiburg im Breisgau: Fillibach, 2003.

Wieser, Dorothee. *Literaturunterricht aus Sicht der Lehrenden: Eine qualitative Interviewstudie*. Wiesbaden: VS Verlag für Sozialwissenschaften, 2008.

Chapter 11

CAN YOU HEAR MY VOICE?

Participatory Research as a Method for Reclaiming Children's Agency in the Archive

EMILY MURPHY

The archive is often described as a site of encounter, a place where fact and fiction collide to illuminate those from the present about the past (Burton 2005: 2). Whether or not it induces a "fever" in this search for clues about the voices captured within its stacks, the archive introduces questions about how to work with and narrate the stories it contains. This is especially true with children's archives, or the original materials created and produced by the young and deemed valuable enough to save in special collections.[1] These unique collections of archival material raise concerns about the potential for children's agency, or the ability of children to have control over the narratives of childhood that emerge from the archival record when working with historical materials: What methodologies can we use to ethically engage with archival records created by young people? How, in effect, do we listen to children's voices from the past? To answer these questions, it is necessary to turn to the children's archive itself. Here, I draw on two archival records, both by individuals who were forced to flee from their home countries but where both time and perspective play an important role in the interpretation of these voices and the stories that they tell.

The first record is a letter by author and illustrator Esphyr Slobodkina, who is most famous for her picture book *Caps for Sale* (1940). In a letter to her editor, Slobodkina writes about fleeing Russia with her family to Northern China before eventually immigrating to the United States in her early twenties. She begins: "When we left Russia, we landed in the Far-Eastern Russian part of Vladivostok. At that time the Russian ruble was still worth quite a bit, so we came there well-dressed, well-heeled, and well-connected. However, the city was terribly overcrowded with similarly well-off refugees, and so we soon landed in a suburban villa [in Manchuria]" (Letter to Lillian, December 10, 1967).

She explains in this same letter how her forced migration shaped her girlhood and her notion of citizenship and belonging. Describing herself as a lovestruck girl hanging on the heels of a young Chinese man who worked in their kitchen, Slobodkina adds, "Seeing our determination to hang around his kitchen, he threw us occasionally a bit of information, a snatch of a song, a part of a story, or corrected our pronunciation of a Chinese word." Slobodkina uses these childhood memories to defend the authenticity of the folktales she retells in *The Flame, the Breeze, and the Shadow* (1969), yet her story of migration, compelled by the rise of the Russian Civil War in 1917, meant that this experience left a deep impact on her, evidenced by her return to this same part of her life story in multiple letters in her archive.

In contrast to Slobodkina's exchange with her editor, a letter written by a group of children from a school in Indiana provides details about their Vietnamese classmate—a child named Puch who formed part of the first major wave of Vietnamese refugees following the fall of Saigon in 1975. The children urge author Ezra Jack Keats (best known for *The Snowy Day*) to write a book featuring this boy. Puch, they write, "comes from Vietnam and could not speak English at first either [like Juanito in *My Dog Is Lost*]" (Thompkins Elementary School, n.d.).[2] Suggesting ways for Keats to tell Phuc's story, they add, "Maybe you could call it *Happy Phuc*. You could tell about the first snow that Phuc saw." As the children relate Phuc's first encounter with snow, a story that takes a mere four sentences to finish, they describe Phuc's joy at seeing snow, his delight in tasting it and in sharing it with his classmates. Stripped of Phuc's voice, however, it becomes difficult to discern if these details are more reflective of the joy of Phuc's peers.

Unlike Slobodkina, we know little about Puch and what his experience of immigration was like, much less how much he felt he fit in with his predominately white classmates. Yet what the comparison of these traces of childhood indicates is the value of developing interdisciplinary methods for reading and recovering the archived voices of children as a way of mapping transnational experiences of childhood. Framing these experiences within the context of war and the forced migration that often results from it, I will discuss how to make a case for a participatory research approach to the children's archive, one that combines the stories contained within it with the stories that continue to exist in the communities with a stake in these materials, providing a new way to interpret the traces of childhood that exist in archives. Because these traces often emerge as scraps or fragmentary pieces of a child's life story, it is imperative to take this community-led or collective approach in narrating these materials. In this respect, my argument aligns with that of Nina Christensen, who, in part I of this volume, discusses how "relational agency" is central to the way children communicate their experiences to others, including in their interactions with adults. Similar to the other authors in this section who offer a methodological lens for considering children's agency, I am interested in the archive as a collaborative space where children are authorities on their lived experience (see Ford Smith 2017; Hamer and Murnaghan and Kulkarni and Owens in part IV of this volume). I share with them an understanding of "agency" as children's ability to assert control over the structures and institutions that frame their voices, particularly in relation to their knowledge and understanding of their lives and the world they inhabit. In considering the ways in which children's voices emerge through the archived materials left behind by them—letters, exercise books, artwork, and other scraps of memorabilia—I argue for the importance of bridging archival theory in the humanities with participatory research in the social sciences as a way of ethically engaging with these voices and, in doing so, relinquishing some of the curatorial power typically bestowed on adults when it comes to managing the narratives of childhood that emerge from the historical records found in the archive.

The notion that the archive has the potential to disrupt, or unsettle, adult conceptions of childhood is certainly not new, nor is the fact that the very voices most impacted by these narratives are the ones most difficult to find. As Karen Sánchez-Eppler relates in her influential essay, "In the Archives of Childhood," the researcher's desire to trace and pin down documents that evidence the lived experience of historical children is often one that goes unfulfilled (2013: 219). She gives the example of Carolyn Steedman, most well known for her study of the child acrobat Mignon in *Strange Dislocations* (1995). In a separate essay, Steedman details her long search to discover a document, even a scrap, that might prove the existence of Henry Mayhew's Little Watercress Girl: "My own romance is that I may find this child, that there is enough evidence in her narrative, that there is enough detail of her life and the life of her household, to trace her" (qtd. in Sánchez-Eppler 2013: 219). Steedman's search for the Little Watercress Girl is thwarted by a lack of sufficient evidence, but this does not stop her from attempting to create a narrative that imagines what her life may have been like. In one of her earlier accounts of this young girl's encounter with Mayhew, Steedman relates how "it was here and during this month that we may assume he met the Little Watercress Girl (though it is possible that the interview took place a month or so later, in January 1851)" (1995: 117). Drawing on newspaper articles and other materials left behind by Mayhew, Steedman begins to weave an intricate narrative of missed encounters with the Little Watercress Girl, moments where she knows she likely appeared but where she is never speaking.

As Steedman's account indicates, the archive does not always offer up the material that researchers are most desperate to find, failing to provide empirical evidence that tracks and traces the lives of children. Even when these materials are available, there remain questions about how to read or interpret the childhood experience documented in them and to what extent we might trust the voices of the children who authored them. Key scholars in childhood studies, including Sánchez-Eppler, have sought to attend to this concern, drawing on decades of debate within the field about adult and child power relations, beginning with that most famous of lines by Jacqueline Rose that "children's fiction is impossible" (1984: 1). Yet what I have found fascinating in my own foray into interdisciplinary work is the fact that these very same conversations appear again and again among researchers within the social sciences as they try to document and chart childhood experience in a different manner that attempts to both quantify and qualify what it means to be a child and how children are awarded agency in society, if at all.

In an article by children's geographer Matej Blazek, he describes the challenges of completing a participatory research project in a small, deprived neighborhood in Slovakia, where he met two boys, Martin, age nine, and Peter, age eleven, while acting as a youth worker on the streets. In reflecting on his interactions with the younger of the two boys, Blazek writes, "I found it difficult to integrate this story [about Martin's brother Peter] into my overall interpretive framework. Most troubling to the analysis was that I had no direct evidence from Martin—he never explicitly expressed to me his feelings over Peter or his new friends" (2013: 25). Blazek, who is describing his conversations with Martin following Peter's removal to a juvenile detention center, notes how Martin frequently provides vivid details about his brother that he could not possibly know due to the lack of contact with Peter as confirmed by family members and other adults within the community. In his consideration of these narrative accounts, Blazek argues for a broader definition of children's "voices," which involves an interpretive framework that considers a child's actions and other forms of embodied experience alongside their words (30).

What Blazek's account reveals is that working with children, in an effort to discover their voice, is always a process of negotiation. This becomes particularly imperative when considering transnational experiences of childhood, especially in the case of those impacted by war and forced to flee their homes, as both Slobodkina and Phuc were. While much of my work has focused on children as global citizens, I choose in this essay to adopt the term "transnational child" precisely because these were children who were shaped by movement beyond the nation, not as part of an educational initiative or national effort to foster global community (and the world peace that was supposed to come along with it) but rather as means for survival to escape persecution or the violence of war. If the global child secures a utopian vision of world peace, the transnational child puts this vision at risk, threatening to undo the borders and boundaries that are essential for propping up this vision.

If we return to the archive, turning to a different letter by Slobodkina that is dated much earlier than her exchange with her editor, we can see some of these ideas at work. Slobodkina, who had very strong opinions about what children were capable of when it comes to reading, relates what she calls "the story of my life" at the request of one of her young fans, a girl named Mary. Slobodkina confesses to Mary, "It would take much too long a time to tell you all about what happened to my Family in those years. I'll only tell you that things did not go so well for us many a time and that was the time when we were neither well clad nor well fed, or well housed" (Letter to Mary, April 19, 1954). While Slobodkina begins her letter to Mary by relating her family's comfortable exit from Russia, enabled by their wealth at the time, she also cites how this comfort led both children and adults to ignore the dangers involved in fleeing the war, adding that they "had a wonderful time of it" and that "we were never what is called 'refugees.'" This letter is curious for a few reasons. First, Mary, as the initiator of this exchange, is very nearly erased. Slobodkina opens the letter by saying, "I hope this letter reaches the right girl because I could not read your last name too well. You know, it got rubbed off a little by the time it got into my hands." Second, it is one that reveals more about Slobodkina's own childhood experience than the more formal exchange with her editor, Lillian. In that same letter, Slobodkina did not mention any challenges or difficulties associated with her migration to China, instead presenting an idealized childhood of mischief, fun, and play.

While the voice that changes register here is, in fact, that of the adult author, Mary finds her way into the archive again in response to a request (this time by *Young Wings* magazine editor Ruth Hoyer) for a biographical sketch. Dated January 24, 1955, not even a year after her response to Mary, Slobodkina rejects the offer to retell the story of her life, the same one she had told so easily to her young fan. She adds, "I hope you will forgive me for sending you instead this copy of a letter I once have written for a real little girl who wrote me a very nice 'fan' letter. I hope it sounds more natural than if I tried to do an article for some 'abstract' children. Of course, if it is too long or does not suit the purpose, you may change it in any way you like."

The letter, which was published in the June 1955 issue of *Young Wings* in revised form with Slobodkina listed as the author, is where Mary disappears yet again. Details about Slobodkina's arrival to China following the crash of the Russian ruble are rearranged to provide a simple account of her daily life, such as where she attended school or private art classes. The stark difference between these two versions, the public one for the "abstract child" and the private one for the "real child," draws attention to the dangers of trusting even the "adult" voice. Just as in the case study with Martin, the young boy who created imagined narratives about his older brother Peter, we cannot read a single account of Slobodkina's experience of migration as a child, for even a cursory look at the letters and published materials that relate this period of her life underscores that the details were constantly changing, even if the main events remained the same; indeed, it is ironically the child, a fan who she hardly knew beyond the single letter they exchanged, who draws out the personal detail of hardships that she frequently withheld from adults in her professional relationships.

So far, I have undertaken a fairly straightforward textual analysis of these materials, informed as they are by childhood studies scholarship. But what happens when the methodologies found in the social sciences, and especially those associated with participatory research with children, reorient our position in relation to these texts? For this example, we need to leave Mary behind and return to Phuc, the little Vietnamese boy who is the subject of a letter to Keats. In the few archival items relating to Phuc, we only know that his classmates perceived him as happy. Indeed, their suggested story title, "Happy Phuc," is a reflection of their views. Upon examination of the class photo that accompanies this oversized letter, Phuc's image seems to secure this version of the story. At the center of the class photo, Phuc does indeed seem happy, a huge smile on his face (*Thompkins Elementary Yearbook* photograph, 1975–76). Yet if we pick up on the few details we are given, such as the fact that upon his arrival Phuc knew little English, a different story begins to emerge.

In a 1976 newspaper article from the *Evansville Courier*, Phuc appears again. "Phuc Phom, a first grader, is 'reading up a storm' just through working in reading groups in his own class and having daily lessons with the remedial reading teacher" (Brown 1976: 9). The article adds other important details, such as the fact that there are a total of "43 Vietnamese students in Evansville, but more children are expected" and that these students are dispersed in the school system, with eighteen being the largest group of children at any one school (9). Moreover, the attitudes of the teachers vary quite widely, with one commenting that they are glad the bilingual tutors previously employed are gone because "their presence causes the children to rely too much on Vietnamese." This report, coupled with other accounts of refugee children in similar situations, suggests that while Phuc may have been a diligent reader, he may not have necessarily been happy.

Now, some of you may be thinking, "But these aren't *children's* voices!" And you're right. They are not, by strict definition, all documents featuring children's voices if by "voice" we mean a text produced and authored by a child. Yet the children's archive always raises suspicion about who is speaking, and just as in participatory research in the social sciences, I'm not convinced that is reason enough to stop listening. Those in children's literature will be familiar with the turn back to the child, initiated in large part by a wave of scholarship known either as "childhood" or "children's" studies and recognized by such influential essays as Marah Gubar's "Risky Business: Talking About Children in Children's Literature Criticism" (2013). Bearing these arguments in mind, when I look at materials like that of Mary or Phuc, I am also thinking about how biases about what counts as an authentic voice can actually lead to the silencing of others (see Spyrou 2011).

Because I have the advantage of a rather broad range of children's materials collected over time through visits to special collections across the United States,[3] I was able to begin to see the patterns that emerged in how these children spoke or used their voices: many of them, for instance, would ask an author for their photograph (see "Selected Fan Letters, Lois Lenski" 1964). There were also materials that seemed to put the child's voice at risk due to adult interference, such as one where a caregiver writes a letter on behalf of a young boy (Kissel, June 26, 1956). Similarly, a set of letters from schoolchildren demonstrate the extent to which copying was involved in the production of the child's voice, though, as in this particular case, the teacher flags the "original" content to distinguish it from this copied material (Robinson, January 29, 1981). There are also other items, drawings or paintings (see Individual Correspondence n.d.), which do not have any words to interpret but still constitute a reflection of that child and their experience: Do these materials count as part of the voice we should be listening to as scholars?

I would argue that they do. If we return to Phuc once again, we can see why interpreting the mediated voices of children is imperative. Like Mary, Phuc nearly disappears from the archival record, in part because the name of the school, Thompkins Elementary, is recorded (including in the printed class photograph) as Tompkins without an "h." In addition, Phuc's surname, recorded in the article I began with as Phom, was, in fact, the common Vietnamese surname Pham. When making this correction, two additional results from 1975 to 1976 turn up in the local paper for Evansville. In one,

Phuc is described as "looking forward to his first Thanksgiving" (November 26, 1975: 1). Listening to the stories of the "hardships" of the pilgrims, Phuc is described as being thankful for the opportunities he has in the United States, along with his parents who immigrated with him and the "thousands of Vietnamese refugees who are spending their first year in a new land."

While the author of this small report dwells on how Americans should be thankful for their freedom, reinforcing national values, what makes this brief report so valuable is one line that tells Phuc's story. As the author relates, Phuc, moved by the story of the Pilgrims, raises his hand and says, "Me a Pilgrim. Me come here for freedom, too." The line, edited slightly for the title, clearly serves to uphold national values that reflect back an image of an "exceptional nation" that are central to narratives of US empire (see Kaplan 2002 and Pease 2009). Yet it still gives us a small window into Phuc's life through *his* words, finally allowing him to speak instead of being spoken about by others. While in his speaking there are power relations that frame and limit our ability to interpret these words, they begin to unsettle the adult assumptions about "foreign" refugee children flooding into small American towns like Evansville.

Phuc, in his refusal to see himself as different from the Pilgrims, and by relation, other Americans, suggests that he, too, belongs, and not just because he is a voracious reader or is beginning to grasp the English language. As he challenges the binary of domestic and foreign that the local newspaper presents, Phuc seems to be urgently and insistently asking, "Can you hear my voice?" If we draw on some of the historical methods Steedman employs to trace the life of the Little Watercress Girl, we can begin to get a fuller answer; yet, as I will soon reveal, to trace Phuc and other voices like his requires a careful and slow development of the relationships required in participatory research practices.

For this particular case, I merge traditional participatory approaches, such as the model put forward by Justyna Deszcz-Tryhubczak in her study of children's rights (2016), with similar practices within the archive. Participatory approaches employed by social scientists focus on engaging and working with children or other members of a community on a shared project, a goal shared by those involved in managing archives. A participatory archival practice prioritizes the voices of those with a right to the record, collaborating with the owners of these records, and sharing curatorial control in a process that involves organizing, framing, and narrating the original materials that make their way into the archive (Gilliland and McKemmish 2014: 1). Rooted in social justice movements, those who uphold a participatory archival practice acknowledge the rights of multiple parties to the record, including decisions about what *not* to include in the archive. In the case of the Keats item, this involves a complex network of individuals, from the teacher who is writing the letter to the children who are drafting it orally to Phuc himself, whose life is the subject matter of the letter. While I have not been able to track down all these individuals, I want to model what such an approach might entail and how it begins to shift the conclusions we might draw about material in the children's archive.

To do so, then, we must begin with Evansville, as the site where the letter is drafted and created, going back to the mid-1970s when Phuc and children like him were just beginning to settle in the area after fleeing Vietnam. In newspaper reports from the *Evansville Courier*, a similar narrative of the model minority is created, focusing on the speed at which young Vietnamese refugees manage to adapt and integrate into the school system and local community. In one report about siblings Anh and Binh Tran, for instance, the children are described as quiet and mild-mannered, with the teacher claiming that her class of first graders has had this good behavior rub off on them. The report describes how the Tran siblings, who were thirteen and fourteen at the time, swiftly and repeatedly fold origami and induct the younger schoolchildren into the intricacies of this Japanese art. "Binh and Anh," the reporter underscores, "speak little English, and as they teach, they speak practically not at all" (Folz 1976: 19). The reporter contrasts this silence with that of the younger children, who quietly watch in amazement as the little origami figures come to life, and in doing so, begins to transform the reason for Binh and Anh's silence as well. Not necessarily failing to speak due to lack of knowledge of the English language, they are instead presented as experts quietly concentrating on their work. The little paper figures are described as "intricate art" that is made with "a few expert folds and tears." In closing, though, the reporter makes a familiar turn to reframe the children as well-integrated Americans, noting how they have "Americanized" their names and adopted the Western practice of putting their surname last.

The report on the Trans reveals that Phuc's own story of immigration is not unique; indeed, many like it could be found in newspapers across the United States at the time, focusing specifically on Vietnamese refugees as the model minority. Yet what I find interesting about the reports specific to Evansville is how the variation in that experience is depicted. Unlike the Trans, who are cast as quiet adopters of American culture, Phuc loudly and insistently demands his place within the nation. While those in Evansville were curious about the stories behind these children, this curiosity was typically framed as a defense of American culture. In one opinion column, for example, Rev. Joseph Ziliak, a pastor in the neighboring town of Newburgh, ruminates on the loss and growth of young people's lives following a tragic highway accident resulting in the deaths of twenty-seven young people. Contrasting this catastrophic loss with the success of a young Vietnamese woman, Anh Tran, who published one of the first studies on how long men and women spend in bathrooms as a way of informing architectural design, Ziliak begins to turn to questions about Tran's origins: "What I do not know about the report," he begins, "is the personal history of this young woman Anh Tran. It would seem she is a Vietnamese by cultural background. Did she come here after harrowing difficulties in escaping from her homeland? Is she alone or did her family also make it here? Someday I may find out" (1988: 7). As with the previous reports, Ziliak finishes by questioning how Tran's life might have differed had she failed to learn English and integrate into American culture, using this as a benchmark of success and solidifying the fact that Tran represents the "good immigrant."

Ziliak's opinion piece appeared in 1988, over a decade after the report about the Tran siblings who, at the time, were in their teens. Anh, who bears the same name as the woman in Ziliak's op-ed piece, was thirteen, and it's reasonable to assume that she could be the same Tran, although given the commonness of both her given name and surname, without further evidence, this cannot be guaranteed. Indeed, no mention of the young woman's hometown is included, with the focus instead on her university affiliation. Ziliak's attempt to reach back into the past and construct a narrative about Anh raises questions about how to track down and trace the "personal history," as he calls it, of those whose lives are presented only in scraps or fragments—a question that is central to any venture into the children's archive. In attempting to pursue more lines of connection to Phuc, for example, it became necessary to turn away from historical records to community knowledge in the town of Evansville. This approach, which involves a slow process of carefully developing connections within the community that can help illuminate the historical records linked to the children's archive, provides oral and written accounts that complement the fragmented narratives of the young lives within the archive. In relation to shifting the agentic power back over to Phuc, it demonstrates how dependent the interpretation of these records is on the communities from which they emerged and the extent to which it remains imperative to be attentive to the colliding voices that emerge from these records, including the power dynamics between children and adult gatekeepers and the context surrounding moments where the child's agentic power is revealed. In the case of Phuc, it provides a beginning point to see where he and his family ended up and the extent to which their lives became embedded in the Evansville community, with the ideal end result being to connect with Phuc himself to allow him to provide his own interpretation of the records relating to the letter from his former elementary school, the one that ended up in the archives of Keats.

To follow up on these archival traces, I began making community links in Evansville, beginning with the Vanderburgh County Historical Society. My inquiry was met with a swift reply from Terry Hughes, the president of the Society and a former educator in the Evansville school district. The answer was short and professional, promising to pass on my inquiry to the board of directors at the VCHS, but a second, much more personal reply quickly followed. With Hughes's permission, I share an excerpt from this email:

> I had two of the students in a different school across town from Thompkins, Ahn and Bing Tran [sic]. Neither spoke English when they came, but both had an incredible work ethic. Bing [sic], especially, was able to transfer his knowledge of the universal language of mathematics into great success. After they left Howard Roosa elementary school, I lost track of them, but no doubt they continued on their trajectory of success. (email to author)

While Hughes was not familiar with Phuc, his knowledge about the Trans, who also became examples of "success stories" in Evansville, provided guidance for tracing the lives of recently immigrated children to Evansville. The Trans, much the same as Phuc, have inconsistencies in their reported stories that could make it difficult to verify that each new document was indeed about the same child. In the case of the Trans, an incorrectly mentioned school name made it at first appear as if there were another set of Tran siblings. Yet in working with Hughes, I was able to confirm the relationship between the sparse documents I had so far, reaffirming the value of being able to draw on community knowledge to piece together such narratives. This shows that when taking a participatory approach to the archive, particularly in the case of refugee children, it can sometimes be necessary to work with those with relationships to the owners or subjects of these records—not privileging these narratives over that of the child, but rather using them to continue to piece together evidence to provide a fuller narrative of their life story.

That said, this was only the beginning of the network of relationships needed in a participatory approach to the archive. While helpful in providing the contextual information I was seeking about the experience of Vietnamese immigrants in Evansville, providing a glimpse, at least, into how white residents of the town perceived them in an educational setting, I had yet to turn up any new information about Phuc. His voice remained hidden for the time being. Aware that the Evansville Library collected local memorabilia, including yearbooks from all the major high schools, I contacted the reference librarian asking if any of these records might contain further proof of Phuc's life in Evansville. Through this search, I learned about the high school Phuc would have likely attended based on where he went to elementary school, but despite searching the stacks, the librarian helping me could find no record of Phuc in the yearbooks dating back to the time when he would have been in high school. Unlike the Tran siblings, who can be found in these yearbooks, Phuc and his family did not seem to settle in Evansville (see Tran 1981). Indeed, a further record documenting residential addresses shows that the Phams only resided in their home at 905 Stonebridge Road for a brief period (Evansville Residential Directory, 1977).

Unable to trace and contact Phuc, as I had hoped to do when I first set out on my research journey—though lessons from other similar efforts have taught me that this can be a long process that still has the potential to yield results—I was left with a closed story similar to Slobodkina's public narrative of her escape from Russia. With only the most rudimentary details, I could only say that Phuc and his family fled Vietnam in the first wave of refugees following the fall of Saigon in 1975, that they had likely transited through one of the major refugee camps in the United States before receiving sponsorship by a member of the Evansville community, and that, following their arrival, their son, Phuc, became one of the many examples of the town flourishing, in part due to its successful integration of these newly immigrated refugees.

As disappointing as such an ending might be, it is useful to examine how, once Phuc's narrative is disentangled from the literary archive, his story shifts and takes on new meaning. As part of the Ezra Jack Keats collection, housed at the de Grummond Children's Literature Collection at the University of Southern Mississippi—the record mentioning Phuc is a small file that appears alongside a set of school correspondence to Keats. Some of these archival materials, like the letter featuring Phuc, are written from a group perspective, while others are individually drafted, though still written in a classroom setting. Typical of fan mail, these letters are filled with admiration for Keats and his books, including the craft that went into making his distinctive illustrations. Children cite favorite books and gush over the collage technique employed by Keats, even re-creating this same technique in their own artwork before sending it to the author/illustrator. Framed alongside these letters, the traces of Phuc's life become overshadowed by the educational responses to Keats's work, directing, as one might imagine they would, attention back to the author and his life's work.

The arrangement and framing of children's material is particularly imperative, for it raises questions about what a children's archive is and how we might approach it as researchers in the field of children's literature. Collections like the de Grummond emerged in the mid-twentieth century, largely in response to a desire to preserve and save the original materials of children's authors and illustrators for educational purposes (see Murphy 2014). Lena de Grummond, the founder of this collection, used these materials to instruct her library science students. But today, with the expansion of the field and theoretical and methodological shifts, one of the most important being the turn to the interdisciplinary field of childhood studies, the materials gathered up about children's lives, often in the form of fan mail and letters, become just as valuable as the dummies, sketches, and editorial correspondence found in the stacks of the archive. Indeed, there are new collections emerging, such as the Italian collection Exercise Book Archive, which are dedicated to exclusively collecting this material as a way of informing conversations about the lived experiences of children from the past. As these new collections emerge and put forth collecting missions that diverge from earlier intentions to showcase the creative process of children's authors and illustrators, a creative and flexible methodology for collecting, displaying, and working with these materials must emerge in turn.

So what, to return to my opening statements, might a participatory approach offer in these instances? Participatory research in practice seeks to work with living communities, giving, in the case of children, an increased amount of agency over how their voices are represented and interpreted by adults. Although this approach is not possible to apply exactly as intended in the case of historical research, particularly depending on the time period in which one is working, the focus on relationship-building with those with a stake in the record gives life back to these materials. This can be a frustratingly slow process—but, in all fairness, so is participatory research. Often done over long and intense periods of time with a small group or specific local community, participatory research reaches its limit when it comes to trying to track down large amounts of data. It is best suited, in these cases, to develop what historians call "microhistories," or richly detailed histories about the creators of historical records that are instructive for key questions in the field (Magnússon and Szijártó 2013: 4–5). A microhistory such as Phuc's story, if followed to the end, has the potential to reveal more about the experience of Vietnamese immigrants during the tumultuous first wave of refugees following the fall of Saigon in 1975. It provides real-life accounts that supplement fictional narratives by writers such as Thanhha Lai, who has written about her own childhood memories of this challenging period

of transition through her award-winning children's book *Inside Out &*
Back Again (2011).

In the case of Slobodkina's memories, her accounts of transnational flight
as a child provide a very different lesson. Because the literary archive is built
to reveal more about the author—and in this case, Slobodkina is quite the
character, who was intensely devoted to retelling her life history as a way
of preserving her memory—there is more available than the little scraps
provided about Phuc's life. Yet despite the voluminous amount of archival
material in her collection, Slobodkina's voice becomes entangled with the
voices of young readers of her work, often in uniquely interesting ways, as in
the case with Mary. Though writing as an adult, her reflections on her childhood and the way that these reflections emerge through these engagements
with the "real child" (the children who sent her fan mail) return to questions
about voice in historical research raised by scholars such as Nell Musgrove,
Carla Pascoe Leahy, and Kristine Moruzi. As Musgrove et al. remark in their
essay on conceptual and methodological challenges to recovering historical
children's voices, "a major challenge for historians seeking children's voices
is to avoid categorical confusion and unproblematic binaries" (2019: 11).
The example provided by the authors is the difference between "voice" and
"agency" (12), where "voice" equates to the "opinions, emotions and behaviours of young people" and "agency" involves the child actively making their
own decisions in the face of societal influences that seek to shape their lives
(12). In making this key distinction between these two terms, Musgrove et al.
draw attention to the interventions of other key scholars in the field, such as
anthropologist Spyros Spyrou, who has already spoken extensively about the
dangers of recovering children's voices without a thorough consideration of
the frameworks in which these voices appear (see Spyrou 2011).

CONCLUSION

Archival research is always a risky business, particularly in instances where
the child's voice becomes so entangled with that of the adult that it is difficult
to discern who is speaking. In cases where correspondence continues over
a period of time, there are also instances where the child no longer recognizes themselves in their previous writings or artistic work.[4] In seeking to
navigate the risks associated with recovering historical children's voices, it is
imperative to consider how interdisciplinary practices, such as the participatory archival research approach I have modeled, can both reframe children's
original materials and provide an avenue for more ethical engagements with

these voices. This approach, when coupled with interpretative strategies found in history and literature, enables researchers to reposition the child's voice within the community where it originated, asking, as microhistorians do, larger questions that emerge from the network of relationships connected to these young lives. While I don't believe that a participatory approach is the only means of completing this type of archival research, I certainly think it is one method worth adding to our repertoire for reconstructing the lives of children from the past.

NOTES

1. See Murphy 2023 for more on the "children's archive," a term I have coined both as a means to describe the unique archival materials produced by children and a signpost of different methodological approaches necessary for interpreting these materials.

2. While there is no date on the letter, a school photograph that was taped on the original is dated 1975 to 1976, and with the references to snow, it was likely between December 1975 and February 1976, based on snowfall patterns in Indiana.

3. I refer here to the Kerlan Collection of Children's Literature and the de Grummond Children's Literature Collection, though I have since conducted further research at smaller regional collections in the US and the UK that confirm my assertions here. A special thanks goes to the de Grummond Collection for funding the research that appears in this essay.

4. In correspondence with British author Beverley Naidoo, a teenage girl remarks that "it was hard for me to believe it was me that wrote the letter" in a fan letter written to the author a mere three years earlier. See Rahman, June 25, 1990.

REFERENCES

Blazek, Matej. "Emotions as Practice: Anna Freud's Child Psychoanalysis and Thinking—Doing Children's Emotional Geographies." *Emotion, Space and Society* 9 (2013), 24–32.

Brown, Janice. "Viet Students: Math Great, English Improves." *Evansville Courier and Press.* (Evansville, IN), January 24, 1976, 9.

Burton, Antoinette. "Introduction: Archive Fever, Archive Stories." In *Archive Stories: Facts, Fictions, and the Writing of History*, edited by Antoinette Burton, 1–24. Durham NC: Duke University Press, 2006.

Deszcz-Tryhubczak, Justyna. "Using Literary Criticism for Children's Rights: Toward a Participatory Research Model of Children's Literature Studies." *The Lion and the Unicorn* 40, no. 2 (2016), 215–31.

Evansville Residential Directory. Evansville, IN: Vanderburgh County Public Library, 1977.

Folz, Edna. "Refugees Teach Dexter Students Old Japanese Art." *Evansville Courier and Press* (Evansville, IN), February 25, 1976, 19.

Ford Smith, Victoria. *Between Generations: Collaborative Authorship in the Golden Age of Children's Literature.* Jackson, MS: University Press of Mississippi, 2017.

Gilliland, Anne, and Sue McKemmish. "The Role of Participatory Archives in Furthering Human Rights, Reconciliation and Recovery." *Atlanti: Review for Modern Archival Theory and Practice* 24 (May 2014), 78–88.

Harrison High School. *Harrison High School Yearbook: Legend 1981.* Evansville, ID: 1981. Evansville Digital Yearbooks Collection. Vanderburgh County Public Library. Accessed March 12, 2023. https://digital.evpl.org/digital/collection/evayearbook/id/14877/rec/22.

Hughes, Terry. "Evansville History—Vietnamese Refugees." Email to author. November 14, 2022.

Individual Correspondence, n.d. Ezra Jack Keats Collection, box 102, folder 6. The de Grummond Children's Literature Collection, University of Southern Mississippi, Hattiesburg, Mississippi.

Kaplan, Amy. *The Anarchy of Empire in the Making of U.S. Culture.* Cambridge, MA: Harvard University Press, 2002.

Keats, Ezra Jack. Collection. The de Grummond Children's Literature Collection, University of Southern Mississippi, Hattiesburg.

Kissel, Jon. Letter to Esphyr Slobodkina, June 26, 1956. Esphyr Slobodkina Collection, box 4, folder 4. The de Grummond Children's Literature Collection, University of Southern Mississippi, Hattiesburg.

Lenski, Lois. Collection. The de Grummond Children's Literature Collection, University of Southern Mississippi, Hattiesburg.

Letter from Thompkins Elementary School, circa December 1975 to February 1976. Ezra Jack Keats Collection, box 104, folder 3. The de Grummond Children's Literature Collection, University of Southern Mississippi, Hattiesburg, Mississippi.

Magnússon, Sigurður G., and István M. Szijártó. *What is Microhistory? Theory and Practice.* London: Routledge, 2013.

"Me Pilgrim, Me Here for Freedom." *Evansville Courier and Press* (Evansville, IN) November 6, 1975, 1.

Murphy, Emily. "The Anarchy of Children's Archives: Citizenship and Empire in the Global 1930s." *Journal of American Studies* 57, no. 5 (2023), 677–99.

Murphy, Emily. "Unpacking the Archive: Value, Pricing, and the Letter-Writing Campaign of Dr. Lena Y. de Grummond." *Children's Literature Association Quarterly* 39, no. 4 (2014), 551–68.

Musgrove, Nell, Carla Pascoe Leahy, and Kristine Moruzi, editors. *Children's Voices from the Past: New Historical and Interdisciplinary Perspectives.* Cham, Switzerland: Palgrave Macmillan, 2019.

Naidoo, Beverley. Collection. Stories: The National Centre for Children's Books, Newcastle upon Tyne.

Pease, Donald E. *The New American Exceptionalism.* Minneapolis: University of Minnesota Press, 2009.

Rahman, Asma. Letter to Beverley Naidoo, June 25, 1990. Beverley Naidoo Collection, BN/12/02/01/02. Seven Stories: The National Centre for Children's Books, Newcastle Upon Tyne, UK.

Robinson, Antoine. Letter to Ezra Jack Keats, January 29, 1981. Ezra Jack Keats Collection, Box 104, Folder 14. The de Grummond Children's Literature Collection, University of Southern Mississippi, Hattiesburg, Mississippi.

Rose, Jacqueline. *The Case of Peter Pan, Or the Impossibility of Children's Fiction*. Philadelphia: University of Pennsylvania Press, 1984.

Sánchez-Eppler, Karen. "In the Archives of Childhood." In *The Children's Table, Childhood Studies and the Humanities*, edited by Anna Mae Duane, 213–37. Atlanta: University of Georgia Press, 2013.

Selected Fan Letters, Lois Lenski, 1962. Lois Lenski Collection, box 1. The de Grummond Children's Literature Collection, University of Southern Mississippi, Hattiesburg, Mississippi.

Slobodkina, Esphyr. Collection. The de Grummond Children's Literature Collection, University of Southern Mississippi, Hattiesburg, Mississippi.

Slobodkina, Esphyr. Letter to Lillian, December 10, 1967. Esphyr Slobodkina Collection, box 2, folder 2. The de Grummond Children's Literature Collection, University of Southern Mississippi, Hattiesburg, Mississippi.

Slobodkina, Esphyr. Letter to Mary, April 19, 1954. Esphyr Slobodkina Collection, box 1, folder 1. The de Grummond Children's Literature Collection, University of Southern Mississippi, Hattiesburg, Mississippi.

Slobodkina, Esphyr. Letter to Ruth C. Hoyer, January 24, 1955. Esphyr Slobodkina Collection, box 4, folder 4. The de Grummond Children's Literature Collection, University of Southern Mississippi, Hattiesburg, Mississippi.

Slobodkina, Esphyr. "Using Scissors to Make Pictures." *Young Wings: The Junior Literary Guild*, June 1955.

Spyrou, Spyros. "The Limits of Children's Voices: From Authenticity to Critical, Reflexive Representation." *Childhood* 18, no. 2 (2011), 151–65.

Steedman, Carolyn. *Strange Dislocations: Childhood and the Idea of Human Interiority, 1780–1930*. Cambridge: Harvard University Press, 1995.

Thompkins Elementary Yearbook photograph, 1975–76. Ezra Jack Keats Collection, box 104, folder 3. The de Grummond Children's Literature Collection, University of Southern Mississippi, Hattiesburg, Mississippi.

Tran, Anh. *Harrison High School Yearbook: Legend 1981*. Evansville Digital Yearbooks Collection. Vanderburgh County Public Library. Evansville, Indiana. https://digital .evpl.org/digital/collection/evayearbook/id/14877/rec/22.

Ziliak, Joseph. "As May Ends, Thoughts Turn to Youth." *Evansville Courier and Press* (Evansville, IN), May 21, 1988, 7.

Chapter 12

EXPLORING THE MUSEUM AT NIGHT

Young People's Agency and Citizenship in Museum-Related Children's Literature and Programming

NAOMI HAMER AND ANN MARIE MURNAGHAN

In children's literature and media, museums act as significant sites for stories of children's agency, adventure, and independence. The popularity of these fictional narratives reveals how adult authors and child readers fantasize about children's agency as active citizens in social and cultural life through museum spaces. Museums act as an apt stage for this fantasy, becoming a refuge for both adults and children alike in children's texts, as places of mystery and delight. Thus, museums act as stand-ins for all human knowledge, from the prehistoric dinosaurs to the art of great global masters to the diverse customs and costumes of a range of places historically and geographically. The representations of museums we see in some fictional texts stand in stark contrast to children's lived experiences in contemporary museums, where their presence is monitored, their actions curtailed, and their participation limited by rigid pedagogic agendas geared toward young visitors. Activist movements of decolonizing and queering the museum (Coombes and Phillips 2020; Sullivan and Middleton 2019) highlight the challenges that people of color and 2SLGBTQIA+ communities have brought to existing museum narratives but often omit or downplay the potential role of young people as curators and active citizens in these spaces. Critical children's museology (Patterson 2021) has emerged to address some of these gaps in integrating children's perspectives into critical museum research, and we situate our work within this framework and broader ones seeking participatory approaches to children's engagement in public life (see Parker, Murphy, and Kulkarni and Owens in this volume).

This chapter will explore the spaces between the fantastical representations of museums in children's literature and museum programming inspired by these literary representations and how these spaces hold the potential for critical interventions. We particularly draw attention to the fantasies of nighttime at the museum and the museum sleepover to unpack questions and contradictions of child agency and citizenship both inside and outside of these texts. Through a discussion of Elaine Lobl Konigsberg's *From the Mixed-Up Files of Mrs. Basil E. Frankweiler* (1967) and Milan Trenc's *The Night at the Museum* picture book (1993), in addition to recent texts such as Karen LeFrak's picture book *Sleepover at the Museum* (2019), we explore how children's agency and citizenship are both absent and present in these texts and what this means for child readers and museum programmers. We discuss the associated programming around these texts in their own museums and beyond to highlight how children's citizenship is both imagined and enacted. Despite the promise of the inspiring texts and fictional narratives, the programming occurs within the constraints of museum rules and regulations, and critical interventions are limited. We argue that museums are significant sites for analyses of children's citizenship as they represent both the past of national heritages and as potentially liberatory venues for imagined futures (Mai and Gibson 2011), and we highlight some questions to encourage a more critical citizenship for young people. This space of critical reimagination holds promise for children to engage their own experiences and knowledge with the broader society in a more participatory and active form. Monica Patterson (2021: 331) argues that critical children's museology is distinctive as an approach in its "upending the patronising view of children as merely passive recipients of museum content and programming, and focusing instead on their capacities for cultural production, critical interpretation, and curatorial innovation." While many fields have argued for participatory, decolonized, and queered museums, they have not taken children's perspectives and contributions seriously, and our approach aims to challenge that perspective by mining the fantastical texts for their glimmers of critical thought.

CITIZENS-IN-TRAINING: THE MUSEUM IN CHILDREN'S TEXTS

Children's citizenship is a fraught concept; it is assumed and expected, something that needs to be learned and is not equivalent to adult citizenship with its voting rights and legal privileges (Jans 2004). As a characteristic that is imbued by birth in a region by documented citizens, children's citizenship is often a given. Citizenship, in the guise of civics, is a common set of courses in the middle years of education, where lessons about politics, laws, and social responsibilities highlight the knowledge that citizens are expected to have. In Canada, for example, civics and citizenship are taught as part of both primary and secondary school required curricula (Ontario Ministry of Education 2022). The citizenship test that many countries require adults to take to obtain citizenship supposedly contains the breadth of knowledge around geography, history, and politics that a young person would learn in their primary and secondary years. At the same time, children cannot vote, engage in legal wage labor, or own property in most Western democracies and are expected to belong as a dependent to a family unit, which will provide for their needs and training.

Gerard Delanty (2000) argues that contemporary citizenship can be broken down into rules, responsibilities, identity, and participation. Children are thus trained as citizens through school, family, and cultural institutions like museums. Alongside the child-saving movement of the twentieth century, much of the earliest children's programming in museums had the notion of good citizenship at its core (McCreary and Murnaghan 2019), where good citizens were moral, cooperative, and educated. Since the adoption of the United Nations' *Convention on the Rights of the Child* (1989), children's participation in society at large has been foregrounded and children's participation in museums increasingly valued (Mai and Gibson 2011), yet the importance of regulating children's behavior in museums is still seen as paramount (Hamer, 2019). Agency has thus arisen as a counterpoint to citizenship: it is not enough to be a passive citizen, following rules and regulations in one's day-to-day life. Active citizenship implies taking a role in working together to build a stronger social fabric (Isin and Turner 2002). Adopting a different perspective to Rosoff (part I of this volume) in terms of the government's failure to consider children's perspectives, here we argue that children's agency, their choices, viewpoints, and contributions, are increasingly being valued, while participatory endeavors attempt to integrate multiple stakeholders in rewriting national narratives (Phillips 2011) and contributing to public discourse (Harris and Manatakis 2013).

Many children's texts, particularly picture books, explore the first set of citizenship elements of rules and responsibilities in museums, where these unique parapublic spaces act as sites for education between the home and school (Serafini and Rylak 2021). Consequently, many picture books set in museums model social lessons of behavior and learning in public spaces. In the *Maisy Goes to the Museum* picture book (Cousins 2009), Maisy is taught how to act in a museum with limited highlights of museum collections. In *Curious George Museum Mystery* (Rey 2017), based on the PBS show of the same name, Curious George and the Man with the Yellow Hat engage in an educational game at the museum by following clues to solve a mystery of a missing bone. *Arthur Lost in the Museum* (Brown 2005) and *Peppa Pig and the Day at the Museum* (Astley and Baker 2015), among many other picture books set in museums, highlight the importance of following museum rules such as not eating in the gallery. Perry Nodelman (2018) describes how engaging with the art museum is different from engaging with picture books: you can touch, play with, bite/rip picture books while museums have an intended mediated distance between the patron and the art and artifacts. Betül Gaye Dinc and Ilgim Veryeri Alaca (2021) build on Nodelman to examine how nonfiction picture books on art museums and artists may supplement and support young people's learning in art museums through guided play in picture book form. However, while these nonfiction texts extend the embodied experience of artwork at the museum, they continue to maintain a controlled distance from the artifacts. Even Grover, in *Grover and the Everything in the Whole Wide World Museum* (Stiles and Wilcox 1974), who is on an immersive itinerary through the museum of the whole wide world, is still a model for a relatively passive yet participatory patron; immersed, yes, but not free to explore at his own pace or interest—he doesn't have agency over his engagement. Like Grover, young people are encouraged to consume, fantasize about immersion, and explore some hands-on interaction with objects in educational programs—but their interactivity is disciplined and confined. Comparatively, in a 1983 (American) Public Broadcasting System special, *Sesame Street at the Met: Don't Eat the Pictures*, Cookie Monster does indeed try to eat some of the pictures in the gallery but is repetitively, musically reminded in the reprised theme song "Don't Eat the Pictures." However, the most disruptive moment is when he sings about his fantasy of consuming a Modigliani painting of a nude that is described in the language of delicious food, and he is almost drooling to eat it. The disruption here is the articulation of the hyperbolic fantasy that pushes boundaries of acceptable social behavior, but ultimately, Cookie Monster is a rule-abider.

These rules and responsibilities are seen to enable the second set of citizenship practices, those of knowledge acquisition of national and global histories and artistic and scientific knowledge. Children are taught how to behave like ideal museum patrons who are good middle-class consumers of knowledge and heritage. These texts geared at young people also assume readers and patrons where children from diverse backgrounds are often not represented (or only superficially) unless related to the contents of the exhibits themselves that may focus on Black, Indigenous, or other people of color in terms of colonial histories and cultures. The specific subject matter varies by museum, but often art, science, as well as national and global heritage are the main areas of study, couched in global frames of the classics and canons. In colonial contexts, histories prefer the narratives and perspectives of the colonizing culture, writing the exoticized other into dependent and subordinate roles (Murnaghan and McCreary 2016) and often as relics of the past instead of citizens of their own nations and cultures. However, as discussed above, museums increasingly incorporate silenced knowledge and topics that have been pushed aside. As alluded to above, the children's picture book genre has replicated this topical focus in terms of Grover's *Everything in the Whole Wide World Museum* and other books that highlight how children's museum visits can encourage them to be enlightened and well situated for global citizenships.

AGENCY AND CITIZENSHIP IN *THE MIXED-UP FILES . . .* AND *THE NIGHT AT THE MUSEUM*

In order to explore these questions of agency and citizenship in museum-related children's literature, we have chosen two important North American cultural texts in *The Mixed-Up Files of Mrs. Basil E. Frankweiler* (Konigsburg 1967) and *The Night at the Museum* (Trenc 1993). These two focus texts extend beyond the models of citizenship and education in the museum picture books to pose wider questions about agency in these contexts. These texts offer different plots, narrative structures, and critical receptions and point more to the extremes of this literature than its general character. On the one hand, *The Mixed-Up Files . . .* is a Newbery Medal–winning mystery book of children's literature, beloved by librarians, that has continued to be included on best books for children lists for over fifty years. Its film adaptations have featured award-winning actors Ingrid Bergman (1973) and Lauren Bacall (1995) in the role of Mrs. Basil E. Frankweiler, the narrator whose gravitas acts as a foil for the youthful insouciance of the runaways. This tale offers suspense and a child-oriented perspective on a runaway adventure fantasy, where the sibling protagonists are portrayed as capable, independent, and resourceful in their weeklong visit to the Metropolitan Museum of Art in New York City.

Comparatively, *The Night at the Museum* is a short picture book that follows one night in the life of Larry, a newly hired night guard at the American Museum of Natural History in New York City. Not particularly well known or well received, the title is more recognizable by its adaptations, both as a bestselling eponymous novelization by Leslie Goldman (2006) and the live action, computer animated, fantasy-comedy film franchise that includes *Night at the Museum* (2006), *Night at the Museum: Battle of the Smithsonian* (2009), *Night at the Museum: Secret of the Tomb* (2014), and *Night at the Museum: Kahmunrah Rises Again* (2022), which expands and alters the tale and where the story and the characters get the Hollywood treatment. *The Night at the Museum* (1993), in its original picture book form, is void of children's agency. The eight children that appear in the drawings appear only as observers, relegated to contently looking at dinosaur bones and the sleeping night guard. While children are encouraged to identify with the child-like night guard, they are imagined as citizens-in-training, with their current existence as obedient children holding the hands of their adult companions.

The Mixed-Up Files of Mrs. Basil E. Frankweiler presents agency in the behavior and language of Claudia and Jamie Kincaid, who leave their Greenwich, Connecticut home by train, scheming to travel, gather food, find sleeping arrangements, wash their clothes and bodies, and, most of all, elude the adult gaze inside the Metropolitan Museum that would send them home. While they attempt to get away from their parents and have fun, they find themselves entangled in a mystery to solve, finding clues and using their research resources. This novel is a fantasy of the museum at night as both a protective, safe space for two children who need a place to hide in Manhattan and one of excitement, evasion, mystery, and rule-bending antics. The young protagonists have a moderate level of agency and freedom to explore, but the protective space of the museum is underlined by pedagogic imperatives of museums as educational sites for young people. While the young people have agency without parental authority or supervision, they practice self-discipline, following other social rules of the space. Moreover, the text is a fantasy of idealized child patrons who learn about the artifacts, follow tours, sit quietly in galleries, and try to research artifacts like real-life curators. *The Mixed-Up Files . . .* invites readers to imagine running away from home and sleeping in the exhibits while also engaging in a relatively educational archival mystery. Zimmerman observes: "The children are not so much running away from home as they are running toward a richer sense of self in context, and they choose museums as the best places to find what they seek. These child protagonists come to know themselves in relation to objects and displays they find in museums. They are observers and would-be curators, but they are also objects themselves" (2015: 45). But how would this fantasy text be different if Claudia and her brother were represented as visible minorities, not wealthy, white, well-educated suburbanites with upper-crust New York cultural knowledge and behavior modeled at school and home? What if they were young people who were not fully physically mobile and would not be able to hide or access the exhibits in a particular way or young people who were adolescents (often coded as more dangerous or labeled "at-risk" youth)? Even young people who did not have the same curatorial, archival, and academic curiosity or social currency and ingenuity would not have been able to blend in at the museum or to understand why to prioritize certain objects or artifacts in the central mystery around the fabled Michelangelo's *Angel*.

The experience of running away is focused on the young siblings; however, the narrator is an adult, Mrs. Basil Frankweiler—reinforcing this fantasy of agency as an adult one. Claudia says:

> "But, Mrs. Frankweiler, you should want to learn one new thing every day. We did even at the museum." "No." I answered, "I don't agree with that. I think you should learn, of course, and some days you must learn a great deal. But you should also have days when you allow what is already in you to swell up inside of you until it touches everything. And you can feel it inside you. If you never take time out to let that happen, then you just accumulate facts, and they begin to rattle around inside of you. You can make noise with them, but never really feel anything with them. It's hollow." (Konigsburg 1967: 153)

This exchange illustrates a contradiction between the adult's fetishization of a slower experiential immersive learning that is often idealized as child-like, while Claudia, the child, wants to follow the adult structure of didactic, fact-based learning even in her runaway experience. Mrs. Frankweiler, the omnipotent narrator of the book, instructs the children in an embodied form of knowledge, one that they feel, and chooses to overlook the feelings of insecurity that the museum might lead them to have.

The opening page of *The Night at the Museum* shows Larry the night guard's pleasure looking up in the mirror as he dresses in his "wonderful new uniform with shiny brass buttons" with open boxes of tissue paper on the floor and his arms spread as he delights in the image, that of "a general, or a policeman, or a pilot" (Trenc 1993: 1). The masculine, protective identities presented in the text contrast with the childlike image of the guard dressing up, with his scrolly, mauve, oval mirror, socked feet, arms spread and fingers raised, with a delighted smile and closed eyes conjuring make-believe or a dress-up moment of glee. The oblique angle of the mirror in the drawing does not reflect back to him the character in the book, but the angle brings the reader into a triangular formation where they act as the mirror reflecting Larry and his image alike. This explicit reflection invites the reader to see what it would be like to be a museum guard, the notion gesturing to the idea that, unlike a curator with specialized knowledge and training, anyone (even a child!) could be a museum guard. As a blue-collar job, this text points to a less-rarified employment with the museum for one who has not necessarily gained all the knowledge that the museum claims to teach.

As Larry arrives at the museum's main hall, he is greeted by the chief guard, a man with a bushy gray mustache who is stouter and stands taller than Larry. The chief guard refers to Larry as "my boy" and gives him an "easy task" to watch over the dinosaur skeletons for the night. Larry is reassured by the chief, as a parent who is putting their child to sleep might do, that "everything will be okay. I'll check on you in the morning" (Trenc 1993: 4). Larry's small stature is again emphasized, having to reach above his head for the large door's handle as he closes the door. On the facing page, Larry falls asleep with a smile on his face, slumped in his chair beneath the museum's emblematic Tyrannosaurus rex skeleton in the entry hall.

When Larry wakes up, the dinosaurs appear to be gone, and he sets out on a quest to find them, their location a mystery to solve. On his tour through the museum's various exhibit halls, the other guards smile at him and ask for his help with "little jobs," which Larry completes dutifully, finding large bones in every exhibit and learning that sometimes the dinosaurs "wander off if you're not careful" (Trenc 1993: 5). Larry's childlike carelessness is emphasized and his newness to the job reinforced. After learning that all the exhibits come out for the night to stretch their legs, Larry is shocked to observe the feeding and care of all the animals coming to life. William Clark, of the Lewis and Clark exhibit (whose adult figures are sepia-toned, playing cards and drinking coffee in the staffroom), refers to Larry as "little fellah" and reveals the joke: that the dinosaurs were playing hide-and-seek with Larry as an initiation ritual.

At the end of the night, Larry calls "Olly-olly-ox-in-free [sic]," and the dinosaurs return to their places in exhibits for the day, just in time for the museum's visitors, including six of the eight children featured in the book, to arrive. The chief guard returns and asks Larry to cover the job of a day guard out sick since he (sarcastically) "had a tough job napping among the dinosaurs" (Trenc 1993: 24). The story ends with the adage aimed at the child readers of the text: "So if you see a guard asleep when you visit the museum, don't wake him up. He might be recovering from a very difficult night," facing an image of two children smiling at Larry sleeping in his guard's chair, while the exhibit gorilla in the background shushes the reader to keep the secret about what really happens at night in the museum.

The utility of this text in understanding agency is how Larry's childlike character demonstrates common adult relations to children: being chided to be careful, being teased when facing new situations, being belittled in their use of diminutive language, being tricked and deceived by the dinosaurs, and being asked to keep secrets when faced with unusual knowledges like the whole museum coming alive at night. While children's agency is absent in this text, unlike *The Mixed-Up Files*, the notion that children, as outsiders to museum professions, could provide the museum with a useful contribution through their subject positions lies in wait. Can their unfamiliarity with museum protocol allow them to see, or shine a flashlight on, ways that museums could become more open to critical inquiry? Could their good faith approach to searching for answers lead to new analyses for old puzzles of interpretation? Could their willingness to believe that there are some inherent qualities in artifacts lead them to emotionally informed readings or more participatory understandings of the interplay between artifact and action?

Following the popular and profitable success of the first *Night at the Museum* film based on Trenc's text, with its box office gross of half a billion dollars worldwide, *A Night at the Museum* events and programming spread from New York's American Museum of Natural History (AMNH) around the world.[1] Many of these events follow the same format, with flashlighted self-guided tours invoking both the notion of an illicit night visit (or the night guard's preferred tool for their nightly rounds) and the uncovering of a mystery or other collection of clues. Some museums have events that run all night, knowing that children's excitement around being in the museum exceeds their ability to sleep. Often known as museum sleepovers, these events are generally expensive, with prices around $150 per person for the family sleepover events and $350 per person for the adults-only version at the American Museum of Natural History (2023), whereas smaller regional museums have costs as low as sixty dollars per person. Some museums have a one-on-one policy for adults and children and others allow up to five children per parent, for example, the Royal Ontario Museum in Toronto, Canada. The age ranges for these programs are also prescribed, with the AMNH allowing ages six to thirteen, and on Scout nights, six- to sixteen-year-olds are welcome. Reviews of these programs generally remark that the museums are cold, yet the children enjoy the experience of staying up late and snacking, the search and find activities, and the films that are shown in the galleries where the patrons sleep. Apart from the museum being dark and the time being night, children are not allowed to transgress the museum's rules, enter many of the galleries, or see the museum exhibits come to life despite the programs' titles (and the fictional texts they are all familiar with). The sleepover rules are extensive and registration is required, and dinner and breakfast are often provided. Since the beginning of the COVID-19 pandemic, some of the sleepover events (including at the AMNH) have been canceled, while the adult evening museum programming has recently resumed, although many museums have reopened these events as lucrative attractions for their growing memberships.

On the fiftieth anniversary of *The Mixed-Up Files*, the Metropolitan Museum of Art in New York hosted a program where young museum visitors were invited to superficially consume the museum and elements of the book in multiple and heavily structured ways, including a classic educational activity of collection and finding objects and exhibits mentioned in the book, followed by the remediation of the same activity through a social media scavenger hunt and a selfie station to reenact the "iconic" book cover. The program concluded with the literal consumption of a book cookie inspired by Konigsberg's novel (bringing us full circle back to Cookie Monster from *Don't Eat the Pictures* described above but following the rules of appropriate consumption). Nina Simon in *Participatory Museum* (2010) discusses different modes of participation designed by curators and offered to museum patrons. Following Simon's framework, the fiftieth-anniversary events offer a superficial level of participation primarily focused on collection or consumption rather than a contributory or critical engagement with the museum exhibits or the narrative of the novel. As observed by Hamer, there is "a gap between critical work in children's literature scholarship and the curatorial decisions made in the planning of children's book exhibits. This is doubly true for those exhibits that prioritize creative hands-on engagement and immersive experiences of the story worlds over critical engagement with discursive representations" (2019: 397). This is particularly true of texts and programs around the museum at night, when fantasies about the museum space and collections are at the center of the activities.

Karen LeFrak, an author and composer, wrote *Sleepover at the Museum* (2019), a picture book and orchestral accompaniment that exemplifies the line walked between didacticism and fantasy in museum sleepover programs. Since so many children could no longer experience the night at the museum programming, they can through Mason, the lead character in this tale who celebrates his birthday at the sleepover program at the American Museum of Natural History with his two friends for the child readers (and listeners). The dreamy illustrations by David Bucs highlight some of the beloved sites in the museum, like the blue whale and the long, dark hallways filled with cases. Alongside the story about the children solving riddles in a scavenger hunt and following the map of the museum included in the book are corny trivia quips about exhibits provided by the children as they contemplate which hall they should sleep in if they win the scavenger hunt. The children's headlamps and bedrolls on their backs in the illustrations point to the real-life encounter in the museum sleepover, which echoed the fantastical encounter in the film, which was based on the picture book. The New York Philharmonic debuted the orchestral piece, introduced on YouTube by Grammy-winning producer David Foster (New York Philharmonic 2020) as part of the "Fun at the Phil" family programming. The dramatic music highlights the imaginative fantasies that come to life in the children's experience of their night at the museum, eventually settling on sleeping beneath the blue whale, although in their dreamscapes, they rest on the whale's head as he swims in a pod.

HOW CHILDREN'S CITIZENSHIP CAN TRANSFORM MUSEUM PROGRAMMING THROUGH TRUTH-TELLING AND RECLAMATION

Inside our chosen texts, children and museums are presented both realistically and fantastically, reinforcing assumptions about child learning, participation, and curiosity but also representing child protagonists with varying levels of agency in their engagement. However, outside the texts, children's programming at museums has cultivated a more domestic relationship between children and museums through the museum sleepover but intentionally establishes a distance between young people and their direct engagement as active contributors to the museum knowledge and cultures. While museums inside the texts tend to be more fantastical, where children get to sleep, play, and hide their belongings in the exhibits (in Konigsburg's text) or see the museum come to life in the adaptation of Trenc's text, the fantasies of their active citizenship in participating in museum programming and curation have been limited. We argue that we can use the fantastical representations of children's nights at the museum to enhance the experience of children's museum programming. One of the central aims of critical children's museology (Patterson 2021) is to take children's perspectives and contributions seriously, and our approach aims to mine the fantastical texts for their examples of critical thought as a way to return to the museum programming with an emphasis on young people's agency in the museum space.

While museum studies have begun to reimagine the museum with a focus on civic engagement and dialogue in the public sphere, in Simon's (2010) words as "participatory," very few programs for young people invite rigorous participation or critique. Young people are not encouraged to challenge or question the museum as an institution through the disruptions proposed by the decolonizing or queering the museum movements.

Sullivan and Middleton discuss how historically museum curation exemplified "[a]n attempt to create a grand narrative which was at once didactic, encyclopedic, objective, ethnographic, and intended to educate a 'genuinely interested' liberal, bourgeois audience" (Sullivan and Middleton 2011: 46). The texts and programs discussed in this chapter show how museums continue to sustain the educational elements of creating a grand narrative. There are a few textual examples in the genre, such as the picture book *How the Sphinx Got to the Museum* (Hartland 2010), that illustrate how artifacts are created, collected, and brought to the museum millennia later, but this text does not delve directly into the political issues around the recent rise in repatriation of objects that were gathered through specious methods during colonial acquisitions.

The National Film Board of Canada's animated film *This Is Your Museum Speaking* (Smith 1979) presents an early example of how a filmic text used the museum at night to show some of the ways objects may voice untold histories. Perhaps one of the first children's films to feature the museum's dinosaur skeleton coming to life, this "soft-sell educational piece" (Maltin 1980: 78) invited children to accompany a night guard and his dog to work and experience the exhibits coming to life, guided by Muse, the goddess of the museum. The puzzled night guard does not see the value in the artifacts before his tour guide encourages him to "take what you do know and use your imagination." As an antidote to the adage that "technology is the future," paintings, costumes, and artifacts speak to the guard and let him know that the artifacts belonged to real people. A pair of moccasins transport him to a precontact moment before European settlers began to settle and trade in North America (bringing disease and violence to these communities), noting that the museum itself is located on Indigenous land. Breaking the fourth wall and looking directly at the viewer, the night guard begins to see how history is embedded in his own city. And the museum's cartographic icon marks it as common to all cities instead of a specified location as in the texts described above.

More recent multiplatform performance work has taken acts of language and cultural reclamation far beyond this. An album by Jeremy Dutcher, a Wolastoqiyik member of the Tobique First Nation, draws upon archival recordings of traditional Maliseet songs at the Canadian Museum of History not known by young community members (Brocklehurst 2018). The Museum of Vancouver's exhibit "There is Truth Here: Creativity and Resilience in Children's Art from Indian Residential and Day Schools," curated by Andrea Walsh, drew upon children's artwork created at residential schools as a form of truth-telling:

"There is Truth Here" brings a new line to bear on the role of art as part of children's knowledge, identity, and experiences of Indian Residential and Day Schools. Through paintings, drawings, sewing, beading, drumming, singing, and drama produced by children and youth who attended schools in British Columbia and Manitoba the exhibition seeks to contribute in vital and new ways to dialogues and initiative about truth telling, reconciliation, and redress in Canada. (*Museum of Vancouver* 2019)

The exhibit included audio and video testimonies by the child artists as adults and, in some cases, their own children who responded to this work decades later, particularly in terms of the role of art as therapeutic, reflective, and critically engaging during a period of trauma. Here, we can see real engagement with serious issues of critical importance to a more realistic perspective on Canadian heritage. By incorporating children as agentic actors who create art, who interpret art, and who contribute to contemporary culture, these museum programs are highlighting the best of participatory approaches. By working with adults instead of having to evade them (*The Mixed-Up Files . . .*) or pretend to be them (*Night at the Museum*), children's points of view can contribute to the museum to make richer exhibits that reckon with reality.

WAYS FORWARD: CHILDREN AS ACTIVE CURATORS AND CITIZENS

Ellen Yates and colleagues (2022) have offered that museums can indeed incorporate children's perspectives into museums by focusing on the notion that children are "experiencers" instead of patrons. As Emily Murphy, Sonali Kulkarni, and Emilie Owens argue in part IV of this volume, youth's presence and participation in the public sphere, both in the physical archive and in the virtual world of BookTok, is vital to their sense of agency and citizenship. The fictional texts we have discussed here seem to support this proposition, where children's fantasies about the spaces blur the boundaries between (sleepover) dreams and realities. But what would museum programming that challenges museum narratives and narratives about children's passive citizenship look like? Monica Patterson (2021) has pointed to the "Anything Goes" exhibit at the National Museum in Warsaw, Poland, as a superb example where museum curators supported children's lead in designing and executing new technology to make children's fantasies come to life. Children's interest in spooky lighting and violent themes were represented in many of the galleries, with animations bringing new immersive techniques and nontraditional layouts to the display of artifacts. Children's imaginative labels, replete with spelling errors and in their handwriting, accompanied traditional didactic labels beside the artifacts. From activity-based installations like huge crossword puzzles to simple stairs to allow smaller bodies to view artifacts more closely, the exhibit manipulated the traditional notions of citizenship: there were indeed new rules and new ways of educating in this child-directed exhibit. At the same time, some of the children's suggestions were limited by adults' safety concerns about suspending furniture from the ceiling or concerns about propriety over the children's desire to make bedsheets with prints from a painting of a decaying female body. Patterson (2021: 341) points to the importance of "sharing institutional authority with children" and engaging young people in the process of curation, not just assuming they all want dinosaurs to come to life, pharaohs to talk to them, and to swim alongside the blue whale in their dreams. These realistic contributions help to move the work forward, highlighting how considering children's agency requires working with, instead of on, children.

NOTE

1. Helsinki's Night of the Arts in 1989, Berlin's The Long Night of Museums in 1997, and Paris's Nuit Blanche in 2001 were some of the precursors to these types of night events, although these focused on a visit (not a stay) and a network of museums and other cultural venues open at night and less family-oriented programming.

REFERENCES

Astley, N. and M. Baker. *Peppa Pig and the Day at the Museum*. Massachusetts: Candlewick Press, 2015.

Brocklehurst, Sean. "'Deep Listening': How Jeremy Dutcher Crafted His Fascinating Polaris Prize–Winning Album." CBC News. Last modified September 18, 2018. https://www.cbc.ca/news/indigenous/national-jeremy-dutcher-interview-polaris-prize-wolastoq-1.4820825.

Brown, Marc. *Arthur Lost in the Museum*. New York: Random House Books for Young Readers, 2005.

Civics and Citizenship Curriculum and Resources. Ontario: Ontario Ministry of Education, n.d. Accessed January 11, 2023. https://www.dcp.edu.gov.on.ca/en/curriculum/canadian-and-world-studies/courses/chv2o/overview.

Coombes, Annie E., and Ruth B. Phillips, editors. *Museum Transformations: Decolonization and Democratization*. New York: Wiley, 2020.

Cousins, Lucy. *Maisy Goes to the Museum*. London: Walker Books, 2008.

Delanty, G. *Citizenship in a Global Age: Society, Culture, Politics*. Buckingham: Open University Press, 2000.

Dinc, Betül Gaye, and Ilgim Veryeri Alaca. "Interacting with Nonfiction Picture Books in Art Museums." In *Verbal and Visual Strategies in Nonfiction Picture Books: Theoretical and Analytical Approaches*, edited by N. Goga, S. H. Iversen, and A. S. Teigland, 236–49. Oslo: Scandinavian University Press, 2021.

"Don't Eat the Pictures: Sesame Street at the Metropolitan Museum of Art." Children's Television Workshop. Directed by John Stone. New York. 1983.

From the Mixed-Up Files of Mrs. Basil E. Frankweiler. Directed by Marcus Cole. 1995. Kansas City: Signboard Hill Productions, film.

From the Mixed-Up Files of Mrs. Basil E. Frankweiler. Directed by Fielder Cook. 1973. Montague, NJ: Westfall Productions, film.

Goldman, Leslie. *Night at the Museum: The Junior Novelization*. New York: Barron's Educational Series, 2006.

Hamer, Naomi. "The Hybrid Exhibits of the Story Museum: The Child as Creative Artist and the Limits to Hands-on Participation." *Museum and Society* 17, no. 3 (2019), 390–403. doi:10.29311/mas.v17i3.3256.

Harris, Pauline, and Harry Manatakis. *Children as Citizens: Engaging with the Child's Voice in Educational Settings*. New York: Routledge, 2013.

Hartland, Jesse. *How the Sphinx Got to the Museum*. New Jersey: Blue Apple Books, 2010.

Isin, Engin F., and Bryan S. Turner. "Citizenship Studies: An Introduction." In *Handbook of Citizenship Studies*, edited by Bryan S. Turner and Engin F. Isin, 1–10. California: Sage Publications, 2002.

Jans, Marc. "Children as Citizens." *Childhood* 11, no. 1 (2004), 27–44. doi:10.1177/0907568204040182.

Konigsberg, E. L. *From The Mixed-Up Files of Mrs. Basil E. Frankweiler*. New York: Atheneum Books, 1967.

LeFrak, Karen, and David Bucs, illustrator. *Sleepover at the Museum*. New York: Crown Books for Young Readers, 2019.

Mai, Lea, and Robyn Gibson. "The Rights of the Putti: A Review of the Literature on Children as Cultural Citizens in Art Museums." *Museum Management and Curatorship* 26, no. 4 (2011), 355–71. doi:10.1080/09647775.2011.603930.

Maltin, Leonard. "Leonard Maltin from Ottawa." *Film Comment* 16, no 6 (1980), 78–79.

McCreary, Tyler, and Ann Marie F. Murnaghan, "The Educational Work of a National Museum: Creating Knowledgeable Young Citizens in Ottawa, Canada." *Children's Geographies* 17, no. 6 (2019), 635–48.

Murnaghan, Ann Marie, and Tyler McCreary. "Projections of Race, Nature, and Ethnographic Childhood in Early Educational Cinema at the National Museum of Canada." *Geografiska Annaler: Series B, Human Geography* 98, no. 1 (2016), 37–53.

New York Philharmonic and Karen LeFrak. "Sleepover at the Museum." YouTube. 2020. Accessed January 11, 2023. https://www.youtube.com/watch?v=kYduhFQBuS4&t=81s.

Night at the Museum. Directed by Shawn Levy. 2006. Los Angeles, CA: Twentieth Century Fox. Film.

Night at the Museum: Battle of the Smithsonian. Directed by Shawn Levy. 2009. Los Angeles, CA: 21 Laps Entertainment. Film.

Night at the Museum: Secret of the Tomb. Directed by Shawn Levy. 2014. Los Angeles, CA: 21 Laps Entertainment. Film.

Night at the Museum: Kahmunrah Rises Again. Directed by Matt Danner. 2022. Burbank, CA: Walt Disney Pictures. Film.

Nodelman, Perry. "Touching Art: The Art Museum as a Picture Book, and the Picture Book as Art." *Journal of Literary Education*, no. 1 (2018), 6–25. doi:10.7203/jle.1.12085.

Patterson, Monica. "Toward a Critical Children's Museology: The Anything Goes Exhibition at the National Museum in Warsaw." *Museum and Society* 19, no. 3 (2021), 330–51. doi:10.29311/mas.v19i3.3393.

Phillips, Louise. "Possibilities and Quandaries for Young Children's Active Citizenship." *Early Education & Development* 22, no. 5 (2011), 778–94. doi:10.1080/10409289.2011.59 7375.

"Plan Your Visit." American Museum of Natural History. Accessed January 4, 2024. https://www.amnh.org/plan-your-visit/sleepovers.

Serafini, Frank, and Danielle Rylak. "Representations of Museums and Museum Visits in Narrative Picturebooks." *Libri et Liberi* 10, no. 1 (2021), 45–62. doi:10.21066/carcl. libri.10.1.3.

Simon, Nina. *The Participatory Museum.* California: Museum 2.0, 2010.

Stiles, Norman, and D. Wilcox. *Grover and the Everything in the Whole Wide World Museum.* New York: Random House Books for Young Readers, 1974.

Sullivan, Nikki, and Craig Middleton. *Queering the Museum.* New York: Routledge, 2019.

"There is Truth Here." Museum of Vancouver. Accessed January 11, 2023. https://museum ofvancouver.ca/there-is-truth-here.

This is Your Museum Speaking. Directed by Lynn Smith. 1979. Ottawa: National Film Board of Canada. Film.

Trenc, Milan. *Night at the Museum.* New York: Barron's Educational Series, 1993.

Yates, Ellen, Judith Szenasi, Amanda Smedley, Kayla Glynn, and Michelle Hemmings. "Children as Experiencers: Increasing Engagement, Participation and Inclusion for Young Children in the Museum." *Childhood* 29, no. 1 (2022), 58–74. doi:10.1177/09075682211064429.

Zimmerman, Virginia. "The Curating Child: Runaways and Museums in Children's Fiction." *The Lion and the Unicorn* 39, no. 1 (2015), 42–62. doi:10.1353/uni.2015.0008.

Chapter 13

YOUNG ADULT AGENCY ON BOOKTOK

A Practice Theory Inquiry into Young Readers' Active Reshaping of Digital Literary Criticism on TikTok

SONALI KULKARNI AND EMILIE OWENS

The reader is the space on which all the quotations that make up a writing are inscribed without any of them being lost; a text's unity lies not in its origin but its destination.

—ROLAND BARTHES, *THE DEATH OF THE AUTHOR*, 1967

In August 2020, author Adam Silvera found himself in an enviable situation: several years after the release of his YA novel *They Both Die at the End* (2017), it witnessed a significant surge in popularity and sales, at once exciting and confounding the author. It quickly became apparent that the second life of Silvera's novel was the result of a viral "trend" on BookTok in which young readers made and uploaded short videos of their reactions to the ending of the novel, speaking to its cathartic nature. #BookTok compiles a wide range of similarly bookish videos in which young readers review, recommend, and rate books, discuss problematic content, and so on (Harris 2021; Jerasa and Boffone 2021). Although adolescents uploading videos on a social media platform is a seemingly straightforward practice, the case of BookTok demands an investigation of the new ways in which young people are positioning themselves as knowers and active agents in the literary sphere. We respond to this demand by drawing attention to young readers' use of TikTok to express their opinions about books and the ways in which self-positioning as literary knowers relates to or contrasts conventional forms of literary criticism.

Our research is motivated by the pervasive nature and relevance of Book-Tok in (post-)pandemic literary zeitgeist. Since its international release in September 2017, TikTok has become one of the most downloaded apps in the world, with over one billion users in the second quarter of 2022 (Mohsin 2022). #BookTok, in its own right, has over seventy-seven billion views globally and is one of the most popular hashtags on TikTok (TikTok 2022). As a result, "Best of BookTok" displays are now commonplace in online and offline bookstores, featuring books that are most talked about on the platform. These include a significant portion of YA novels by authors such as Silvera, Sarah J. Maas, and Alice Oseman. This is unsurprising since, at the time of writing in 2022, over 47 percent of TikTok users are between ten and twenty-nine years old, indicating the popularity and importance of the platform in youth culture (Dean 2022).

Conventionally, the meteoric rise of digital platforms such as TikTok has been understood by reading researchers and cultural commentators through a lens of anxiety concerning a decline in positive reading behaviors (Carr 2010). This is due to the supposed "End of Books" (Coover 1992) at the hands of the digital. While several of the concerns expressed by the detractors of internet use by young people merit urgent attention, generalizations about the largely *negative* effects of the internet and the digital sphere abound (see Twenge, Martin, and Spitzberg 2019; Natanson 2018), leading to a false binary between the digital and the literary. This is not to say that the contours of reading and book culture have remained unchanged within the evolving media landscape. They have changed consistently, leading to new forms and modes of reading (Andersen et al. 2021). Consequently, scholarly discourse is likewise moving toward an understanding of reading as a "situated phenomenon that evolves in the intersection of media developments, literary trends, and social practices" (Andersen et al. 2021: 136). This intersection is aptly illustrated by the case of BookTok, where the confluence of media developments and changing reader practices create a new set of opportunities to reexamine youth reading.

For said reexamination, we will focus on *media practices*, a theoretical method suitable for articulating the nuanced changes wrought to social and cultural spheres—for example, that of literary criticism and appreciation—by digital media technologies such as TikTok. This method decentralizes the focus from either the media as a text or the user as an audience and allows instead for an approach that acknowledges a range of behaviors on and associated with media by individuals and groups within a given context. So, in this instance, rather than focusing on what is *happening to an individual as a result of TikTok*, we are invited by practice theory to consider what *an individual is doing in relation to TikTok*. Given that the notion of agency— understood as the central tenet of this volume—relies upon the ability of an individual to make choices and act for themselves (Cavazzoni et al. 2021;

Robson 2007), this emphasis on the active work of *doing* is well suited to comprehensively examining young people's agency within the digital literary sphere. In keeping with the overall theme of part IV of this volume, we argue that by taking this approach to the examination of the digital literary space of BookTok, we can begin to better understand how young people are using TikTok (and similar technologies) to exercise readerly agency and demonstrate their literary knowledge, shifting and ultimately expanding *what it is to know* about books and literature within the digital sphere.

CURRENT TRENDS IN BOOKTOK RESEARCH

BookTok may be a relatively new phenomenon within the broader literary sphere, but it has nevertheless been the subject of numerous studies. Broadly speaking, current publication on the topic of BookTok can be divided into three categories: non-literature-oriented (and often celebratory) consumer research; pedagogical research, focusing on literacy development; and library-related studies. Within the first and most populated category, numerous articles have appeared in publishing-oriented journals that focus on the transformative potential of BookTok as a tool for book marketing (McIlroy 2022; Stewart 2022), for detailing its role in turning books from the backlist into bestsellers (Stewart 2021; Vatner 2022), or for exploring the broader influence of TikTok's viral nature on the commercial positioning of books (Delemos 2021). While many of these consumer research–oriented reports are positive in tone, citing the commercial successes already seen on BookTok, there are also more cautionary articles suggesting that this digital literary trend cannot be relied upon for consistent success (Apple 2022; O'Sullivan 2022). Site-specific investigations of the relationship between BookTok and the publishing industry also exist: Paula Cuestas et al. (2022) have explored the changes wrought by BookTok's viral trends in Argentina, concluding that shifting reading practices, especially among young female TikTok users, are influencing the national publishing landscape.

Occupying the second category are a handful of studies that emphasize the potential of BookTok in service of broader literacy development among young people. Trevor Boffone and Sarah Jerasa, for example, have undertaken research on BookTok in relation to youth literacy within queer reading communities (Boffone and Jerasa 2021), as well as the out-of-school reading practices of young people (Jerasa and Boffone 2021). They conclude that it is essential to recognize adolescents' use of TikTok as an authentic form of reading and literary engagement. Brenda K. Wiederhold (2022) has

also written from a psychological perspective on the potential of Book-
Tok to reignite an enjoyment of reading among young people, and Michael
Dezuanni et al. (2022) have examined how the reading practices of young
people—their engagement with the concept of literacy but also their experience of book-related culture more broadly—are influenced by digital trends
such as BookTok and Bookstagram.

Third, and finally, is the category of research relating to library studies that
explores how TikTok—and more specifically, BookTok—can help develop
strategies for book collection at a public and private level. Though some of
these studies offer a similarly celebratory perspective as those suggesting Book-
Tok will change the world of publishing and sales for the better (Kelly 2022;
Roberts 2021), there have also been critical approaches that seek to better
understand how the digital literary world of BookTok might shape the practices of librarians as curators of reading experiences. In a brief article for the
Association of College and Research Libraries, Dina Mashiyane (2022) highlights the importance of taking account of book trends across digital platforms
such as BookTok in creating a diverse, relevant, and engaging library collection.
The platform, she argues, can be used to "build a collection appealing to the
TikTok generation of library users to entice and nurture their leisure reading
behaviours" (450). This sentiment is reflected in an earlier, more in-depth
research article by Margeret K. Merga (2021), who undertakes an analysis of
how reader advisory services—notably those of libraries—can utilize content
on BookTok to enhance their informational offering to young people, thus
contributing to their broader reading practices. She writes the following:

> Libraries' reader advisory services for young people can use these
> findings from analysis of BookTok content to build young reader
> friendly spaces and give greater primacy to current popular com-
> monalities informing recommendations, such as emotional response
> in readers' advisory services. Further research could explore how such
> interventions are received by young people who are both members
> and non-members of the BookTok community to determine their
> broader utility. (Merga 2021: 8)

While these studies, especially those in the latter two categories, are clearly
relevant to the field of children's literature, it is notable that across this
research landscape the emphasis is placed primarily on how BookTok promotes, relates to, takes away from, or can serve the broader aims of reading promotion; in short, these are perspectives that focus on *literacy*. And
while acknowledging that this focus is urgent within our field, we seek to

move instead toward an understanding of BookTok from the perspective of reader agency and literary criticism. How do young people express their opinions about the books they read? And how do their ways of positioning themselves as literary knowers relate to or contrast conventional forms of literary criticism? Taking such questions as a point of departure, we propose an expansion in scope from considerations of *literacy* on BookTok to a conceptualization of *the literary* on BookTok to emphasize young people's use of digital media to create spaces for active participation in literary discourses to which they may have been previously denied access.

EPISTEMICS OF THE DIGITAL LITERARY SPHERE

BookTok represents only the most recent noteworthy instance of book-related content online. In 2022, the internet hosted many books in pdf and audio form, as well as countless examples of what Simone Murray fittingly refers to as "book talk," "book review websites, self-cataloguing library networks, author home pages, publishers' portals, online book retailers, archived writers' festival panel sessions, and recorded celebrity author readings" (2018: 1). The term she uses to account for the complexity of this now-rich history of books and book-related activities on the internet is the *digital literary sphere*, arguing that literary scholars must take account of the digital realm in order to comprehend how their area of focus is transformed, and transforming, in a contemporary media landscape. In further research, she also stresses the need to "cease conceptualising the analogue and digital as ontological opposites" and focus instead on their interdependence and mutual revivification (Murray 2021: 971). Such a conceptualization of understanding reading and book culture as *a part of*, and not in opposition to, the larger media ecology is not always reflected in scholarly and popular discourse on the topic. For instance, Robert Coover (1992), among several others, prophesied the "End of Books" at the hands of the internet, fearing that the codex was an outdated type of technology. In hindsight, this pronouncement presents itself as a form of "media panic": an intensely negative popular reaction to new media that are perceived to threaten a normative way of life (Drotner 2013: 18). In this case, cultures of reading. This is not to say that reading and book culture has gone unaffected by technological developments. As Murray rightly states: "While the central tenet of 1990s-style digital futurism—the death of the book—has failed to materialise, digital processes and platforms undeniably infiltrate the global book industry at every stage: from production . . . to consumption (reader reviews, fan fiction, bookish social networking, amateur booktubing, bookstagramming)" (2021: 971).

The infiltration of digital platforms and processes in literary consumption is of particular relevance to our exploration of young readers' agentic reshaping of literary criticism via BookTok as it has opened a wide range of avenues for ordinary readers to exercise their critical voices, shifting the ways in which criticism is written and read, as well as the role it plays in the literary field (Neima 2017: 51). Conventional forms of literary criticism are characterized by a strict hierarchy between author, critic, and reader, with the latter playing a largely passive receptive role. The critic, in this case, is usually a professional employed by newspapers and magazines. The mediation of reading and reception through the internet, however, has resulted in the collapse of the author-critic-reader triad, creating a "horizontal network of lay readers, who can take the decision of what should be published and read in their own hands" (Neima 2017: 52), also discussed in this volume by Schulz. Such conceptualizations feed into the idea of a cultural democracy where critical authority has shifted from the few to the many. Unsurprisingly, this popular enfranchisement has been met with enthusiasm and alarm in equal measure; some cultural commentators express concern about "the degradation of literary taste" as a result (Sutherland 2006, n.p.). Murray (2018) provides further nuance in this polarized debate, stating succinctly, "We are witnessing the literary critical equivalent not of an absolute monarchy nor a proletarian revolt, but something poised ambiguously in between" (Murray 2018: 113).

We agree with Murray in that the state of contemporary literary criticism is indeed ambiguous, with elite professionals and amateurs occupying different but complementary positions within the literary field, compelling a renegotiation of our ideas of expertise and agency. And even though we are decidedly not in the midst of a proletarian literary revolt, the power vested in lay readers to determine the success of a particular book is significant enough to merit further discussion on readerly agency, a discussion that takes into account new platforms and ways of exercising critical authority. The case of Silvera's novel presented above makes this abundantly clear. Particularly, this "non-elite reception" (Allington 2016: 258) of literature comprises atypical forms of literary criticism such as vlogging (as seen on BookTube) and personal and affective reviews (as seen on Goodreads). And while the atypical nature of such cases as BookTube and Goodreads, for instance, has been studied (see Steiner 2008; Allington 2016; Jaakkola 2019), BookTok has gone largely unnoticed as a platform for literary criticism. Moreover, scholars such as Luke Neima and Daniel Allington discuss issues of democratization wherein lay readers—who were previously excluded from literary criticism—find an avenue for exerting influence on literary taste. Notably, however, another category of readers that has been consistently excluded from mainstream literary criticism is missing from these scholarly discussions: children and young adults.

The present volume demonstrates that the discussions on the voice of children and young adults that are missing in the scholarly work cited above increasingly take center stage in current children's literature studies. A result of the decisive "childist turn" in the field, this focus on the child as an agentic being challenges the image of the powerless child that had come to define the power dynamics central to children's literature. In fact, so dominant was such an image that Swedish scholar Maria Nikolajeva conceptualized children's literature as "a unique art and communication form, deliberately created by those in power for the powerless" (2010: 8). A wide range of theoretical discussions have since consistently problematized this scholarly imagination of the child (see Gubar 2013; García-González and Deszcz-Tryhubczak 2020; van Lierop-Debrauwer 2022). We build on this burgeoning strand of research within our field to propose a reexamination of BookTok and young readers' use thereof to position themselves as rightful literary knowers and commentators in ways that are hitherto unrecognized.

We particularly turn to Helma van Lierop-Debrauwer's (2022) recent contribution, in which she rereads key research from her illustrious career through the lens of onto-epistemic (in)justice (Murris 2013). The concept of onto-epistemic (in)justice derives from Miranda Fricker's (2007) work on epistemic injustice.[1] Ian James Kidd, José Medina, and Gaile Pohlhaus (2017) define epistemic injustice as "those forms of unfair treatment that relate to issues of knowledge, understanding, and participation in communicative practices" (1). For example, the systemic disregard for the medical narratives and symptoms of women by healthcare professionals would amount to epistemic injustice since their position as *knowers* is not respected. Building on this, Karin Murris (2013) recognizes that, much like women in the above example, children have been historically disregarded as knowers solely as a function of their *being a child* and introduces the related term *onto-epistemic (in)justice*. This concept has since been operationalized by Joanna Haynes and Murris (2019), Macarena García-González and Justyna Deszcz-Tryhubczak (2020), and van Lierop-Debrauwer (2022) in relation to children's literature. The latter explicitly includes young adults in this category and applies the concept to their role as literary critics. For example, van Lierop-Debrauwer writes of the decision in the Netherlands to establish a national children's jury in 1988 to adjudicate children's books awards; at the time, detractors argued that including children as judges was a threat to

critical standards since they are too young to read and evaluate books critically, an argument that displays ageist ideologies rooted in onto-epistemic
injustice. She also draws a striking parallel between the alarmist narrative
developed around these child juries and the fear of degradation of literary
standards due to digital criticism by lay readers. In both cases, those conventionally bearing the power to shape literary shapes and standards display
anxiety over critical authority shifting to those previously excluded.

In BookTok, we find a phenomenon that is not only digital but also primarily driven by young people's participation. By means of short and engaging videos, young readers create content that reviews/recommends books
that they read, dramatizes the contents of the book or even their reading
experience, or, in their most abstract form, presents the aesthetic of a particular book. Explaining the popularity of such literary content, an article
in *The Guardian* states:

> BookTokers capture the "visceral reaction" to a book, which doesn't
> come across in a written review, Horrox [publicity manager of Silvera's
> novel] says. "There's something about the fact that it is under a min-
> ute. People who are consuming this content want stuff that's quicker
> and snappier all the time—you watch a 32-second video and some-
> one's like: 'This book has LGBTQ romance, it's really heartbreaking,
> it's speculative fiction.' And then the viewers think: 'Oh, OK, those are
> all things that I'm interested in. I'll go buy it.'" (Flood 2021: n.p.)

This proclamation of BookTok's ability to capture visceral reactions aligns
with Ann Steiner's (2008) observation that literary criticism online is decidedly personal, intimate, and affective. Murray (2018) places this affective turn
in opposition to literary academe's "palpable unease with literary affect" (126).
The informal space of BookTok challenges this unease and uses affect as one
of its main tools (see Martens et al. 2022). Against the backdrop of the above
discussion on the onto-epistemic injustice faced by young people as knowers
of the literary, in the following analysis, we examine how—among other practices—affect is wielded by young readers in their literary-epistemic practices
on BookTok. We argue that these evolving practices unearth unconventional
forms of literary knowing and exemplify young readers' active reshaping of
the digital literary criticism on BookTok. To examine this in further detail, we
propose an approach borrowed from media studies that brings an emphasis
on *practice* to the fore.

In his book *Media, Society, World*, Nick Couldry writes the following:

A practice approach starts not with media texts or media institutions but from media-related practice in all its looseness and openness. It asks quite simply: what are people (individuals, groups, institutions) *doing in relation to media* across a whole range of situations and contexts? How is people's media-related practice related, in turn, to their wider agency? The outcome, potentially, is a new paradigm for media research. (Couldry 2012: 37, emphasis original)

Understanding practices as the basic units of study for researching digital media—such as TikTok or, more specifically, BookTok—thus foregrounds an emphasis on the user and their *choices* and how the relationship between those choices over time begins to shape the structure of the media themselves; namely, how user agency can and does influence media technologies, not only the other way around. Couldry states that the aim of this is to "establish . . . the new principles by which practices related to media are demarcated . . . [by looking] closely at what people are doing, saying and thinking in relation to media" (2012: 40). So, rather than conducting a traditional analysis based in the deconstruction of a media text as a digital object—in so doing, conceptualizing it as a *discrete entity* with the ability to effect a user wholesale—we can use an analysis based on an understanding of practices to focus instead on the complex *relationships* between the digital media as a text and the individual human user as a member of a broader social world.

This is of particular relevance to young people's engagement with media; as cultural anthropologist Mizuko Ito notes, there is a tendency within children's media studies to "fetishize technology as a force with its own internal logic standing outside of history, society and culture" (2008: 402). She argues that research that seeks to comprehensively examine the role of digital media in childhood must instead cultivate an "understanding of *practice* and *participation* from the view of young people" (411, emphasis mine). To this end, Stine Liv Johansen has created a model for applying the principles of practice theory to children's media specifically, building on the work of Couldry and other mediatization scholars to identify the ways in which "media are being used by children to anchor physical practices . . . and communities" (2017: 8). Her ethnographic study of how children use the video-sharing website YouTube operationalizes the principles of practice theory laid out by Couldry—identifying what the young people in her study were doing and saying in relation to YouTube—to draw conclusions about their agency in pursuing what interests them and participating in their communities. This attests to the utility of practice theory in examinations of agency vis-à-vis young people.

Approaching the study of digital media in this way allows us to conceptualize how young people choose to make use of technologies to carve out space for themselves within set cultural frameworks that are otherwise adult-centric and adult-controlled. Johansen's work emphasizes the way in which "aspects of mediatized play . . . challenge these set frameworks . . . for instance, children can use the iPad to communicate without adult permission or restriction" (2017: 8). As children and young people develop the skills to use these technologies, so too do they begin to develop practices that challenge, subvert, or entirely avoid existing adult power structures; "social media and video sharing platforms (act) . . . for better and for worse, as a sort of online 'bicycle shed,' a space where play culture can take place *outside the reach of the adult gaze*" (9, emphasis mine). Though this research was published one year before the launch of TikTok in the international market, Johansen's argument regarding the liberatory potential of children's digital media practices has become even more salient in light of the ubiquity of the app and its intense popularity among children in particular. The fact that any child who has learned the basic functions of a smartphone can first record and then post a TikTok video has several significant implications for the cultural frameworks that formerly governed, for example, the literary sphere.

READER PRACTICES ON BOOKTOK

It has been noted that selecting videos for analysis on TikTok presents certain distinct challenges (Owens, 2024); famously, the application decides which videos will be shown to any given individual using a complex recommendation algorithm that takes into account a wealth of information such as age, location, gender, and previous TikTok browsing habits like the amount of time spent watching one particular video or the frequency with which certain other types of videos are scrolled past (TikTok 2020). In the interest of both expediency and continuity, we selected videos that are a part of the viral trend relating to Silvera's novel *They Both Die at the End* (2016), used as an illustrative example at the beginning of the chapter. The method for selection was as follows: the words "they both die at the end" were typed into the search function of TikTok. The second and third videos that appeared at the top of the search results were analyzed. The reason for this was to get a fair and accurate snapshot of the trend without first "screening" the videos and skewing the analysis toward content that the authors predetermined would speak to the aims. The videos can be viewed by scanning the following QR codes.

Figure 13.1. QR code for Video A by @abbysbooks

Figure 13.2. QR code for Video B by @hua.b

Operating within the critical framework laid out above that highlights the digital sphere as a potential space where youth can both exercise their knowledge of literature and also be recognized for that knowledge by the literary community, our practice analysis of this video thus first conceptualized *knowing itself* as a practice. What Miranda Fricker (2007) calls epistemic authority, having sufficient power to possess and share knowledge, may helpfully be understood in this context as precisely those thoughtless or habitual sets of actions that Couldry and Johansen identify as media practices. That is, though in both videos the creators may not have overtly intended to demonstrate their authority in knowing about books, the way in which they have chosen to use the app to create these particular videos exemplifies a routine relationship with both literature and TikTok as well as the interaction of the two, which nevertheless succeeds in firmly establishing their knowledge for the viewer.

This is demonstrated elegantly in the very first scene of the first video (hereinafter Video A in the absence of titles on TikTok), in which user abbysbooks shows herself holding the book to the camera under the text "reading they both die at the end in one day." Whether or not she did actually read the titled book in one day as the text suggests, the fact that she has chosen to open with this premise acts as an establishment of her familiarity and skill with the act of reading; we as viewers are meant to understand that she can, and routinely does, read an entire novel in one day. This runs counter to the expectation by adults that younger individuals are less experienced or capable readers—a belief that is closely tied to those historical understandings of child readers as powerless that are currently being called into question by the childist turn cited above—and asserts her ability as a skillful reader, a trait which must necessarily inform the practice of *knowing* for a critic of literature at any level.

Though the video opens with this fairly typical assertion of agency in *knowing*, namely an establishment that this young TikTok user possesses the required skill set as a knower, which in this case includes the ability to skillfully read a novel, the rest of the video exemplifies the practice through a different set of routine behaviors relating to reading, one which, as yet, has gone underrecognized in its authority with regards to the literary episteme. At the 0:10 time stamp, the screen shows a hand holding the book open, but there is also text on the screen that reads, "I'm already attached this isn't going to end well"; one second later, the text on the screen changes to read, "all the feels already." Later in the video, at 0:17, we see abbysbooks's face again, looking pained and into the distance off camera. The text on the screen at this point reads, "why do I read books that I know will break me." Rather than through the demonstration of reading skill or literary accomplishment, all these brief textual inclusions indicate an assertion of agency to know based instead on the intense *experience* of reading. More specifically, in making these statements, the creator is demonstrating an emotional relationship with the book in question, which serves to underwrite the practice of *knowing* about it: because abbysbooks had a lot of intense feelings while reading *They Both Die at the End*, she has the right to comment on it critically. Indeed, the video ends with a close-up of her face with tears rolling down her cheek, suggesting that just by having experienced these emotions, she has become an authoritative critic of the book.

As a practice, this type of *knowing* aligns with Steiner's (2008) emphasis on affect discussed above, moving away from traditional literary criticism and formally authorized literary response, which is functionally devoid of emotion (Moody 2011: 48). Professional reviews of books have long relied on an assertion of their own objectivity as a form of authority; there has indeed already been debate within the realm of digital literary criticism as to whether exploring the emotional effect of a book on the reader is of value to the reviewing process (Rebora et al. 2021: 231). In Video A, however, there can be no doubt that abbysbooks's feelings about the novel inform her opinion of it; indeed, her crying face serves as the ultimate proof to other readers that this was an experience worth having. Thus in this video, and countless other BookTok videos like it, *knowing* becomes more than factual knowledge and critical understanding. The practices of this young user as she "reacts" to and demonstrates her fundamentally affective personal experiences with Silvera's text potentially present a new literary episteme grounded not in technical know-how or analytical skill but instead in the reality of human affect. Rather than being limited to the realm of specialty knowledge or official expertise on books, the power to critique literature is, at least in this space, expanded to include individuals who have powerful emotional experiences with books.

The second video by user hua.b—hereinafter Video B—makes use of an entirely different set of visual and storytelling tools but similarly succeeds in exemplifying how literary knowledge and expertise are established through affective experiences with books. In this instance, hua.b capitalizes on an existing BookTok trend that consists of re-creating the "aesthetic" of a particular text using a collage or pastiche of images to the accompaniment of an (often romantic or sad) song. As the viewer, we are made aware of this at the opening sequence of the video, where the text on the screen reads, "THE AESTHETIC OF:" and below is placed a copy of the book showing its title: *They Both Die at the End*. Thus, we know that hua.b will be creating with us her own version of how Silvera's novel functioned as an *aesthetic* experience. Following the opening sequence, a number of still images appear on screen in rapid succession, including images of a city skyline at night, a hospital bed, a house on fire, a graveyard, a telephone booth lit up at night, the inside of a subway car, and various images of teenage boys laughing together and enjoying each other's company.

Unlike Video A, Video B does not directly share any information about how and why it was read; it is left to the viewer to assume that hua.b has in fact read it based only on the images she has chosen to include in her collage (though this assumption is of course helped by the caption of the video which reads " ⚠ spoiler ⚠ ," indicating that the video contains information about the end of the book). In this way, the authority to know about *They Both Die at the End* is, at least in part, assured by the viewer of the video, who makes an active appraisal of the "aesthetic" portrayed by hua.b in her choice of images. The practice of *knowing* on BookTok thus becomes a relationally established power: it functions only when both video creator and video viewer agree that the portrayal of, and thus knowledge about, the novel is informed and accurate. This suggests that, on digital platforms favored by young people, literary authority is established and maintained collectively and on an ongoing basis.

There are key visual similarities between Videos A and B which point to a particular language of BookTok that we might begin to establish in our critical approach. First, both videos show the book itself on screen, emphasizing the aesthetic qualities of reading in equal measure to its entertainment qualities. But, more importantly, both videos show the relevant novel framed lying on the top of a bedspread. From this we can ascertain that engagement with BookTok likely happens as a broader part of what youth scholars have termed "bedroom culture" (Harris 2001; Lincoln 2013; Steele & Brown 1995). From this perspective, BookTok makes up a part of the broader practice by which "young people engage with culture and . . . within which they find the resources to explore their emerging sense of identity" (Lincoln 2016: n.p.). One critical difference between the videos is that in Video A, abbysbooks primarily films herself as she reads and reacts to the book; though there are sequences where only the book is filmed, for the majority of the time, her face is on the screen. By contrast, in the *Aesthetic* Video B, we never see hua.b, or any other figure, on the screen. The video is composed of one long shot featuring the book (as previously mentioned, lying on a bedspread) followed by a sequence of still images from sources unknown. From this, we can ascertain that although BookTok may work as a relevant feature in the identity development processes of young people, wherein, perhaps, young people are able to try on the role of literary knower, there is no need to *act performatively* in order to participate in this role. In other words, the practice of self-representation is not a requirement of BookTok. This means that a young person can be a BookTokker and, in so doing, demonstrate their agency within the realm of the literary as knowledgeable and authoritative on the subject of books and book criticism without having to display their own image or represent themselves physically in any way. This potentially "lowers the bar," allowing access to a form of authoritative power which is not granted on digital media platforms where self-representations via performances and selfies are the main agentic currency (Rettberg 2014; Abidin 2016).

CONCLUSION

The aim of the final cluster of essays in this volume is to explore systems of engagement within which young people experience and are afforded agency in relation to literature and culture. This chapter has focused on the potential of the popular digital platform TikTok as one such "system" and delved into its potential to expand the literary episteme in a way that allows for young people to act as knowledgeable and authoritative on the topic of books: in short, for them to exercise agency as literary critics in new and formerly unrecognized ways. By taking an approach based in the theory of media as practice to the potentialities inherent in an onto-epistemic (in)justice lens on the digital literary sphere (as it is manifest in young people's engagement with books via the BookTok trend), we have suggested that one notable instance of this expansion can be seen in the increasing emphasis on reader affect; that is, a consideration of the feelings and emotional experiences of the person engaging with the book as an integral part of *knowing* about literature. We believe that this is but one of the ways in which BookTok works to challenge traditional knowledge structures that have historically and traditionally impeded the ability of young people to do literary criticism, much less be understood as authorities within broader book culture, and that further exploration of the topic would elicit a great deal many more examples of these shifts to the literary episteme vis-à-vis young readers.

There are, however, significant challenges to this area of research that merit noting alongside these exciting possibilities. As Neima (2017) has noted, a seemingly infinite volume of criticism online has given rise to the new critical role of aggregator: this is the person (or, more often in recent times, algorithm machine) that collects a select sampling of works from this abundance of critical voices and presents it to the average reader. In the case of BookTok, this aggregator is a "highly sophisticated algorithmic recommender system" (Kaye et al. 2022: 58). Known colloquially as well as in the literature as "the TikTok algorithm" (see Boffone 2021: 7; Schellewald 2021: 1438), this system works as a blackbox (to return to the language of Murray) that ultimately constructs *different* hierarchies of power from those that were originally in place within the realm of digital literary criticism and, indeed, book cultures more generally. While we acknowledge that BookTok may in some ways be opening up new avenues for certain young people to possess and act on agency as literary knowers, in doing so, it may well be simultaneously closing avenues to this type of power for others. We mention this not to discourage further study of BookTok but merely to problematize overly optimistic claims concerning the democratization of literary cultures on the internet that our study might suggest. As Murray writes, "Literary culture in the twenty-first century is still characterised by hierarchies, but they are notably plural, more loosely defined, and demonstrably more in flux than in the pre-digital era" (Murray 2018: 140). This take offers a more nuanced understanding of digital literary criticism that should foreground further research into the topic of BookTok. As these digital platforms continue to make their way into the day-to-day lives of individuals worldwide, we as researchers have an obligation to understand the complex ways in which they relate to—restricting, expanding, informing, or reinforcing—the agency of young people. The way in which youth in particular learn to operate as citizens of this hyperconnected reality will shape not just the realm of the literary, but, in fact, structure the social world as we know it.

NOTE

1. Although the term was coined in Fricker's seminal monograph, roots of ideas surrounding suppression of voice of certain categories of people can be found in the intellectual work by scholars of color such as Anna Julia Cooper and Gayatri Chakravorty Spivak (see May 2014).

REFERENCES

Abidin, Crystal. "Visibility Labour: Engaging with Influencers' Fashion Brands and #OOTD Advertorial Campaigns on Instagram." *Media International Australia* 161, no. 1 (2016), 86–100. doi:10.1177/1329878×16665177.

Allington, Daniel. "'Power to the Reader' or 'Degradation of Literary Taste'? Professional Critics and Amazon Customers as Reviewers of *The Inheritance of Loss*." *Language and Literature: International Journal of Stylistics* 25, no. 3 (2016), 254–78. doi:10.1177/0963947016652789.

Andersen, Tore R., Stefan Kjerkegaard, and Birgitte Stougaard Pedersen. "Introduction." *Poetics Today* 42, no. 2 (2021), 131–47. doi:10.1215/03335372-8883164.

Apple, Chelsea. "Managing Expectations." *Publishers Weekly* 269, no. 17 (2022).

Boffone, Trevor, and Sarah Jerasa. "Toward a (Queer) Reading Community: BookTok, Teen Readers, and the Rise of TikTok Literacies." *Talking Points* 33, no. 1 (2021), 10–16. doi:10.58680/tp202131537.

Boffone, Trevor, editor. *TikTok Cultures in the United States*. London: Routledge, 2022.

Carr, Nicholas G. *The Shallows: How the Internet is Changing the Way We Think, Read and Remember*. New York: W. W. Norton & Company, 2010.

Cavazzoni, Federica, Alec Fiorini, Cindy Sousa, and Guido Veronese. "Agency Operating Within Structures: A Qualitative Exploration of Agency Amongst Children Living in Palestine." *Childhood* 28, no. 3 (2021), 363–79. doi:10.1177/09075682211025588.

Cetina, Karin K., Theodore R. Schatzki, and Eike Von Savigny, editors. *The Practice Turn in Contemporary Theory*. London: Routledge, 2000.

Coover, Robert. "The End of Books." *New York Times* web archive. Last modified 1992. https://archive.nytimes.com/www.nytimes.com/books/98/09/27/specials/coover-end.html.

Couldry, Nick. *Media, Society, World: Social Theory and Digital Media Practice*. Cambridge: Polity, 2012.

Cuestas, Paula, Giuliana Pates, and Victoria Saez. "El fenómeno booktok y la lectura en pandemia: jóvenes, pantallas, libros y editoriales." *Austral Comunicación* 11, no. 1 (2022). doi:10.26422/aucom.2022.1101.pat.

Dean, Brian. "TikTok Statistics You Need to Know." Backlinko. Last modified July 1, 2024. https://backlinko.com/tiktok-users.

Delemos, Raquel S. "TikTok for Viral Book Marketing." *Publishers Weekly* 268 (2021).

Dezuanni, Michael, Bronwyn Reddan, Leonie Rutherford, and Amy Schoonens. "Selfies and Shelfies on #Bookstagram and #Booktok—Social Media and the Mediation of Australian Teen Reading." *Learning, Media and Technology* 47, no. 3 (2022), 355–72. doi: 10.1080/17439884.2022.2068575.

Drotner, Kirsten. "The Co-Construction of Media and Childhood." In *The Routledge International Handbook of Children, Adolescents, and Media*, edited by Dafna Lemish. London: Routledge, 2013.

Flood, Alison. "The Rise of BookTok: Meet the Teen Influencers Pushing Books up the Charts." *The Guardian*. Last modified June 25, 2021. https://www.theguardian.com/books/2021/jun/25/the-rise-of-booktok-meet-the-teen-influencers-pushing-books-up-the-charts.

Fricker, Miranda. *Epistemic Injustice: Power and the Ethics of Knowing*. Oxford: Oxford University Press, 2007.

García-González, Macarena, and Justyna Deszcz-Tryhubczak. "New Materialist Openings to Children's Literature Studies." *International Research in Children's Literature* 13, no. 1 (2020), 45–60. doi:10.3366/ircl.2020.0327.

Gubar, Marah. "Risky Business: Talking about Children in Children's Literature Criticism." *Children's Literature Association Quarterly* 38, no. 4 (2013), 450–57. doi:10.1353 /chq.2013.0048.

Harris, Anita. "Revisiting Bedroom Culture: New Spaces for Young Women's Politics." *Hecate* 27, no. 1 (2001), 128–38.

Harris, Elizabeth. "How TikTok Became a Best-Seller Machine." *New York Times*. Last modified July 6, 2022. https://www.nytimes.com/2022/07/01/books/tiktok-books -booktok.html.

Haynes, Joanna, and Karin Murris. "Taking Age out of Play: Children's Animistic Philosophising Through a Picturebook." *Oxford Literary Review* 41, no. 2 (2019), 290–309. doi:10.3366/olr.2019.0284.

Hjarvard, Stig. *The Mediatization of Culture and Society*. London: Routledge, 2013.

Ito, Mizuko. "Mobilizing the Imagination in Everyday Play: The Case of Japanese Media Mixes." *The International Handbook of Children, Media and Culture*, 2008, 397–412. doi:10.4135/9781848608436.n24.

Jaakkola, Maarit. "From Re-Viewers to Me-Viewers: The #Bookstagram Review Sphere on Instagram and the Uses of the Perceived Platform and Genre Affordances." *Interactions: Studies in Communication & Culture* 10, no. 1 (2019), 91–110. doi:10.1386 /iscc.10.1-2.91_1.

Jensen, Kelly. "AS SEEN ON #BookTok: Inspiring Young Readers, TikTok Is a Boon to Books." *School Library Journal* 68 (2022), 28.

Jerasa, Sarah, and Trevor Boffone. "BookTok 101: TikTok, Digital Literacies, and Out-of-School Reading Practices." *Journal of Adolescent & Adult Literacy* 65, no. 3 (2021), 219–26. doi:10.1002/jaal.1199.

Johansen, Stine L. "Everyday Media Play." *Conjunctions* 4, no. 1 (2017), 1–10. doi:10.7146 /tjcp.v4i1.103493.

Kaye, D. Bondy Valdovinos, Jing Zeng, and Patrik Wikström. *TikTok: Creativity and Culture in Short Video*. Cambridge: Polity, 2022.

Kidd, Ian James, José Medina, and Gaile Pohlhaus. "Introduction to the Routledge Handbook of Epistemic Injustice." In *The Routledge Handbook of Epistemic Injustice*, 1–9. New York: Routledge, 2017.

Lincoln, Siân. "Media and Bedroom Culture." In *The Routledge International Handbook of Children, Adolescents and Media*, edited by Dafna Lemish. London: Routledge, 2013.

Lincoln, Siân. "Bedroom Culture: A Review of Research." In *Space, Place and Environment: Geographies of Children and Young People*, edited by Karen Nairn, Peter G. Kraftl, and Tracey Skelton, 1–19. Singapore: Springer, 2016.

Lundby, Knut. *Mediatization of Communication*. Berlin: Walter de Gruyter, 2014.

Martens, Marianne, Gitte Balling, and Kristen A. Higgason. "#BookTokMadeMeReadIt: Young Adult Reading Communities Across an International, Sociotechnical

Landscape." *Information and Learning Sciences* 123, no. 11/12 (2022), 705–22. doi:10.1108/ils-07-2022-0086.

Mashiyane, Dina. "From the Horse's Mouth: BookTok as a Collection Development Strategy in Academic Libraries." *College & Research Libraries News* 83, no. 10 (2022). doi:10.5860/crln.83.10.459.

May, Vivian M. "'Speaking into the Void'? Intersectionality Critiques and Epistemic Backlash." *Hypatia* 29, no. 1 (2014), 94–112. doi:10.1111/hypa.12060.

McIlroy, Thad. "The Future of Book Marketing: Promoting Books Today Demands a Deep Understanding of How Social Media, and BookTok in Particular, Works." *Publishers Weekly*, 2022, 269.

Merga, Margaret K. "How Can BookTok on TikTok Inform Readers' Advisory Services for Young People?" *Library & Information Science Research* 43, no. 2 (2021). doi:10.1016/j.lisr.2021.101091.

Morton, Timothy. *Hyperobjects: Philosophy and Ecology After the End of the World*. Minneapolis: University of Minnesota Press, 2013.

Mohsin, Maryam. "10 TikTok Statistics You Need to Know in 2023" (new data). Oberlo. Last modified September 12, 2023. https://www.oberlo.com/blog/tiktok-statistics.

Moody, Nickianne. "Entertainment Media, Risk and the Experience Commodity." In *The Richard and Judy Book Club Reader: Popular Texts and the Practices of Reading*, edited by Jenni Ramone and Helen Cousins, 43–58. Farnham: Ashgate, 2011.

Murray, Simone. *The Digital Literary Sphere: Reading, Writing, and Selling Books in the Internet Era*. Baltimore: Johns Hopkins University Press, 2018.

Murray, Simone. "Secret Agents: Algorithmic Culture, Goodreads and Datafication of the Contemporary Book World." *European Journal of Cultural Studies* 24 no. 4 (2021), 970–89.

Murris, Karin. "The Epistemic Challenge of Hearing Child's Voice." *Studies in Philosophy and Education* 32, no. 3 (2013), 245–59. doi:10.1007/s11217-012-9349-9.

Natanson, Hannah. "Yes, Teens Are Texting and Using Social Media Instead of Reading Books, Researchers Say." *Washington Post*. Last modified August 20, 2018. https://www.washingtonpost.com/news/inspired-life/wp/2018/08/20/for-american-teens-texting-and-social-media-are-replacing-books.

Neima, Luke. "Fragmentation and Aggregation: The Future of Criticism?" In *The Digital Critic: Literary Culture Online*, edited by Houman Barekat, Robert Barry, and David Winters, 50–58. New York: OR Books, 2017.

Nicolini, Davide. *Practice Theory, Work, and Organization: An Introduction*. New York: Oxford University Press, 2013.

Nikolajeva, Maria. *Power, Voice and Subjectivity in Literature for Young Readers*. London: Routledge, 2009.

O'Sullivan, Joanne. "Boon or Burden? Two Years into the BookTok Phenomenon, Its Success Stories Stun, but Not All YA Authors See Benefits." *Publishers Weekly* 269 (2022), 21.

Owens, Emilie. "Teens on TikTok: Understanding Young People's Digital Agency as Practice." *International Research in Children's Literature* 17, no. 2 (2024), 174–88. Accessed November 18, 2022. doi:10.3366/ircl.2024.0562.

Pink, Sarah, Heather Horst, John Postill, Larissa Hjorth, Tania Lewis, and Jo Tacchi. *Digital Ethnography: Principles and Practice*. Thousand Oaks, CA: Sage, 2015.

Rebora, Simone, Peter Boot, Federico Pianzola, Brigitte Gasser, J. B. Herrmann, Maria Kraxenberger, Moniek M. Kuijpers, et al. "Digital Humanities and Digital Social Reading." *Digital Scholarship in the Humanities* 36, Supplement 2 (November 2021), ii230–ii250.

Rettberg, Jill W. *Seeing Ourselves Through Technology: How We Use Selfies, Blogs and Wearable Devices to See and Shape Ourselves.* London: Palgrave Macmillan, 2014.

Roberts, Elly. "The Rise of BookTok." *School Librarian* 69 (2021), 27–28.

Robson, Elsbeth, Stephen Bell, and Natascha Klocker. "Conceptualizing Agency in the Lives and Actions of Rural Young People." In *Global Perspectives on Rural Childhood and Youth: Young Rural Lives*, edited by Ruth Panelli, Samantha Punch, and Elsbeth Robson. London: Routledge, 2007.

Russell, Sam. "Page Turner: BookTok Is Brilliant." *The Spectator*, 2021.

Schellewald, Andreas. "Communicative Forms on TikTok: Perspectives from Digital Ethnography." *International Journal of Communication* 15 (2021), 1,437–57.

Silvera, Adam. *They Both Die at the End.* New York: Simon & Schuster, 2017.

Steele, Jeanne R., and Jane D. Brown. "Adolescent Room Culture: Studying Media in the Context of Everyday Life." *Journal of Youth and Adolescence* 24, no. 5 (September/October 2022), 551–76.

Steiner, Ann. "Private Criticism in the Public Sphere: Personal Writing on Literature in Readers' Reviews on Amazon." *Participations* 5, no. 2 (2008).

Stewart, Sophia. "How TikTok Makes Backlist Books into Bestsellers." *Publishers Weekly*, September 3, 2021.

Stewart, Sophia. "U.S. Book Show: How TikTok Is Transforming Book Marketing." *Publishers Weekly*, May 24, 2022.

Sutherland, John. "John Sutherland Is Shocked by the State of Book Reviewing on the Web." *The Telegraph*, November 19, 2006. Accessed January 11, 2023. https://www.telegraph.co.uk/culture/books/3656629/john-sutherland-IS-SHOCKED-BY-THE-STATE-OF-book-Reviewing-on-the-web.html.

TikTok. "A New Way to Tap into the #BookTok Community." Newsroom, TikTok. Last modified September 20, 2022. https://newsroom.tiktok.com/en-us/a-new-way-to-tap-into-the-booktok-community.

TikTok. "How TikTok Recommends Videos #ForYou." Newsroom, TikTok. Last modified June 18, 2020. https://newsroom.tiktok.com/en-us/how-tiktok-recommends-videos-for-you.

Twenge, Jean M., Gabrielle N. Martin, and Brian H. Spitzberg. "Trends in U.S. Adolescents' Media Use, 1976–2016: The Rise of Digital Media, the Decline of TV, and the (Near) Demise of Print." *Psychology of Popular Media Culture* 8, no. 4 (2019), 329–45.

van Lierop-Debrauwer, Helma. "Children's Literature: A Joint Venture." *International Research in Children's Literature* 15, no. 3 (2022), 249–63. Accessed November 18, 2022. doi:10.3366/ircl.2022.0465.

Vatner, Jonathan. "The Literary Dimensions of TikTok." *Poets & Writers* 50, no. 5 (2022), 17–18.

Wiederhold, Brenda K. "BookTok Made Me Do It: The Evolution of Reading." *Cyberpsychology, Behavior, and Social Networking* 25, no. 3 (2022), 157–58. doi:10.1089/cyber.2022.29240.editorial.

ABOUT THE CONTRIBUTORS

Daniela Brockdorff obtained a Master of Arts degree in Modern and Contemporary Literature and Criticism from the University of Malta in 2013, following a Bachelor of Arts (Hons.) degree in English. Since then, she has dedicated most of her time to teaching language and literature at the postsecondary and tertiary levels and is currently part of the CASP team at the University of Malta, delivering sessions on communication and academic skills. Her research and writing interests tend to focus on the broader theme of humanity as mediated through narratives, dwelling on the ontological need and desire for the reconstruction of self and identity through storytelling.

Nina Christensen is Professor in Children's Literature and Head of Centre for Children's Literature and Media at Aarhus University, Denmark. Her research interests include the history of children's literature, the interaction between children's literature and concepts of childhood, and picture books. With Charlotte Appel, she coauthored *Children's Literature in the Nordic Worlds* (2021) and *On the Trail of Children and Books* (2023, in Danish), about children's books and media and reading practices in Denmark from 1750 to 1850. She was coeditor of the second edition of *Keywords for Children's Literature* (2021, with Philip Nel and Lissa Paul) and *Transnational Books for Children 1750–1900* (2023, with Charlotte Appel and M. O. Grenby). She coedits the book series *Children's Literature, Culture, and Cognition* with Elina Druker and Bettina Kümmerling-Meibauer and is cofounder of the Erasmus Mundus Master's program Children's Literature, Media and Cultural Entrepreneurship.

Jill Coste received her doctorate in 2021 from the University of Florida, where she concentrated on children's and young adult literature. Her research examines activist agency in young adult literature, focusing particularly on contemporary fairy tale retellings and their intersections with other forms of speculative fiction, such as the dystopia. Her work has appeared in the journals *Women's Studies* and *Girlhood Studies* and in the edited collections *Beyond the Blockbusters: Themes and Trends in Contemporary Young Adult Literature* and *Race in Speculative Young Adult Fiction*. She teaches first-year writing at Elizabethtown College.

Katrin Dautel graduated from the Universities of Tübingen, Bonn, and Florence and was awarded her doctoral degree from the University of Malta, where she is currently employed in the role of Senior Lecturer in German language and literature. Her main research areas are German contemporary literature with a special focus on space constructions, island fictions, and migration. Her latest publications include the article "Of Worms and Birds: Approaches to the Island Between Practice and the Imaginary" (University of Tübingen Press 2021) and the monograph *Räume schreiben. Literarische (Selbst)Verortung bei Tanja Dückers, Jenny Erpenbeck, and Judith Hermann* (Peter Lang 2019).

Justyna Deszcz-Tryhubczak is Associate Professor of literature and cofounder of the Centre for Young People's Culture and Literature at the Institute of English Studies, University of Wrocław, Poland. She is also a member of the Centre for Research on Children's and Young Adult Literature at the University of Wrocław. She published *Yes to Solidarity, No to Oppression: Radical Fantasy Fiction and Its Young Readers* (2016). *Intergenerational Solidarity in Children's Literature and Film* (2021), which she coedited with Zoe Jacques, was awarded the 2023 Edited Book Award from the International Research Society for Children's Literature. She also coedited (with Irena Barbara Kalla) *Children's Literature and Intergenerational Relationships: Encounters of the Playful Kind* (2021) and *Rulers of Literary Playgrounds: Politics of Intergenerational Play in Children's Literature* (2021), as well as (with Macarena García-González) *Children's Cultures After Childhood* (2023) and (with Terri Doughty and Janet Grafton) *Children's Literatures, Cultures, and Pedagogies in the Anthropocene: Multidisciplinary Entanglements* (2025). She is a Fulbright Fellow, a Marie Skłodowska-Curie Fellow, and a grantee of the Polish Foundation for Science and the Polish National Agency for Academic Exchange.

Giuliana Fenech is Senior Lecturer in the Department of English at the University of Malta, specializing in work involving children's and young adult literature and citizenship, agency, creative protest, and activism. She combines research with cultural and artistic community projects involving stories, multimedia, cultural heritage, and youth. In May 2022, Giuliana convened the circuit conference The Child and the Book, themed "The Role of the

Child as Citizen: Constructing Childhood Through Agency and Activism"
in Malta. She is Principal Investigator of an Erasmus K2 HED project called
Seen and Heard: Young Adult Voices and Freedom of Expression. Additionally, Giuliana runs a storytelling organization, Lignin Stories, which works
with diverse groups of children and youths in Malta and across Europe.

Naomi Hamer is Associate Professor in the Department of English at
Toronto Metropolitan University (Canada). Her publications examine the
cross-media adaptation of children's literature with a focus on picture books,
mobile apps, and children's museums. She is the coeditor of *More Words
About Pictures: Current Research on Picture Books and Visual/Verbal Texts for
Young People* (eds. Hamer, Nodelman, and Reimer 2017) and *The Routledge
Companion to Media and Fairy-Tale Cultures* (eds. Greenhill, Rudy, Hamer,
and Bosc 2018). Dr. Hamer's current research on international story museums
extends from an SSHRC-funded joint research project, "Curating the Story
Museum: Transmedia Practices, Participatory Exhibits, and Youth Citizen-
ship," with Dr. Ann Marie Murnaghan (York University).

Irena Barbara Kalla is Associate Professor, Head of Dutch Studies, and
Coordinator of the Centre for Research on Children's and Young Adult Literature at the Faculty of Letters, University of Wrocław, Poland. She has
published on Dutch and Flemish literature, on interactions of literature and
digital media culture, and on intergenerational relationships (*Rulers of Literary Playgrounds: Politics of Intergenerational Play in Children's Literature*,
Routledge, 2021; *Children's Literature and Intergenerational Relationships:
Encounters of the Playful Kind*, Palgrave, 2021, both with J. Deszcz-Tryhubczak). From 2020 to 2023, she was a member of the research team in the
project "21st-Century Literature and the Holocaust." In 2022, she was elected
as an honorary member of Koninklijke Academie voor Nederlandse Taal en
Letterkunde (Royal Academy of Dutch Language and Literature, KANTL),
Belgium/Flanders, where she serves as Chair of the jury KANTL Children's
and Young People's Literature Prize.

Anne Klomberg is a PhD candidate at Tilburg University, the Netherlands.
Her thesis centers on embodied outsiderhood in adolescent fiction. She
explores how interactions between material embodiment and (aeto)nor-
mative discourses construct adolescents as outsiders and how this alleged
outsiderhood subsequently affects adolescents' sense of self, their agency, and
their experience of space. Anne obtained her Master of Arts degree in Children's and Young Adult Literature at Tilburg University in 2017, then did a

research traineeship at the Dutch Reading Foundation. With Dr. Sara Van den Bossche, she coauthored a book on ethnic-cultural diversity in Dutch youth literature: *Jeugdliteratuur door de lens van etnisch-culturele diversiteit* (2020).

Sonali Kulkarni is a PhD Researcher at Tilburg University. In her PhD, she focuses on reading in the (post-)digital age. In particular, she examines the practices of and motivations for adults rereading children's and young adult literature within the context of attention economies. In addition to her PhD, Sonali has been researching BookTok since the early years of the phenomenon. She was an Erasmus Mundus scholar and followed the International Master in Children's Literature, Media and Culture from 2019 to 2021 at the universities of Glasgow, Aarhus, and Tilburg. She has taught courses related to children's and young adult literature at Tilburg University in the Netherlands and the University of Antwerp in Belgium.

Elizabeth Leach-Leung received her PhD from the University of Cambridge where her thesis, *Representations of Dyslexia Across Genres in Children's and Young Adult Literature*, received the Faculty of Education Doctoral Student Excellence Prize. In addition to children's and young adult literature and disability studies (particularly dyslexia studies), her areas of academic interest include genre studies, media studies, Disney studies, new adult literature, posthumanism, and creative writing for children and young adults. She is an associate editor for the *International Journal of Young Adult Literature*, and her work has been published in several journals including *Children's Literature in Education*, *International Research in Children's Literature*, and *Jeunesse: Young People, Texts, Cultures*.

Ann Marie Murnaghan is Associate Professor in the Department of Humanities at York University. Her previous research analyzed how the material cultures of play and playgrounds influenced discourses of childhood and children's identities in early twentieth-century Toronto. In her current research, Murnaghan examines how museums act as sites of children's informal education and how integral these are to the formation of children's identities using film studies, critical museology, and participatory, playful methodologies.

Emily Murphy is Senior Lecturer in Children's Literature at Newcastle University (UK), with research interests in international children's literature, childhood studies, and global citizenship education. Her monograph, *Growing Up with America: Youth, Myth, and National Identity, 1945 to Present* (University of Georgia Press, 2020), was the winner of the 2021 International

Research Society for Children's Literature Book Award. She has published essays in *The Lion and the Unicorn*, *Children's Literature Association Quarterly*, *Jeunesse*, and the *Journal of American Studies*, as well as in several edited volumes. Currently, she is working on a new book project titled *The Anarchy of Children's Archives: Children's Literature and Global Citizenship Education in the American Century* and a British Academy– and Nuffield Foundation–funded grant called "Beyond the School Gates: Children's Contribution to Community Integration."

Emilie Owens is a Doctoral Research Fellow with the Department of Media and Communications at the University of Oslo. She has a background in communications and media research, as well as in children's literature, media, and culture. Her current project is focused on undertaking ethnographic research to better understand where and how the social worlds of teenagers are shaped by digital media using the popular video-sharing application TikTok as a case study.

Nicola Parker is a specialist in children's literature and human rights. She worked with Amnesty International for over twenty years, cocreating books and literary projects through a human rights lens. These include *We Are All Born Free: The Universal Declaration of Human Rights in Pictures* (2008) and "Words That Burn" (2016), a spoken word resource for school students to explore and express human rights through poetry. On behalf of Amnesty International, she coauthored with Angelina Jolie and Geraldine Van Bueren *Know Your Rights and Claim Them: A Guide for Youth* (2021) and wrote *These Rights Are Your Rights: An Empowering Guide for Children Everywhere* (2024). From 2016 to 2022, she was Chair of Trustees of the Centre for Literacy in Primary Education (CLPE) and is on the steering group of Reflecting Realities, an annual survey of ethnic representation in British children's books. She is a trustee of English PEN.

Patrycja Poniatowska, PhD (2000), lectured on Early Modern Literature and Culture at the Institute of English Studies, University of Wrocław, Poland, and published on Dutch and English Renaissance literature, including *"As You Are Well Pronounced by All External Warrants": Women's Bodies and Women's Places in 17th-Century Dutch and English Drama* (2006). Currently, she is an editor and a translator for works such as J. Zylinska, *Bioethics in the Age of New Media* (2013); R. Shusterman, *Myślenie ciała, Thinking Through the Body: Essays in Somaesthetics* (2016); M. Wójcik-Dudek, *Reading (in) the Holocaust: Practices of Postmemory in Recent Polish Literature for Children* *and Young Adults* (2020); Ł. Smuga, *Queer Rebels: Rewriting Literary Traditions in Contemporary Spanish Novels* (2022); and D. Koczanowicz, *The Aesthetics of Taste: Eating Within the Realm of Art* (2023).

Meg Rosoff was born in Boston, MA (USA), educated at Harvard University and St. Martin's College of Art, London, and has lived in London since 1989. She is the author of ten novels and nine books for younger readers and has won or been shortlisted for twenty-four international literary awards, including the National Book Award in the US, the Carnegie Medal in the UK, and Germany's Deutscher Jugendlitetaturpreis. She was awarded Sweden's Astrid Lindgren Memorial Award in 2016, is a Fellow of the Royal Society of Literature, and is an honorary Fellow of Homerton College, Cambridge University.

Farriba Schulz is Senior Lecturer in the Institute of Education at Humboldt-Universität zu Berlin and Universität Potsdam. She was the Visiting Professor of Primary Education in the Department of German at Technische Universität Dresden, Germany, and worked as a guest lecturer at Freie Universität Berlin. Her main research interest centers on the construction of childhoods, (visual) literacy and inclusion, and working collaboratively with schools, libraries, museums, the International Literature Festival Berlin (ilb), and artists. She has worked on several projects that explore issues of diversity and inclusivity in children's literature, including an international research project with Maureen Maisha Auma and Melanie Ramdarshan Bold. She is a jury member of the GEW literature award Lesepeter; a member of the advisory board of the circuit conference, The Child and the Book; a coeditor of the book *Political Changes and Transformations in Twentieth and Twenty-First Century Children's Literature* (2023), and since 2023, the Humboldt-Universität zu Berlin coordinator and academic lead in Seen and Heard: Young People's Voices and Freedom of Expression (https://seenand heardproject.eu/).

INDEX

www.ingramcontent.com/pod-product-compliance
Lightning Source LLC
Chambersburg PA
CBHW030357270326
41926CB00009B/1149